The Rhetoric of History

UNIVERSITY OF OKLAHOMA PRESS : NORMAN AND LONDON

The Rhetoric of History

Savoie Lottinville

By Savoie Lottinville

Life of George Bent: Written from His Letters by George E. Hyde (editor, Norman, 1968)

Soldier in the West: Letters of Theodore Talbot During His Services in California, Mexico, and Oregon (editor, with Robert V. Hine, Norman, 1972)

Paul Wilhelm, Duke of Württemberg, *Travels in North America, 1822–1824,* Translated by W. Robert Nitske (editor, Norman, 1974)

The Rhetoric of History (Norman, 1976, 1990)

Thomas Nuttall, *A Journal of Travels into the Arkansas Territory During the Year 1819* (editor, Norman, 1980)

Herbert Butterfield: The Ethics of History and Politics, with Kenneth W. Thompson (Washington, D.C., 1980)

Library of Congress Cataloging-in-Publication Data

Lottinville, Savoie, 1906–
   The rhetoric of history.

   Bibliography: p. 231.
   Includes index.
   1. Historiography. I. Title.
D13.L67   907'.2   75–19418
ISBN 0–8061–2190–4

To Helene

Pro aris et focis

Preface

My copy of *Eve's Diary* by Mark Twain (1905) contains the author's inscription:

> 'Tis noble to be good. 'Tis nobler still to teach others to be good—and much less trouble.

From a similar conviction, born of writing a good many hundreds of letters to authors in the toils of serious historical construction, I have concluded it is high time to give systematic form to my ideas on the craft of writing history. And to make sure that the resulting book is not confused with many others which contain "writing" in their titles, but deal, actually, with historical research, bibliography, and intellectual styles in the pursuit of man's past, I have called it *The Rhetoric of History*. Its sole purpose is to help the person committed to history to become an effective writer in that inviting field.

There is a belief, more widespread than many people suppose, that historical research is an end in itself. It finds support in the heavy emphasis given the research function in American graduate schools. Here the thrust is towards a thorough mastery of the critical method in the finding and analysis of historical fact. Writing, while it is not neglected in the familiar forms of the book review, the historical essay, and even the early venture into the journal article, leaves the dissertation and the book to the end. The time for learning historical narration, analysis, portraiture, the management of historical time and place, and, above all else, conceptualization, is often too late. It is as if the mastery of historical writing techniques is expected to come to the young historian without analysis, simply from reading history. Effective historical writing is rarely developed in this painless fashion.

Carl L. Becker complained mildly more than half a century ago that, even in the historical journals, reviewers were reviewing bibliographies rather than historical works as such. Later, he wrote with great skill about the rhetorical tasks of the historian. But the most striking examples from his own drafts did not appear until a decade after his death. What they tell us is what every writer tells us in life, that writing must be understood and it must be practiced as a discipline, as exacting as the research which forms its base and as elusive as achievement in any of the other arts.

The Rhetoric of History offers no formulae of universal application. But it does contain principles and a number of illustrative examples. They suggest solutions to specific problems. But as the student of historical episodes knows, all episodes are unique. Equally, the writing about individual episodes must find and develop its own uniqueness. Gross failure occurs when narration, to take one essential, is not understood as a technique, or analysis, to take another, breaks under the weight and disorganization of its details. Good history will always be good writing, provided it is joined with sound data, critically examined.

SAVOIE LOTTINVILLE

The University of Oklahoma
Norman, Oklahoma

Acknowledgments

The helpfulness of several friends in history and letters has chastened the thought expressed in the individual chapters of this book and refined many of its less apt expressions. Among them, Professor John S. Ezell of the University of Oklahoma read all of the chapters in manuscript. Lawrence S. Poston, Jr., Professor Emeritus of Modern Languages in the University of Oklahoma, gave my short translations from French his critical attention. W. Foster Harris, Professor Emeritus of Journalism in the University of Oklahoma, whose *The Basic Formulas of Fiction* I had copy-edited not at all at the University of Oklahoma Press when it was being published, gave me the benefit of his wisdom for the chapter on narration.

The chapter on bibliographies and edited documents had the critical scanning of Charles L. Camp, the co-compiler of *The Plains and the Rockies, 1800–1865*; Professor Donald Jackson, the editor of the Papers of George Washington at the University of Virginia; and Professor Thomas D. Clark of Indiana University.

Mr. Gaylord Donnelley, chairman of the board of R. R. Donnelley and Sons Company, The Lakeside Press, Chicago, very kindly examined my Chapter 10 and gave me valuable suggestions for shaping it into final form, as did also Mr. O. J. Engle, of his technical staff.

Professor Rudolph Bambas, of the Department of English at the University of Oklahoma, not only went over my chapter on words but permitted me to append to this volume his article on the split infinitive, perhaps the most misunderstood entity in the English language.

The section on institutional portraiture in Chapter 5 benefitted from a reading by Daniel A. Wren, Professor of Management and Curator of the Harry W. Bass Collection in Business History at the University of Oklahoma.

My respected and gifted former colleague at the University of Oklahoma Press, Miss Mary Stith, kindly read my forward and backward views of the scholarly publisher's role and expectations in the historical field.

Nothing I have written, however, may be blamed on these worthy practitioners of the higher learning in America. Nor yet upon my graduate students in history at the University of Oklahoma, whose response to modest lessons in writing was both large and rewarding to me.

From a memory sharpened by teaching and the stage, and from successful writing in the creative and musicological fields, my wife Helene Collins Lottinville gave me many valuable insights.

To each and all of these I return "by these presents" my very real gratitude and thanks.

To the many authors and their publishers who permitted me to quote from their copyrighted works (indicated by year below) I also make acknowledgment and express my thanks:

The Clarendon Press, Oxford, for E. F. Carritt, *The Theory of Morals* (1952).
Yale University Press for Charles McLean Andrews, *The*

Acknowledgments

Colonial Period in American History, 4 volumes (1934–38), and Herbert Eugene Bolton, *The Spanish Borderlands,* No. 23 in *Chronicles of America Series* (1921).

Westways, Los Angeles, and Messrs. Rodman Paul, Ray Allen Billington, Richard H. Dillon, W. H. Hutchinson, and John Walton Caughey, for the Symposium on the California Gold Rush (May, 1967).

Harcourt Brace Jovanovich for Vernon Louis Parrington, *Main Currents in American Thought,* 3 volumes (1927–30).

Sir Herbert Butterfield for his *The Peace Tactics of Napoleon, 1806–1808* (Cambridge, England, 1929).

Houghton Mifflin Company for Garrett Mattingly's *The Armada* (1959) and *Renaissance Diplomacy* (1955).

Dodd, Mead and Company for Allan Nevins, *Grover Cleveland: A Study in Courage* (1933), and *Hamilton Fish: The Inner History of the Grant Administration* (1936).

Charles Scribner's Sons for Allan Nevins, *The Emergence of Lincoln,* 2 volumes (1950).

The University of Chicago Press for Marc Leopold Benjamin Bloch, *Feudal Society,* translated by L. A. Manyon (1961).

Peter Smith for Élie Halévy, *England in 1815,* translated by E. I. Watkin and D. A. Barker (1949).

Paul B. Sears, for his *Charles Darwin: The Naturalist as a Cultural Force* (New York, Charles Scribner's Sons, 1950).

Princeton University Press for Arthur S. Link, *Wilson: The Struggle for Neutrality, 1914–1915* (1960).

Little, Brown and Company for Charles W. Ferguson, *Naked to Mine Enemies: The Life of Cardinal Wolsey* (1958).

The University of Oklahoma Press for the many authors and their books cited in footnotes and accounted for in the bibliography appended to the present volume. To the Press my thanks for permissions to quote.

And for an indispensable index, I have to thank Mrs. H. C. Peterson, my former colleague.

SAVOIE LOTTINVILLE

Contents

xiii

The Rhetoric of History

1. Foundations and Concepts

HISTORY is not a problem. The writing of it is. The impulse to record what men have witnessed or received from earlier times on "good authority" is as old as the human voice and the primitive skills of painting and incising on stone, bone, and the skins of animals. It has gratified the curiosity of men from the Paleolithic age to the present day. But the record was never easy to render, whether pictographically, as in the case of the Kiowa Calendar History, or in the more sophisticated and often misleading areas of European diplomacy.

Things are not always as they seem. And telling them as they were is dependent upon structural and stylistic considerations no less than upon finding and assessing the facts. Thus, while the first question for any history seems to be, What happened? the attempt to answer it immediately raises other questions of even more complex issue. What was the background of the event? Who were the immediate principals, and who the more remote? Which dates were significant? What did the event mean? What influence, if any, did it exert upon subsequent developments?

The gathering of data is properly the province of seminars in bibliography and methods. The questions one asks of one's data fall also in that province. Structures and techniques of applying the answers to these questions are the province of this book. The questions asked immediately above suggest the urgency of organizing historical data so that the resulting narrative may escape the twin evils of overdependence upon chronology, on the one hand, and a formless insignificance, on the other. Good history rests, to be sure, on the solid foundations of its research, but memorable history achieves its ends by honest stratagems as old as Xenophon's trick of putting first things first.

In history, scholarship and grace were never enemies, despite a too common tendency today for professional historians to assert a contrary view. And *per contra* no amount of facile writing can make up for the deficiencies resulting from lax scholarship. It is just this interdependence of ascertainable fact and the appropriate form of its historical presentation which makes historical composition one of the most challenging of all disciplines. Here the beginner must face up to his responsibility and the veteran knows he can never escape it.

The reasons are simple. Every historical episode is unique. It urgently requires of the writer an understanding of its internal principle. This is merely another way of stating the need for thought about meaning, which goes by the long but honored phrase, "conceptualization." Without it, nothing happens. Even two armies locked in battle will fail of significance if, through the historian's preoccupation with his narrative, no sense of man-made destiny is understood and conveyed. The backward view, which is the vulgar name for history, cannot succeed if it does not contain this principle essential to its synthesis. With it, most elements will fall into place. Its abuse, however, is known as bias.

Because most developing historians today rightly confine their first ventures to rather clearly defined, manageable areas of history, our principal emphasis will be upon episodes rather than upon the grand sweep of human action and fate. Our task is to get hold of techniques of writing, knowing in advance, from the myriad examples in journals and books recently published, that data-gathering and annotation have become the common property of all who approach history seriously. Equally, historiography—the study of the theories, principles, and techniques of historical research and presentation as contained in the work of major historians—is beyond our purview. Our principal concerns will be directed to getting historical narration and interpretation on paper and avoiding some of the manifold pitfalls which can arise for the historian in language, structures, bibliographical forms, and ethics and literary laws.

The resources for an undertaking such as we now embark upon exist in profusion in the work of historians living and dead who have surmounted these common problems and concerns. They exist also in part in what I can only describe as a worm's eye view of countless representatives of the historical corpus. At this level I have worked for nearly forty years, blue pencil in hand, docking the prolix, smoothing the reckless flow, asking the unanswered question, proposing a better for a worse management of bibliographical techniques. The work of a scholarly editor, however, represents at best a very imperfect art. It always suggests to its practitioner the superior validity of prior teaching, which has the great merit of exposing the young historian to craftsmanship before he takes his first serious steps towards extended historical composition. This experience I have also enjoyed, more for what it has taught me than for the competence it may have conferred upon my students, though nothing in Professor Walter Rundell's massive survey of graduate training implies that historical writing, *qua* writing, is now common in our graduate schools, or ever has been.[1]

In any consideration of priorities, however, it is all but impossible to avoid the conclusion that before writing is, reading must be. And by reading we mean a goodly sampling of "all that man has thought and said and done." This doctrine, little questioned in other eras, has lost most of its force in ours, less from the modern tendency to high specialization than from a partial abandonment, at least, of the humanistic tradition in American and European scholarship. But such neglect can be indulged only at a certain cost—in its worst form by an embarrassing exhibition of cultural unawareness in writing, in its least offensive form, by insights unconsciously missed. From the positive side, wide reading by the historian can be formative of style, perhaps even of a certain wisdom in the management and interpretation of data. For there is scarcely anything in man's historical and cultural experience which has not been examined somewhere, at some time, by someone. It is almost useless to speak of beauty if the speaker has not examined it himself in the poetry, ballad, psalm, and prose epic of peoples from the Athenians to the creative intellects of our own era. The words "heroic" and "heroic peoples" are practically forbidden the historian who is unfamiliar with Homer's *Iliad* and *Odyssey* and Virgil's *Aeneid*. Roland, Beowulf, Chaucer, Shakespeare, Milton, Goethe, Schiller— what do these hold for the historian of man, his societies, and his wars?

1 Walter Rundell, *In Pursuit of American History: Research and Training in the United States, passim.* The syllabus of Professor David Donald's graduate seminar at Johns Hopkins, at pp. 374–78 in this study, indicates a much more than average emphasis upon historical construction, if not upon the rhetoric described in the present book.

The fiction which can be called great is a vast store. But the narrative historian who has missed the naturalistic novel, from Gustave Flaubert, whose *Madame Bovary* gave it birth, to Ernest Hemingway's *The Short Happy Life of Francis Macomber*, may wish he knew it when he finds in a historical character a major and persistent flaw which may be said to lead to his ruin.

The humanistic foundation which lies under history in any of its phases obviously includes much more than the beautiful and the true. It can hardly escape science and technology, even though until recently it was a rare scientist who knew anything about the history of his own specialty. The world from the middle of the eighteenth century became increasingly science-oriented and increasingly dependent upon technology, so that the debates of legislative bodies and the content of newspapers, magazines, and books found more and more to report to a public poorly prepared to honor it or, by its social stratifications, to welcome it.

These are some of the attractions of reading, but there is still another, in philosophical thought, from which at least two of the acceptable assumptions of the Western historian may be drawn. It is customary, of course, to remind those who aspire to write history that the task should be approached without preconceptions or even broad social or political assumptions. It is true that, for those who subscribe to Marx and an inverted Hegel, the avoidance of doctrinal commitment has no bearing. These practitioners, however, are outside our concern. In the West, if we strip away all other assumptions, we still are left with two, without which we can scarcely proceed at all. The first of these is the notion of freedom of choice.

Said Immanuel Kant towards the end of the eighteenth century, While freedom is the *ratio essendi* of the moral law, the moral law is the *ratio cognoscendi* of freedom.[2] Freely rendered, this means that while freedom is the condition of the moral law, the moral law is the recognition of freedom. In politics and law and administration as well as in ethics, freedom is the essential assumption or condition without which the historical construction has no place to go.

The second assumption which I think you may readily accept is a corollary of the first. It says that in historical writing you must exercise the severest possible detachment, overcoming, if you can, the most persistent assumptions and beliefs of your society and era. It is aptly demonstrated in the following quotation, in which E. F. Carritt writes about societies and how we may judge them:[3]

"Infanticide, slavery, and other customs now condemned were suffered by the highly civilized Greeks; as are suttee, polygamy, and suicide by some modern races. To eat your parents, to sacrifice your first born, to refrain from washing; there is hardly anything so monstrous or so trivial that it has not been considered somewhere a duty, though somewhere else a crime. For one man private property is the sacred foundation of society, for another it is the source of all injustice. Plato, the puritan and the greatest of philosophers, advocated the abolition of marriage. And so men are apt to doubt if the duties most accepted today are anything but the prejudices of convention and training. It is not easy to be uninfluenced by surroundings and tradition. Had we been born in another continent we might not have inherited from chivalry an ideal of honour, but might have shuddered at the pollution of our caste or the impiety of taking animal life. The northerner is apt to condemn passion, the southerner to despise calculation. Take no thought for the morrow,

2 John Watson, tr., *The Philosophy of Kant*, 250–58; 271 ff.
3 E. F. Carritt, *The Theory of Morals*, 6–7.

give to everyone that asketh, turn the cheek to the smiter; what is the relation of these maxims to the duties of thrift, of philanthropy, of respect for law?"

In some senses, the corollary is more important than the major proposition, for it redirects our attention to the broadest and, to detached critics in other continents, the most persistent flaw in American historical writing: it is the purely national point of view, at best parochial in its outlook, from a critical point of view still where Edward Augustus Freeman and John Fiske had left it with their belief in the "endless linear progress of man."[4] Any student who approaches a serious writing task in American history will find it difficult to divorce himself from this tendency, which is to be found in countless examplars upon which he will unconsciously draw. But if he can he must imagine himself a man "on a peak in Darien," surveying his episode with the eyes of a visitor of another land, undisturbed by national interests or fate and capable of offering provocative, sometimes even amusing, insights. Thomas Babington Macaulay has commented upon this essential, but in a way which has sometimes been overlooked:

"Most people look at past times as princes look at foreign countries. More than one illustrious stranger has landed on our island amidst the shouts of the mob, has dined with the King, has hunted with the master of stag-hounds, has seen the guards reviewed, and a knight of the garter installed; has cantered along Regent Street, has visited St. Paul's, and noted down its dimensions; and has then departed, thinking he has seen England. He has, in fact, seen a few public buildings, public men, and public ceremonies. But of the vast and complex system of society, of the fine shades of

[4] Allan Nevins, "In Defence of History," in Whit Burnett, ed., *This is My Best*, 1028.

national character, of the practical operation of government and laws, he knows nothing. He who would understand these things rightly must not confine his observations to palaces and solemn days. He must see ordinary men as they appear in their ordinary business and in their ordinary pleasures. He must mingle in the crowds of the exchange and the coffee-house. He must obtain admittance to the convivial table and the domestic hearth. He must bear with vulgar expressions. He must not shrink from exploring even the retreats of misery. He who wishes to understand the condition of mankind in former ages must proceed on the same principle."[5]

In short, to the sin of parochialism must be added another common one, the limited, the incomplete view even from the detached level of pure scholarship. It is one to which the searcher after a thesis or dissertation subject must be peculiarly alert. For the small, well-delimited area usually chosen for exploitation in one of these forms often invites straight-line treatment. Thus an account of the New York Stock Exchange between the years 1890 and 1900 might tell us a good deal about trading, financial crises, and the attitude of government towards the so-called "free market in securities," without ever coming to grips with the character of the traders and the scenes on the trading floor on hectic days. The mistake is not one that a Walter Bagehot or a Vernon Louis Parrington would make.[6] Similarly, there is a natural-science requirement in any undertaking devoted to American exploration from the time of Lewis and Clark forward, and a botanical one for the history of grazing lands, for what was on the land is the prime condition of its being grazed. The internal contradictions in the history of political parties have often been vaguely felt and still more often

---

[5] Thomas Babington Macaulay, "History," *Edinburgh Review*, 1828.

not pursued by those who have chosen to deal with these centers of power in American life.

Individual failures to cope with these conditions and these questions, along with many more like them, have occurred within the last decade and a half. As Macaulay observed in a quite different context, they arise from too narrow a view and less than adequate investigation of factors traditionally (and conveniently) overlooked. And as John Walton Caughey has shown, myth-making in American history flows less from conscious design than from the acceptance of unanalyzed assumptions, whose power to distort is scarcely less than that of incompleteness.[7]

Any attempt in this book, however, to draw up a satisfying casuistical list—a convenient inventory of sins to be avoided—has to be restrained. The task, rather, is a considerably more positive one, i.e., providing a brief manual of historical writing procedures, leaving to competent theorists the large range of historical styles and motivations as conceived by the masters. From this point of view, there can be little doubt about what comes first. Every student has struggled with it early, and all who continue in the profession of "historical faith" struggle with it late. It is, as we have suggested earlier, the conceptualization of their findings. This and this alone affords the basis for starting a paper, a chapter, or a whole book. The Dutch historian Johann Huizinga (1872–1945) wrote in depth about the character, processes, and limitations of conceptualization. Perhaps his most telling statement is his least complex:

"It is not the size of the subject that determines the im-

6 Walter Bagehot, *Lombard Street: A Description of the Money Market*; Vernon Louis Parrington, *Main Currents in American Thought*, III, 7ff.

7 John Walton Caughey, Presidential Address, "Our Chosen Destiny," Mississippi Valley Historical Association, April, 1965, in *The Journal of American History*, Vol. LII, No. 2 (September, 1965), 239–52.

portance of a study: the student of a world-shaking conflict can produce the most short-sighted analysis. The important thing is the spirit in which the work is undertaken. It may sound paradoxical, but in history synthesis occurs to a certain extent in the act of analysis itself, since historical knowledge is primarily a view of something—much as people passing through a landscape absorb its beauty as they go."[8]

Just so the student, as he moves through the landscape of his data—that ever growing assemblage of factual cards— must consciously or unconsciously find there the element or elements that will make his final synthesis possible. In military history, it may be a combination of overextended lines of supply and an unfortunate choice of wheeled vehicles over half-tracks, as in Germany's deployment of her forces against Soviet Russia in World War II.[9] In British colonial history, the unlearned lessons of the American Revolution in the Canadian crisis of 1845.[10] Or in cultural-intellectual history, the failure to perceive that Russia's early rejection of British empiricism was a continuous process, almost inevitable in later Soviet political and social doctrine.[11]

"In particular facts," says Huizinga, "great contexts are recognized; without knowledge of the particular, that of general phenomena becomes dry and lifeless. At just one point in time, in the Roman Empire shortly before the dawn of Christianity, Caesar lived. But Caesar is compre-

8 J. Huizinga, "The Idea of History," in Fritz Stern, ed., *The Varieties of History from Voltaire to the Present*, 300.

9 Major General F. W. von Mellenthin, *Panzer Battles: A Study of the Employment of Armor in the Second World War*, 153.

10 John George Lambton, Earl of Durham, *Report on the Affairs of British North America*, ed. by Sir C. P. Lucas, 3 vols., *passim*.

11 Stuart Ramsay Tompkins, *The Russian Intelligentsia: Makers of the Revolutionary State*, 243ff.

hensible to me only because I can compare him with Alexander and Napoleon. Was I looking for a comparison, the Emperor-General as such? If that were so, I might lay aside Caesar, Alexander, and Napoleon at the end of my research, just as the biologist throws away the remains of his experiment. I was looking for the figure of *Caesar* in its uniqueness, in its difference from countless other figures, in its likeness to a few."[12]

What Huizinga is saying is that it is useless to fight the battle of synthesis *versus* analysis: they occur together. But from at least one point of view, analysis is the heart of business. If you haven't found out what your research data mean, you can't very well write the synthesis entailed in productive historical work. For good or ill, the writing of history is an intellectual occupation, as exacting of thought as any of the other humanistic or social-science disciplines, including that delightful form of history, epistemology, from René Descartes to Alfred North Whitehead.

Conceptualization is many things: point of view; a "justness" which John Dryden called the "foundation of good writing"; a grasp of the unity underlying divergent forces and individuals; the apparent design in an historical episode; and even that grasp of historical reality which emerges from incongruities.[13] Too often in the past it has simply been assumed, when in practice it must be rather fully understood in order to be put to work. But for our immediate purposes, reducing it to its simplest definition —point of view or point of departure for an historical undertaking—we can see it in operation in the work of

12 Huizinga, *loc. cit.*, 298.
13 Citing *The Oxford English Dictionary*, 13 vols., would ordinarily offend the historical rule against accounting for the obvious, but the student will find there meanings and shades for the conceptual tasks in history which are far from obvious.

two American historians writing on the same subject, the Colonial Period. The first is Charles McLean Andrews, who complained in 1933 that previous assaults upon the subject had all started from the wrong point of view, namely the American rather than the English. Here, with the special and the more general data in hand, we have conceptualization at work:

"To the maritime states of Europe that bordered on the Atlantic Ocean in the seventeenth century the lands beyond the western seas were as real a frontier as ever were the regions beyond the Alleghenies to the people of the colonial and national periods in America itself. These European states were old settled communities, each with a vigorous past. They had emerged from the conditions of medieval life and were becoming modern—powerful monarchies with boundaries that were fairly well defined and governments that were taking on more and more a centralized form. In the thirteenth century industry and commerce had been subordinate interests in a world that was largely agricultural and feudal, the affairs of which were controlled in the main by the local communities—boroughs, towns, manors, and communes; but in the sixteenth century these interests were rapidly becoming the concern of the state. Louis XI in France and Henry VII in England saw in trade and commerce the future strength of their kingdoms and became kings of the merchants, encouraging the accumulation of capital and furthering by means of treaties with other states the welfare of those who were engaged in trade beyond the borders. This centralization of control in matters that involved the exchange of commodities and the production of wealth was accompanied by the faint stirrings of a national spirit, for the people were widening the range of their patriotism and were taking part and pride in something more comprehensive than the affairs of their local towns, manor, and parishes."[14]

Andrews, then, sees his problem, and therefore the start of his book, in the following terms: the consolidation of the English monarchy, the replacement of a largely agricultural economy by a manufacturing and trading one, and a readiness for mercantile management of possessions beyond the seas.

Now let us turn to Daniel J. Boorstin, writing in *The Americans: The Colonial Experience* in 1958:

In what amounts to a part-title page opening Book I, Boorstin tells us in just seven lines what his concept is for the colonial period: "America began," he writes, "as a sobering experience. The colonies were a disproving ground for utopias. In the following chapters we will illustrate how dreams made in Europe—the dreams of the zionist, the perfectionist, the philanthropist, and the transplanter—were dissipated or transformed by the American reality. A new civilization was being born less out of plans and purposes than out of the unsettlement which the New World brought to the ways of the Old." We then proceed to a page and a half of atmospheric data introducing Part I, and after that to the opening Chapter 1, which describes the Puritans, the first settlers of New England.

Thus we have conceptualization again, but of an entirely different character from Andrews'. Instead of seeing the colonial experience from the English side and from the concepts of economic causation, aggressive English nationalism, and state interest—mercantilist in character—in colonial development, as Andrews does, Boorstin sets out to answer the question which has always plagued us, as it has

[14] Charles McLean Andrews, *The Colonial Period of American History*, I, 1.

countless European historians, What made the radical difference between American and European character, govern-
mental concepts, and social and economic outlooks in the
century and a half of colonial life?

The one looks at what impelled European states to thrust
out colonially; the other, at the people and the considerations which impelled them to resettle in a wilderness. Of
the two, Boorstin's is the more imaginative, penetrating
concept, and his writing has much more dash and interest.
Both points of view, however, contain large measures of
historical truth and they complement each other.

Boorstin suggests in a number of passages his indebtedness to a great predecessor, Frederick Jackson Turner, who
conceptualized the importance of the frontier in American
development. It was the frontier, Boorstin writes, which
freed Americans from Old-World restrictions and attitudes
—in short, changed the character and outlooks of the mil-
lions who, in time, spread over the better, more temperate
part of the continent. What Turner did not explicitly state
was the relation of this frontier to the development of
Europe long after the better part of the continent was no
longer in European hands. This awaited the late Walter
Prescott Webb of Texas. Webb's concept, formalized in
The Great Frontier, sees the frontier as the economic blood-
bank of the Metropolis, which is the Old World of Europe,
settled, crowded, undersupplied with capital and trade. It
sees the interaction of the frontier in America and elsewhere with the Metropolis and the enormous stimulus it
provided both.

We have in Webb's work a union of two concepts, namely
the importance of the American colonial experiment to
Europe and, second, the influence the frontier had upon

colonials and, subsequently, U.S. nationals. Of the latter, Webb had this to say, "I think the case may be put this way: European institutions and practices wore themselves out against the abrasive frontier grindstone."

Any study of the colonial experience or of a developing American nationalism must answer the questions: What did colonials bring to the American continents? What changes occurred in their outlooks? Why did the changes occur? What peculiarly derived and what peculiarly developed ideas of political and social organization did they put into operation? What were the responses of the mother countries—England, France, and Spain? How did the colonial connections come to be dissolved?

Every historian who has attempted to deal with the colonial experience has had to raise these questions for himself. Most historians have access to essentially the same sets of documents. Yet, if you take three of them, as we have just done, you get three leading but disparate ideas, each with a considerable amount of merit.

There are obvious limitations upon conceptualization. One of them is that there are degrees of conceptualization appropriate to various types of historical undertakings. Some, as in the foregoing examples, demand a grand concept of historical development. But a seminar paper on the occupation of the Cherokee Outlet in Indian Territory by associated cattlemen demands something much less world-shaking. It may be as simple as the challenge of the Indian Office to fence-building by lessees, directed against the American trait of firm lines of control, or it may be the confusions of an Indian nation emerging for the first time as landlord on a grand scale.

Large or small, the historian's concept of meaning is the

device by which he and his readers are enabled to see the forest in spite of the trees. It is another aspect of the "peak in Darien."[15]

15 Literary-critical scholars have long since disposed of what Cortés saw from his "peak in Darien" as that phrase appears in John Keats's poem, "On First Looking Into Chapman's *Homer*." For us, it is figuratively the scholar's contemplative roost.

2. Opening Scenes

CONCEPTS can be highly satisfying but openings are often the stuff of which nightmares are made. There is a temptation to believe that only historians of great skill and experience can make them come off with disarming grace. The adjective here is the telling one, however, for honest craftsmen will usually admit that their grace is truly disarming—it usually costs them much sweat and some blood. The reasons are in part implicit in the historical time scale: working historians today are specialists in relatively limited eras, which, by their very nature, must be deftly separated from all the eras that have gone before and those that are known to have come after. To single out a period in the historical time continuum is to confront a disjunction. The required response is the exercise of any of a number of devices suggesting continuity from what precedes to what is now about to be narrated and described. Of the range of possibilities, Rudyard Kipling had this to say:

> There are nine and sixty ways
> Of constructing tribal lays,
> And every single one of them is right![1]

Clearly, the exercise of imagination in stylistic matters is no less incumbent upon the historian than upon the

[1] Rudyard Kipling, *In the Neolithic Age*.

creative spirits found in letters, criticism, drama, and art. Examples and analysis from some of the more notable historical undertakings will appear later in this book, but immediately we may learn much from a symposium on the California Gold Rush appearing in *Westways* for May, 1967. Here several established historians offer a wide and interesting set of openings to papers, important to us because all of the papers are addressed to the same subject.

Professor Rodman W. Paul, one of the best-known historians of mining, writing under the title, "When Was That Golden Day?" ushers his reader into the quest for credibility by asking him questions:

> How accurate are your recollections of an event that occurred one year ago? Ten years ago? Fifty years ago? As you try to recall an event that you shared with others, do the same remembered details recur to you as to the other eyewitnesses? For those interested in the original California gold discovery of 1848, these questions are not just rhetorical. Most of what we know about that great occurrence is based not on precise and full documents, but rather on a few incomplete contemporary records, plus a mass of reminiscences by participants who gave their conflicting versions long after the event. As any trial lawyer will tell you, the unreliability of the human memory is rivaled only by the discrepancies between accounts of rival witnesses who supposedly had equal opportunities for observation.

What follows in Professor Paul's account is essentially a narrative analysis of the worth of the several fragmentary documentary sources and the several other eyewitness recallings, long after the event, of the discovery of gold at Sutter's Mill. At the close he has established within perhaps a day's tolerance the time of the discovery and the name of the discoverer, James Wilson Marshall. But the minor details, he admits, may never be fully established. At that point, and to close his narrative, he repeats the first two questions with which he began.

A fine example of the professional historian's use of what we call point of view is contained in Professor Ray Allen Billington's opening to his paper, "The Overland Ordeal."

The East heard its first tales of California gold in August, 1848, but for four months remained politely skeptical; too many easterners in the past had fallen prey to western speculators who spread tales of riches as a device to peddle mining equipment or vacant lots. Then came President James K. Polk's message to Congress on December 5. "The accounts of the abundance of Gold in that territory," intoned the clerk as he read, "are of such an extraordinary character as would scarcely command belief were they not corroborated by authentic reports of officers in the public service."

In several succeeding paragraphs, Professor Billington develops the incoming news of gold for an eastern audience gradually converted to belief in what was actually happening in California, until "thousands, tens of thousands, in the East and Midwest closed their shops and began preparing for the journey."

It is important to emphasize that the point of view used in this example is that of eastern residents, and as such is ideal for an opening preceding the overland migration to California in 1849. Later we will have an opportunity to see a variety of uses of point of view, all of which offer two great advantages in openings: (1) they bridge disjunctions in time, place, and personalities or populations, and (2) they seize action at the time of its happening, dramatically but truthfully.

Richard H. Dillon, another thorough professional, who demonstrated his ability to command an audience by publishing a best-selling biography of Meriwether Lewis, chooses another point of view, that of the city nearby, for the opening to his paper, "Life in the City." Here is his opening:

> Sophisticated and self-satisfied, for all of its smallness, San Francisco was skeptical, at first, about the El Dorado rumored to exist in the foothills of the Sierra Nevada. Word of Jim Marshall's discovery was not slow in reaching the tiny "metropolis" of Alta California, but it was slow, indeed, to infect the port's people with gold-fever. Possibly this was because Captain Sutter sent samples to Doctor F. Forgeaud in San Francisco and the good doctor guessed, wrongly, that Marshall had found iron pyrites—fool's gold. Presumably, the word got around.

We may overlook the fact that both Billington and Dillon chose to look at gold-rush developments initially through the eyes of contemporary skeptics. The important thing is that a well-tried formula is demonstrated, and it works. And no student of the tricks of style will miss Dillon's last sentence in the passage quoted above.

That there had been clashes of cultures in California is evident from the pre-conquest papers of Thomas Oliver Larkin, the Mexican War observations of John Charles Frémont and Theodore Talbot, and the memoirs of American occupation by Don Mariano Vallejo, among others.[2] In the symposium under discussion, Professor W. H. Hutchinson, long-established as historian, biographer, and editor of scholarly materials, contributes "Gold as Culture's Catalyst." He begins rhetorically:

2 Thomas Oliver Larkin, *The Larkin Papers*, ed. by George P. Hammond; John Charles Frémont, *Memoirs of My Life*, I; Theodore Talbot, *Soldier in the West: Letters of Theodore Talbot During His Services in California, Mexico, and Oregon*, ed. by Robert V. Hine and Savoie Lottinville; Herbert Eugene Bolton, *Guide to Materials for the History of the United States in the Principal Archives of Mexico*, 286, 288, 337. John A. Hawgood, "The Pattern of Yankee Infiltration in Mexican Alta California, 1821–1846," *Pacific Historical Review*, Vol. XXVII (February, 1958), 27–38.

Culture is a word of many meanings, each as shimmering and restless as spilled quicksilver. Just one of these, *"What we do that the monkeys don't,"* may make guidelines for what follows.

Down eighty slow-paced years, the *Californianos* had adapted Spain's feudal mores to a beneficent wilderness, wherein they raised cattle and families with equal ease while fearing God and honoring their heritage.

Professor Hutchinson continues his explications of the descent of a culture from its Spanish origins in California to the arrival and subsequent conquest of cultural expressions by Anglo-Americans. The opening itself may be described as that of a restless and discerning intellect, in full command of the techniques of getting the reader's attention.

Professor John Walton Caughey, whose distinguished career at the University of California at Los Angeles is too well known to require comment, writes on the "Midas Touch." His opening technique is the use of an exclamation by an eyewitness:

"Boys, by God, I believe I've found a gold mine." The words are Jim Marshall's; the place, Coloma on the South Fork of the American River; the listeners, the crew at work building a sawmill; the time, a January morning in 1848. The exact date is not so clearly fixed, though the most educated guess is the 24th.

The choice of these five openings is intended to illustrate the rather wide latitude offered the historian for the employment of originality, in the first instance, and the swift ways in which people of skill can move from a standing start to action and conceptualization, in the second. The problems and the techniques for overcoming them are not confined to journal and magazine articles, however. The former often appear in their most exaggerated forms in the longer work—the dissertation, thesis, or book.

Sometimes in published histories, more often in dissertations freshly done, we see the non-book being born in the opening paragraphs. With a heavy hand, and often a heavy heart, the author starts his delimited subject without any preparation whatever fixing the historical episode in relation to what went before or what is to come after:

"General Philip Henry Sheridan received orders in August, 1867, to report to his commanding officer and friend, General William Tecumseh Sherman, heading up the Department of the Missouri at Jefferson Barracks at St. Louis, Missouri. The Indian troubles in the West, he was informed, would be part of his charge and responsibility."

Then quickly our author tells about Sheridan's birth, ancestors (some schools insist on carrying them back five centuries), career at West Point, and perhaps not at all his campaigns and responsibilities in the Civil War recently closed. After five or six pages of this begat material, we get Phil Sheridan on a train for St. Louis, without being told where he departed for that city. After that, we get a certain amount of fill-in on Sherman's military and administrative problems, particularly vis-à-vis the Indian disturbances from eastern Kansas to the Powder River Country of eastern Wyoming and Montana. This, too, is taken out of its long prior sequence and dumped into our laps, so that we must flounder in a morass of right-and-wrong without antecedents.

But there is a better way, obviously, and it appears in the late Carl Coke Rister's book, *Border Command: General Phil Sheridan in the West*.[3]

Sunday, April 2, 1865, was a gloomy day in Richmond, Virginia. Heavy clouds hung like moist blankets above the rooftops, and the smoke from chimneys settled earthward. For a

3 Pp. 3–6.

people who had withstood the vicissitudes of four years of war, the darkening weather was small matter. Quietly and serenely they moved in and out of the city. Here and there along the streets men stood in groups exchanging opinions on General Robert E. Lee's chances of saving the city, while housewives busied themselves with preparation for the sabbath.

At mid-morning Jefferson Davis, President of the Confederacy, sat at worship in St. Paul's Church. He had risen early and gone to his offices to examine briefly late reports and dispatches before attending church. The services were well in progress when a messenger hurried down the aisle and handed Davis a letter from Lee. He opened it hastily. The Confederate defenses at Petersburg, south of Richmond, were disintegrating and Richmond must be abandoned at once!

Davis left the church hurriedly and went directly to his executive offices where he found a sombre group of his aides and military men awaiting his decisions. He quickly issued orders for the burning of official records and the destruction of accumulated stores of provisions and war materials.

After a tense day of activity in the Confederate capital, the work was done and by midnight Davis and the officials of government had left Richmond for Danville. Nor had they departed any too soon, for early the following morning General U. S. Grant's vanguard entered the city accompanied by a band blaring, "Rally Round the Flag, Boys." At bitter last it had happened. It was three days before the fourth anniversary of the assault on Fort Sumter, and now the spiritual citadel of Davis and Lee and Johnston had fallen.

Up from Petersburg advanced a man, who perhaps more than any other had contributed to Lee's present misfortune. He was Major General Philip Henry Sheridan, the Yankee military leader, who had turned Lee's flank at Petersburg. Relentlessly he had attacked again and again the weary though still formidable Confederal right, until on the morning of April 1 it had drawn back, thus imperiling the whole Confederate position.

In successive paragraphs, Rister describes Sheridan's continuing pressure on and pursuit of Lee's forces, his capture of Confederate supply trains, and, to the dismay of Lee, his maneuver placing his determined forces on April 8 in front of Lee, squarely across the road to Lynchburg. Lee's surrender occurred the next day at McLean House near Appomattox Court House. "Among those privileged to witness Lee's surrender was the stocky little Sheridan, the pulsating embodiment of that aggressive action which had driven the Confederate commander to his final act. In physical stature, Sheridan was very short, and small; and his arms were said, facetiously, to have been so long that his hands reached below his knees. His Irish parentage was revealed in his face . . . ." After the author's swiftly developed description, we benefit from equally swift descriptions by contemporaries, Sheridan's parentage, family, service prior to the Civil War, and, finally his post–Civil War assignments leading to his duties in the West at Fort Leavenworth in 1867 and after, the central subject of the book.

Analytically, the method of starting the book in this instance is a species of flashback. It starts graphically, even dramatically, with a significant moment of action, and after clearing that action, in which at least the principal historical character and one or more of his antagonists are introduced, it is broken by a couple of blank spaces—a convention understood by practically all readers—and then goes back to antecedents or lays the groundwork for still further and future action. There are many possible variations, most of which can easily be developed by the historian once he has mastered the basic scheme here seen in operation.

In all probability, you have not read or seen a play in which something of the flashback was not employed. The ancient dramatists of Greece and Rome had to use it, quite as much as Shakespeare, Molière, and Eugene O'Neill. It does not occur early in straight narrative or historical writing. It is a relatively recent device for biography of the more scholarly kind, for historical subjects rather severely delimited in time and place, and even for subjects in economic, industrial, and agricultural history. Its virtues in the latter categories are more limited than in narrative history and biography, but it takes no master craftsman to describe the end of one era and the beginning of another on October 24, 1929, from the disastrous jumble of ticker tape flowing from machines at the corners of Wall and Broad streets in New York. Equally, the flashback may be the best device for getting into present action—let us say, the Irish famine of 1845–46—which then quickly moves into the larger economic, political, and industrial foundations for the repeal of the British corn laws; after that into the ensuing political and economic history of the next twenty years to the Second Reform Act of 1867. The flashback, we may repeat, is one of the more sophisticated devices for starting an historical episode. But as technique it cannot stand alone.

If we scan the Sheridan opening again, we see more clearly the supports which sustain the flashback from the General's approaching career in the West. In the first place, we have in fairly highly developed form another device known as scene-making. It contains the contrasting elements of an outward calm in Richmond and an inner misgiving about the city's chances of surviving as the nerve-center of the Confederacy. The increasing suspense, evident in the second paragraph depicting the scene in St. Paul's Church and in the third paragraph detailing the preparations for the abandonment of the city, adds a second element. By the opening of the fifth paragraph, we are ready to account for the military person central to the action before Richmond and in the ensuing book. The narrative account of his actions in the military advance constitutes a third element. Finally, the partly quoted description of Sheridan offers a fourth and very necessary one, too often neglected entirely by writers of history as they address themselves to large issues.

We shall have a good many more encounters with scene-making, the management of historical time, and characterization in later sections of this book. But a flashback of the type here analyzed requires immediate identification of its components, if the example is to serve a useful purpose. Meanwhile, having been exposed to historical scene, we should consider it descriptively and in its two most readily recognizable forms, the first of which was developed in the Sheridan example; the second, as it appears in institutional, national, or other more impersonal forms of historical writing.

A work of history or biography of the narrative genre consists of scenes closely tied to chronology and to place. All of it must be the product of carefully organized research, subject to the most meticulous documentation. But the techniques of writing it do not flow solely from the historical process. They flow from man's long struggle with all other literary forms, some of them fictional, some dramatic, others from description, characterization, and explication. Historical writing, in the final analysis, must employ at one time or another practically all of the devices that have been created since the Assyrians, Babylonians, Greeks, and the Western world's Maya authors committed their heroic and religious accounts and poetry to writing.

Reading, as has been suggested earlier, will reveal the keys: John Galsworthy, the novelist, opening one of his

novels with the wedding of the daughter of a now aging
Soames Forsythe, a widower standing reflectively and alone
as the newlyweds drive away. It is the flashback again. But
what of that memorable opening of another novel; "It was
the best of times, it was the worst of times, it was the age of
wisdom, it was the age of foolishness, it was the epoch of
belief, it was the epoch of incredulity, it was the season of
Light, it was the season of Darkness . . . in short, the period
was so far like the present period . . . ." It was the beginning
based upon ironic explication through valid and undeni-
able opposites. But can anyone who has read Charles
Dickens ever mistake the atmosphere it evokes?

It is but a short step from the narrative scene-opening in
history to the atmosphere or spirit of an episode, even of
an age, in the cultural or literary-historical field. It is often
part of, indeed no more than a few steps away from, the
author's concept of his subject. But in most instances it is
best not done without, for the other possible choices often
appear less than adequate. The cultural-historical series,
The Centers of Civilization, offers us some notable examples of book openings embodying the atmosphere or spirit
of a subject. The purpose in quoting four of them here is
to demonstrate the applicability of this technique, as I say,
one step removed from scene-making, to the second category
of history, i.e., institutional, national, cultural, or other
more impersonal forms.

The first example is from *Antioch in the Age of Theodosius the Great,* by Professor Glanville Downey of Indiana
University:

In July and August of every leap year in the Julian calendar,
visitors journeyed to Antioch in Syria from all over the Graeco-
Roman World. The immediate occasion of their coming was
the quadrennial Olympic Games of Antioch, a festival which

had been established in the Syrian capital as long ago as the time of Augustus (23 B.C.–A.D. 14) and Claudius (A.D. 41–54). These games had in fact by the reign of the Emperor Theodosius the Great (A.D. 379–95) become almost more famous than the original Olympic Games in Greece for which they were named. The festival offered something for everyone—athletic contests of all kinds, horse races, musical contests, declamations, and literary displays. Held in the rainless months when the summer weather was at its best, they had come to be a popular fixture in the world of that day.

But it was not always simply the games that attracted people to Antioch. The city was commonly held to be the finest in the Greek East—the historian Ammianus Marcellinus, himself an Antiochene, called it "the fair crown of the Orient". . . .

The key element in this opening is the movement of people to a city for the enjoyment of sports and scenes and music and art, very much as people do in our own time. For it cannot be said too often that history is nothing without people—it is geology or botany or zoology.

For Richard Nelson Frye of Harvard, the problem of opening his contribution to the Centers of Civilization Series, *Bukhara: The Medieval Achievement*, was greatly simplified by the evidence of greatness supplied by a near-contemporary historian, Juvaini, who fixed the city in its intellectual and religious terms:

"In the Eastern countries Bukhara is the cupola of Islam and is in these regions like unto Baghdad. Its environs are adorned with the brightness of the lights of doctors and jurists and its surroundings embellished with the rarest of high attainments. Since ancient times it has in every age been the place of assembly of the great savants of every religion. Now the derivation of Bukhara is from *bukhar*, which in the language of the Magians signifies 'center of learning.' This word closely resembles a word in the language of the Uighur and Kitayan idolaters, who call their places of worship, which are idol temples, *bukhar.* But at the time of its foundation the name of the town was Bumijkath." So wrote the Persian historian Juvaini about 1260, long after the Mongols had taken and sacked Bukhara. The Golden Age of the city had passed but Bukhara never completely lost its importance even down to the end of the Tsarist empire in 1918.

Many routes were open to John J. Murray of Coe College, a leading authority on the Low Countries, for the start of his book, *Amsterdam in the Age of Rembrandt.* But which force besides artistic and intellectual creativity has dominated the lives of Amsterdamers from the beginning of their settlement on the Amstel? It is unmistakably the sea:

Amsterdam, a city rich in history, outstanding in art, and colorful in appearance, is closely linked with the sea, as indeed is the entire history of the Low Countries. The Dutch say, "He who cannot master the sea is not worthy of the land," and "God made the world but the Dutch made Holland." The same can be said even more appropriately for Amsterdam and the Amsterdamers, for they reversed the process of evolution. In the world there was first the sea and the mire with life and man emerging from the mucky chaos. There was also sea and mire where the Amstel sluggishly emptied into the Zuider Zee—now the IJsselmeer. River and sea joined in a large protective inlet called the IJ or Y. To that place man came. Instead of rising from the mud he built on it a city of poise, of courage, of real beauty, which since the beginning of the seventeenth century has been one of the most unusual cultural centers of the world.

The evident incongruity which Edward Wagenknecht, the distinguished professor of literature at Boston University, found in modern Chicago (his home-city) as "a radiating cultural influence" (a phrase from my Invitation to the Contributors to the Series) emerges loud and clear:

The Rhetoric of History

"Center of Civilization"?—Chicago? The City of Al Capone and "Big Bill" Thompson ("Throw away your hammer and get a horn")? The "Hog Butcher for the World"? The city which achieved a great World's Fair and murdered the mayor at the end of it? which welcomed an archbishop to his new diocese at a civic dinner where a crazy chef put arsenic in his soup? Even so.

There is no use trying to be neutral about Chicago or the land which she inhabits. Nobody ever has been.[4]

Three quarters of a century ago, a young man went down to the University of Oklahoma from Kansas via Harvard, to coach a still unformed football team and to teach literature to students from Oklahoma and Indian territories. Today, hardly anyone doing the undergraduate program at Harvard can escape Vernon Louis Parrington's *Main Currents in American Thought*. I gather that one of the favorite indoor sports at Cambridge is to show, with a certain air of learning, how Parrington exhibited a strong populist bias and that he was not always entirely historical. But we read Parrington for other reasons, his style and his management of a fairly complex literary, intellectual, and cultural development in the United States up to a time shortly before his death in 1929. His style, often rich in metaphors, is characterized by purposeful movement and rhythmical structure. Here is how he lays down a scene to open his account of post–Civil War America in Volume 3 of his classic study:

The pot was boiling briskly in America in the tumultous postwar years. The country had definitely entered upon its freedom and was settling its disorderly household to suit its democratic taste. Everywhere new ways were feverishly at work transforming the countryside. In the South another order was

4 *Chicago*, 3.

32

rising uncertainly on the ruins of the plantation system; in the East an expanding factory economy was weaving a different pattern of industrial life; in the Middle Border a recrudescent agriculture was arising from the application of the machine to the rich prairie soil. All over the land a spider web of iron rails was being spun that was to draw the remotest outposts into the common whole and bind the nation together with steel bands . . . .[5]

Admitting that the perfect historian has yet to be born among us, it remains that Parrington in many passages of *Main Currents* and others of his works is at once an exemplar and the despair of those who aspire to stylistic mastery. Of his sometimes sardonic portraiture, we shall see more later.

The springtime of American or European redevelopment, exemplified for the former by Parrington's scene, inevitably gives way to the heat of political summer, the fall's winds of controversy, and the winter's cold blasts of war. This is not to suggest seasonal rhythms in history or even decennial rhythms. But human affairs are characterized by crises, fed by tensions between kings, statesmen, or peoples; or between those who take positions in law, politics, religion, or taste and those who take contrary positions; or between those who periodically take the field against each other in the ultimately decisive games of war.

When an era chosen for book-length development begins with crisis, it is obviously a matter of good fortune to the historian. I say obviously, but not without the need to qualify. For a scene-opening which capitalizes on crisis in any of the above-indicated forms, or others which will readily come to mind, is far rarer in practice than it should be. I am aware, however, that there have been misgivings

[5] Vernon Louis Parrington, *Main Currents in American Thought*, III, 3.

about the use of this structural device in the writing of history. They began as long ago as in the time of Tacitus (b. A.D. 54–56), whose *Annals* open with action (*"Primum facinus novi principatus fuit Postumi Agrippae caedes"*) and much of whose historical theme was personal conflict and the tragic fate of the Roman Empire in the reign of Tiberius, dramatically presented.[6] The corresponding dramatic bravura in Leopold von Ranke's first book, *Fürsten und Völker, 1494–1514* (1824) has attracted little notice in recent times, perhaps because of the currency of a single but mostly misrepresented phrase from his *Vorrede* to that book, *"wie es eigentlich gewesen."*[7] But it is not bravura we're after. It is simply the legitimate use of historical data for a just historical presentation. We find it in the opening paragraphs of Sir Herbert Butterfield's *The Peace Tactics of Napoleon, 1806–1808,* capturing the scene after the Jena campaign:

The fine show of armies arrayed and kings in proud posture had collapsed into medley and muddle in the twin battles of Jena and Auerstädt. It littered the countryside and strove painfully to sort itself out afresh, as the din subsided and the smoke cleared away. Napoleon, sprawling upon the ground to study his maps, fell into an undignified sleep, and his guard took silent stand around him. Murat, writing to his master, apologised: "Your Majesty will pardon my scribble, but I am alone and dropping from fatigue,"[8] and he who was no weakling blundered the strokes of his pen, as if he had been drunk. The release from the tension of battle liberated the worst elements in the army. The forces of the very victors seemed endangered by indiscipline.

6 Clarence W. Mendell, *Tacitus: The Man and His Work,* 125–37.

7 Leopold von Ranke, *Die Meisterwerke,* ed. by Willy Andreas, I, 3–5 (*Vorrede*), *passim.*

8 *Lettres et documents pour servir à l'histoire de Joachim Murat,* IV, 391 (1910).

Opening Scenes

"The footsteps of the corps d'armée," wrote Soult a few days later, "are marked by fire, devastation, and crimes atrocious beyond belief. The orders of the leaders are despised, the lives of officers endangered, and as a crowning evil the resources and food afforded by the country are destroyed as French Troops come upon the scene."

A stray English traveler who came by soon after the battle found a devastating sight, the ground littered with papers, letters, account books, pamphlets and miscellaneous unwanted goods, while the French rummaged baggage waggons, tossed part of the booty to the country people clamouring around, and with the recklessness of light-hearted soldiery invited all passers-by to stop and share their luck.[9] All was in disarray and men went off to shoot game or to steal poultry, to ransack houses or to pilfer farms. "Never was pillage carried further than in this campaign and disorder extended even to insubordination." The Prussians, in still worse condition, had all their evils complicated by panic. In the morning they had lightened their burdens by throwing away their food, and the end of the battle found them scattering through the villages to satisfy hunger and thirst, digging up potatoes and turnips in the fields, and rushing blindly, officers and men alike, ignorant of the true direction of retreat.[10]

With what scene, what crisis, what confrontation do we begin a book when crisis is at hand? Professor Butterfield of Peterhouse, Cambridge, has surely shown us.

[9] *Private and Confidential . . . Narrative of the Circumstances Which Led to an Interview Between the Emperor Napoleon and G. Sinclair*, by Sir George Sinclair (1826).
[10] Sir Herbert Butterfield, *The Peace Tactics of Napoleon, 1806–1808*, 3–4.

3. Structure: Narration

THERE is an unfortunate but widely held theory that if you know enough about a subject a book about it will largely write itself. Books of history which have resulted from this convenient process are practically unknown. Even a fast start will fail if the runner has no bottom. Aside from the rather fearful burden of research which historical projects impose, they do not lend themselves to easily contrived forms, one of which, the chronological, is sometimes found to resemble the Mad Hatter's advice to Alice, when she asked, "How shall I begin?" "Begin at the beginning," he said, "go on to the end, then stop."

Books—even uncomplicated ones—require what can only be called structure. In this the objective is to make them hang together. However satisfying a seemingly workable structure may be to the historian writing his book, that in itself may not be enough. The structure must fit the requirements of the subject and for bottom, or staying power, it must also convince the reader that he had better not put the book down except for a cause unconnected with its scholarly merit and interest. The first of these two requirements is rooted in the nature of the historical task which the writer has chosen to face up to: Is it basically narrative? Is it descriptive and analytical? Does it require large amounts of exegesis or explication? How great is the element of quantification? Are the foci found in leading persons or in the vicissitudes of an institution? How best should the historian give structure to economic, public-policy, and administrative topics?

There are no easy answers to these questions, for each serious study imposes analysis of its special structural requirements. But for each type of subject, there may be from two to five *possible* courses of development, one of which will prove, when joined with writing skill much above average, to be closer to the ideal than the rest. The evidence of this range of options is contained in the twice-, sometimes thrice-told tales which appear from decade to decade, most of them restudied by reviewers for historical journals, often with something more than a hint of questioning, "Should this really have been done again?"

The test of structural excellence rests as much with the uniqueness of the historian's approach as with the uniqueness of the subject itself. What general and what specific means has he adopted for giving form to his subject? The distressing truth is that historical constructions of high merit tend to conceal by their grace the very architecture which makes them admirable. But there can be little question about the course the tyro must adopt: He must find the uniqueness which characterizes his subject. He must arrive at working drawings for its development. He must give to the ultimate construction his own uniqueness of grasp.

The determination of the first of these considerations is a phase of the historical process—of historical awareness joined with detailed research. The second will be described immediately below. The third is the rich stuff of which historical success is made.

First off, every book-length work of history should contain the following parts:

37

Bastard title, containing, well above center, title and sub-title only.

Title page, containing title, subtitle, author's name, and near foot place of publication, name of publisher, and some-times year date, so written (since you will not know until acceptance of the typescript who your publisher is).

Copyright page, with list of acknowledgments for copy-righted materials reproduced in your own work.

Dedication page (the customary "To My Wife But for Whom . . ." is now giving way to more imaginative senti-ments).

Preface.

Acknowledgments.

Table of contents.

List of illustrations.

List of maps.

Book half-title (just like the bastard title).

The text of the study, arranged in numbered, titled chap-ters.

Bibliography.

Index (to follow after the work has been set into type, proofread, paged, and delivered in page proofs to the author).

The list is conventional and generalized, but it does afford a kind of preliminary outline for the historical-work-to-be. For theses and dissertations, the structure given above is varied somewhat and is best developed in the instruc-tions issued by particular graduate schools and in Kate L. Turabian, *A Manual for Writers of Term Papers, Theses, and Dissertations, Third Edition, Revised* (University of Chicago Press, 1967), a paperback.

In any consideration of working procedures, the question inevitably arises, Shouldn't the development of a title pre-cede the actual writing of the dissertation or book? For many people more or less final titling is indispensable; for others it can be allowed to rest until the main task has been accomplished. But in the end the title is of very great importance: it tells everyone what the book is about; it may assist in the formative stages of conceptualization; and it often affords the author structural notions which would have been vague at best without it. All working titles, however, need careful re-evaluation before the author attempts to interest a publisher in his work. In choosing a title, you should try to satisfy two objectives: (1) What are people most likely to be looking for? and (2) To what extent can you interest them, by title, in getting your book and reading it?

The first objective, stated in question form, points to subject-cataloging in libraries everywhere. The answer to it is best given by example: if the book is an ethnohistory of the Comanche Indians, the best title it can bear, in all likelihood, is *The Comanches*.[1] Library catalogers work from this above-board choice to the further subject classifications important to book users, such as Indians, history, ethnology, folkways, and so on. In history, short, one-punch titles are best. Figurative and alliterative titles are to be avoided, as are plays on words. If we choose *Lords of the South Plains* as the principal title for the book about the Comanches, we have begun the process of burying the book even before it is published. The second objective in titling, of getting people to use your book, is attainable by something of the directness outlined in the foregoing example. And use is the historian's surest avenue to immortality.

[1] Ernest Wallace and E. Adamson Hoebel, *The Comanches: Lords of the South Plains*. Historians may take comfort, as the late Bernard De Voto did, from George E. Hyde, who wrote: "There is no more sense in writing 'seven Oglala' than in writing 'seven Spaniard' or even 'seven western state.'" My own choice in thirty years of editing *The Civilization of the American Indian Series* was regular English plurals over the ethnic kind. Bernard De Voto, *Across the Wide Missouri*, xiv.

From some points of view, more is to be learned about significance, and thereby about structure, from the next important feature of the historian's book, namely its preface, than from any other part, except the text itself. All that we have said about the uniqueness of subject and uniqueness of the author's grasp of it comes to a head here. Conceptualization in its crispest form ought to take place here. A preface is a species of essay, more likely to test the author's skill as writer than almost anything else he may do.

In practice, prefaces are often written after the author has completed the text of his work—a course to which there can be little objection. But too often, after the heat and muddle of extended composition, the preface gets short shrift, so that what appears in print serves small purpose, if any. I do not say that a preface should be written ahead of the text; rather, that a preliminary draft may be useful in the formation of emphasis and ultimate structure, while the final draft, written with all conceptual brilliance, may be allowed to wait until the final chapter is in hand.

A preface is, or ought to be, a distillation. As such it should be relatively short. When these two things have been said, they should suffice. But they will not, for there is no widespread understanding of the form—or forms—in which this distillation should be presented. Certain concepts should be kept in mind as the author begins his preface:

1. Early the question must be answered, Why was it important to undertake this episode in history?

2. Answer the question, What new or different light does this undertaking throw upon the period under consideration?

3. What bearing does this period or episode have upon the periods or episodes immediately before and immediately after?

4. What light does the period or episode throw upon the larger historical movement?

5. If others have covered the same subject before you, what special considerations dictated a new assault upon the problem? (Obviously, hitherto unused or unknown primary sources, as for examples, letters, manuscript memoirs, or archival resources missed by others, which now give new meaning to the subject.)

6. What does the development of your subject do for or against earlier estimates of individual figures, e.g., George III in the contest with the American colonies, as Sir Lewis Namier and Professor Charles R. Ritcheson were called upon to do?[2]

All of these are merely formularies, obviously not to be used seriatim or to the exclusion of questions equally or more important in varying situations. But all of us who read your work have a right to know why, in your opinion, it was important to devote an entire book to the subject of your choice. Moreover, as historian you owe it to yourself to make the statement, for today and possibly for posterity. A preface is a statement of purpose, of need, of new significance. It requires restraint, as when an historical editor discovers that two eyewitness accounts have just shown up in a London attic two centuries after Braddock's defeat.[3] It requires candor, as when the historian of the later Roman Empire tells us precisely what he has chosen to avoid in his account.[4] It may indeed call for explication of the spirit of the age and a glimpse of some of the rascals in it, as when

2 Lewis B. Namier, *England in the Age of the American Revolution*; Charles R. Ritcheson, *British Politics and the American Revolution*.

3 Charles Hamilton, ed., *Braddock's Defeat: The Journal of Captain Robert Cholmley's Batman, The Journal of a British Officer, Halkett's Orderly Book*, xi–xii.

4 A. H. M. Jones, *The Later Roman Empire, 284–602: A Social, Economic, and Administrative Survey*, I, v–viii.

the historian of oil essays an account of personal failure.[5] In almost every case there is room in the background for a hint, at least, of the bearing of a particular book upon the larger issues of historical truth—which are somehow always a trifle in doubt. Not least of all, a good preface is the best answer to the reviewer, who often reviews the book he thinks you should have written.

The superstructure that is to rise from this small but important base requires larger plans and a bolder concept. A simplified plan, represented by a tentative table of contents, will not always provide maximum help. For the character of the subject and the theaters of its development can take at least three forms: the more or less straight chronological, a topical one, or a combination of the two. Ordinarily, the more extended the period under consideration the more logically it lends itself to chronological construction. Similarly, the shorter the period the more it calls for a topical development. And for a study covering a half-century, let us say, devoted to the growth of political and social institutions, a combination of the chronological and topical methods is a first choice. Beyond this point it is unsafe to categorize, since the permutations and combinations open to the gifted will always extend, as in the plots developed by those who create fiction from men's lives, to at least a dozen. But of the character of chronologically developed history, more analysis is needed.

Chronology, which came fairly late in human development, is one of the firm organizational means by which we present history. The last two words in the preceding sentence are, if anything, more important than the first word. For history is also a species of story-telling: what happened

5 John Joseph Mathews, *Life and Death of an Oilman: The Career of E. W. Marland*, vii–x.

is more important than when it happened. We are not long about our historical tasks when we make the discovery that "what happened" is a topical matter and that the topic which gives meaning to the event is significant in spite of, rather than because of, the time limits in which it occurs. Any well developed chronological method, therefore, will contain a high degree of topicality—even though no chapter titles in the table of contents reflect that fact. Topicality is the direct consequence of the questions the historian asks of himself and of his data: What makes the period worth examining? What was at stake? Who advanced and who failed? What was the ultimate outcome? What does this episode mean to the larger fabric of history?

A properly managed chronological structure is Janus-like, one of its faces looks ahead in time, the other back at unfolding events. (The British historian A. J. P. Taylor reminds us that "we know what is going to happen. The characters of our history did not.")[6] Our arrangement of events within the chronology of our episode is the order we give to what we now define as historical narration. This order, this topical development, is what takes mere chronology out of its deep and forbidding trough.

When historical narration is effectively managed, it contains two equally indispensable elements, (1) movement and (2) perspective. The first comes into play when the historian knows intimately and with a high degree of completeness the persons, institutions, events, and conditions contributing action towards an outcome. The second, perspective, which is of larger proportion than outcome, however important the latter may be, imbues in good hands the historical story-telling process or narration. Perspective is a

[6] A. J. P. Taylor, "Fiction in History," *Times Literary Supplement* (London), March 23, 1973, pp. 327–28.

detached word when seen in printed form. In action it is anything but calm and reflective. It is a thing of some excitement and much urgency. It insists that the truth, as the historian has found it, be told—and told with the emphasis it deserves.

In the foregoing, we are not only making a commitment to narrative history as such but we are advancing towards some of the structural problems with which it is beset and their solutions. Narrative history, as distinguished from chronology, is the oldest of our forms: as oral information, it preceded any of the forms of writing, though it early developed many conventions, such as the recitative, the epic poem or prose account of past events, simple and more complex histories of tribes and peoples, and individual warriors' accounts of their exploits in far lands. The conventions were formalized in Homer's *Iliad* and *Odyssey*, the Anglo-Saxon *Beowulf*, and the Maya *Popol Vuh*. Their tellers affirmed that they were true. Today we are less concerned with their absolute claims to accuracy than with their generalized importance as folk-memory and the power of their literary constructions.

After early folk-memory had found its forms and expressions and was later captured in writing, the actual witness of great events set down history—a Thucydides writing about the contemporary Peloponnesian Wars, Xenophon recording in the *Anabasis* his experiences of the great march on and retreat from Artaxerxes II's hosts, and Tacitus coping in the *Annals* with the reign of Tiberius. All of it was in narrative form, the most natural construction open to anyone who felt impelled to preserve the record he had gathered first-hand. A far more serious test of the narrative method appeared with its next phase, the reconstruction of events from records of all kinds rather than from the perspective of the witness who had shared events with his contemporaries.

Chronologically, the next phase actually preceded or appeared contemporaneously with the second, whose representatives recorded what they saw or lived with in a nation at war or in a sea of domestic troubles. Herodotus, who did not know or apply Thucydides' tests of critical worth and the relevance and cogency of historical data, nevertheless gave the first effective demonstration of the historian's task, of narrating the whole past life of man. To the capabilities of a superb story-teller he added the talents of the geographer, topographer, and anthropologist. While his *History* is concerned with the Persian Wars, he was less the student of military affairs than of humans and their society. In a sense, he was bequeathing to his successors what they must accomplish in a narrative form which would satisfy objectives much larger than what happened at various points in the struggle between Greece and Persia.[7]

The command of narrative skill by the Greek historians, from the fifth century B.C. to the second, which produced perhaps their greatest representative in Polybius (198–117 B.C.), grew impressively. But mastery of chronology, which would not be real until the time of Julius Caesar (100–44 B.C.), hampered all ancient historians. With the development of the Julian calendar, the narrative historian had finally achieved command of the essential measurement of periods in the human past. It would not, however, be put to greatest use until much later, whatever the significance of Caesar's *Commentaries on the Gallic Wars*, Sallust's *History of Rome* (which we no longer possess) and *Conspiracy of Catiline*, Livy's *History*, and the *Annals* and *Histories* of Tacitus.

7 Harry Elmer Barnes, *A History of Historical Writing*, 27–30.

To imply that the first historians of the Western world were solely occupied over a six-hundred-year period, from the beginning of the fifth century B.C. to the end of the first century A.D., with the founding and perfection of narrative history is misleading. Many were impelled quite as much by analysis and interpretation, greatly mitigated by their commitments to patriotism and national tradition. Just how far they had gained in mastery over both elements in an often diffuse and confusing past is expressed by Polybius, *Historia* (XII, 25e):

The science of history is three-fold: first, in dealing with written documents and in the arrangement of the material thus obtained; second, topography, the appearance of cities and localities, the descriptions of rivers and harbors, and, speaking generally, the peculiar features of the seas and countries and their relative distances; thirdly, political affairs. . . . The special province of history is, first, to ascertain what the actual words used were; and, second, to learn why it was that a particular policy or arrangement failed or succeeded. For a bare statement of an occurrence is interesting, to be sure, but not instructive; but when it is supplemented by a statement of cause, the study of history becomes fruitful. For it is by applying analogies to our own circumstances that we get the means and basis for calculating the future; and for learning from the past when to act with caution, and when with greater boldness, in the present.

As we have observed earlier, narrative history, as method, is something more than a good grade of story-telling tied to an accurate chronology. It must also contain analysis and interpretation, whether disjoined from the main narrative thread or deftly fused with it. The latter must await subsequent discussion and example (see p. 70ff.). Immediately, however, the bearing, or lack of bearing, of Polybius' statements about the practical and moral uses of history needs at least a critical scanning.

That these proposed uses of history had been critically analyzed by Leopold von Ranke seems clear from the longer passage from which the celebrated *wie es eigentlich gewesen* is customarily lifted:

To history has been assigned the office of judging the past, of instructing the present for the benefit of future ages; to such high offices the present work does not aspire: it intends only to show what really happened [*wie es eigentlich gewesen*].[8]

Von Ranke's "only" (*bloss*) in the statement above is an important adverb, fully indicative both of his modesty and of his historical intent. The whole passage was intended as a corrective of the then current moral and philosophical claims made by many of his contemporaries, as well as by his predecessors. And in doing so it urged the importance of pursuing the narrative and interpretative requirements of history as a learned discipline in its own right.

Few people have said as comprehensively, yet simply, as von Ranke what is required in such a two-fold historical pursuit. The research corpus he described is very close to the lists put before graduate students in history today, fully a century and a half after he wrote:

What, then, are the sources for this new investigation? The fundamentals, the sources of its subject matter, consist of memoirs, journals, letters, diplomatic information, and original narratives of eyewitnesses; other writings were utilized only if they were immediately derived from the foregoing or appeared

---

8 Leopold von Ranke, *Fürsten und Völker: Geschichten der romanischen und germanischen Völker von 1494–1514; die Osmanen und die spanische Monarchie im 16. und 17. Jahrhundert.* Die Meisterwerke, herausgegeben von Willy Andreas. I, 4. Translation *meus.*

of equal value because of some form of original information. Every page will indicate these sources.[9]

Von Ranke further tells us that, in treating the history of the Latin and Germanic nations as the Renaissance drew on (1494–1514), he had consciously chosen a narrative method, taking up one of the states of Europe after another, rather than attempting a diffuse portrait of a continent admittedly in political and religious turmoil. So far so good. But he warned his readers that the high interest with which a literary artist might enliven his story could not be used in a work of history. In a large sense, the father of modern historical writing was setting the two conditions which must be observed by all who followed him: the sources must be, in the main, primary, and the presentation, whether narrative or analytical, must not sacrifice authenticity to charm. The latter, coming from a member of the *Gelehrtenstand,* steeped in literary forms and comparative philology (which he had taught for several years), is all the more noteworthy.[10]

It would be a mistake to say that the century and a half from von Ranke's assertion of the principles of narrative historical writing to today's sophisticated applications is the story of modern historical method. (No innovator in history or politics ever comes home scot-free.) But it is fair to state that a detached type of historical narration became the first choice for most historians as they began their careers, and for many of the more brilliant among them it has remained their only choice. How, then, does it work?

Historical narration always begins with the question, asked of himself by the historian, *How did it happen?* The answer to it, *This is how it happened,* is his response to his readers as well as to himself. *How* in this context indicates

9 *Ibid.,* 4.
10 *Ibid.,* 4.

action. *What*, which precedes it, points to significance. Thus in the narrative historical writing process, the author turns abruptly from the importance of his episode—the *what* which emerged from research and conceptualization—to the even more exciting *how* of telling it as it happened. That this task bears close kinship to that of the writer of fiction is unmistakable. But for both the historian and the master of the novel, the exposition of the processes involved calls for a complete reversal of their respective techniques. In story-telling, whether of the true historical variety or of the fictional mode, the teller sits at the wheel of his vehicle and looks ahead. In exposition, he sits at the tailgate and looks back upon what is receding in the distance. Hence creative writers almost uniformly hold that writing can't be taught, and historians abandon the idea of trying to teach it. The latter rely instead upon successful example, which will work if the student takes fire from the sparks constantly emanating from the good to brilliant narration to which he is exposed. Nevertheless . . .

All successful historical construction of the narrative kind exhibits these characteristics:

It develops the required setting and the time of the historical action. (For the management of scene, see pp. 135–39; for the working of historical time, see pp. 132–35.)

It develops action swiftly and economically through conscious and unremitting attention to the actors in the historical action.

It utilizes such well-established narrative conventions as viewpoint, the plant, characterization, all of the devices of continuity and the maintenance of the suspense implied in A. J. P. Taylor's dictum that historical characters do not know what fate has in store for them.

It treats chronology as unfolding rather than as past time.

It utilizes indirect discourse, when it may legitimately be drawn from documents, as an admissible convention in place of the novelist's dialogue.

It intends to recreate what did in fact take place at the time of its occurrence. Its concern is the now of history, not the was.

Narration clearly requires of its writer, approaching his task for the first time, a rather complete rethinking of the ways in which he must look at past reality. The conventions, the tricks of the trade, are far from obvious, no matter how often the student has seen them in action. There is really no reason why the historian as reader should see them at all— for it is the writer's purpose to tell a story, not to make obvious the devices by which, with varying degrees of skill, he tells it. His management of the action words (verbs), even, is far from ordinary. ("He would answer his critics lamely six months after his overwhelming election" is an example of a future-perfect tense, which keeps action within historical time, the now of present action, as well a narrative plant, preparing the reader for the irony of things to come.) The narrative device of using the viewpoint of a contemporary observer, rather than relying upon the often wearying omnipresent viewpoint of the historian, is a strange and wonderful concept on first encounter. It possesses a verisimilitude unmatched by anything in the backward view taken from other documents. These and all the other devices of immediacy are the tools of the narrative historian.

Nothing, however, will put them at the disposal of the historian as writer if he does not early make a distinction between two types of reading. One is critical and historically informed. The other is analytical. The latter intends to see the whole and the parts of a given historical structure and to know how they were achieved. At least half of the imperfect historical writing of the past quarter of a century can be traced to the failure of this principle, the rest to simple lack of aptitude for an exacting discipline. It is not too much to expect that younger historians, equipped with the analytical canons for an understanding of historical style, will give to its future writing the understanding which, correspondingly, Messrs. Cleanth Brooks and Robert Penn Warren have given to the understanding of poetry.[11] It has been slow dawning upon us all that the search for historical reality is only half the game; the search for historical meaning, captured in writing style, is the other half.

Spain in the Old World and the New, from the close of the Moorish occupation at the end of the fifteenth century to the last quarter of the eighteenth, has offered the historian of narrative bent many splendid opportunities, a number of which have been seized and made memorable. Two of these offer, even in a short sampling, a demonstration of the techniques outlined above. Both were written by mature historians. A third, chosen for the narrative historical questions it raised, is notable for the fact that, within twenty-four hours of its completion as a dissertation and its submission in a fourth carbon copy to a publisher, it had been accepted—ahead of its defense before a doctoral committee!

The first selection is from Professor Herbert Eugene Bolton's now classic volume, *The Spanish Borderlands*, written just over half a century ago:[12]

West as well as east, and somewhere in the north, must lie the waters of the Strait of Anian, that direct passage from the

---

11 Cleanth Brooks and Robert Penn Warren, *Understanding Poetry; Understanding Fiction.*
12 Herbert Eugene Bolton, *The Spanish Borderlands*, 79–86.

Atlantic to China, if indeed the northwestern territory did not actually abut on Asia. So reasoned the Spanish dons. To the northwest, some said, was an island inhabited solely by giantesque Amazons. Inland were the Seven Cities, situated on a great height. Their doors were studded with turquoises, as if feathers from the wings of the blue sky had dropped and clung there. Within those jeweled cities were whole streets of goldsmiths, so great was the store of shining metal to be worked.

Indians were ever great story-tellers, delighting to weave the tales most pleasant to their hearers. It was an Indian slave of Nuño de Guzmán who regaled that credulous official of New Spain with fanciful description of the Pueblo towns of New Mexico. The myth led Guzmán north, to the ruthless conquest of Sinaloa and the founding of Culiacán, still the capital city of that Mexican state.

Then, in 1535, came Antonio de Mendoza from Old Spain to be the first Viceroy of New Spain. Mendoza had soon set his heart on the acquisition of those Seven Cities. The arrival of [Cabeza de] Vaca and his companions in the City of Mexico, out of the mysterious north, in July, 1536, added fuel to Mendoza's desires. An expedition must be fitted out immediately, to be led by Vaca's companion Dorantes—since Vaca himself was resolved to go to Spain. The plan came to nothing for the time being, but Vaca left the Moor Estevanico to serve Mendoza.

Three years passed before Mendoza could prepare another expedition. Francisco Vásquez de Coronado was then (1539) made Governor of New Galicia and military head of the force designed to spread the power of Spain northward. To the Franciscan Fray Marcos de Niza was given the spiritual leadership of the expedition. Fray Marcos had already seen strenuous service, for he had been with Pizarro in the conquest of Peru. He had also written several works about the country. He had high acquirements in theology, cosmography, and navigation; he was a hardy traveler, having tramped from Guatemala to Mexico.

To Culiacán Fray Marcos and Coronado journeyed in com-

52

pany. Coronado there halted to establish his authority over the outposts of New Galicia. Fray Marcos, with the Moor Estevanico, some Mexican Indians, and a few other natives who had come with Vaca's little band to Mexico, went on. Estevanico, having wandered through parts of the Northern land with Vaca, was relied upon not alone to guide the friars but to insure the friendship of the Indians.

At Vacapa, somewhere in Sonora, Fray Marcos paused and, "on Passion Sunday after dinner," sent Estevanico ahead to learn what he could. Should Estevanico hear tidings of but a fair country he was to send to the friar a small cross; for great tidings, a cross "two handfuls long"; and, should he discover a country richer than Mexico, he was to send a great cross. Imagine the pleasureable agitation in the friar's breast, when, four days later, some of the Indians who had gone with the Moor came in bearing a cross "as high as a man" and a message urging Fray Marcos to follow at once. Estevanico had found a new people, who had told him of "the greatest thing in the world." He was now at a town but thirty days' journey from the turquoise doors of the Seven Cities which, he had learned, were called Cíbola; and beyond Cíbola there were other rich provinces, each one of which was "a much greater matter than those seven cities." So, as ever in these tales, the splendor within reach was already dimmed by the splendor beyond! To Cíbola, therefore, the friar set out on the second day after Easter.

He is supposed to have gone directly north up the Sonora valley, though it may have been the Yaqui valley. As he went, from time to time he planted crosses; for "it appeared to me suitable from here on to perform acts of possession." He heard from the Indians on his route more details of Cíbola and of the cities beyond. And he was much surprised to learn that the natives of those cities dressed in habits of gray wool like his own. These were perhaps the blanket garments made of narrow strips of rabbit fur and yucca fiber which are still woven by the Moqui Indians. Through the valley of the San Pedro in Arizona

Fray Marcos continued northward; then, finding that the stream led him too far west, he veered to the northeast and reached the Gila, above its confluence with the San Pedro. Here he learned that Estevanico, with three hundred Indians, was crossing the plains to the northeast, where the Apaches now have their reservation. After a rest, on May 9, 1539, Fray Marcos continued his march to Cíbola, which lay fifteen days beyond. His way now led upward, through rugged country, to a pass not identified, between the Sierra Mogoyon and Sierra Blanca ranges. Bad news met him on the Apache plains. An Indian of the Moor's escort, returning in flight, told him that Estevanico had been seized and made prisoner by the natives of Cíbola.

We know very little about the end of Estevanico, this African who was one of the earliest explorers of North America and had wandered over a greater part of its wilderness than any man before him or than any man for long after him. The Arab was one of a fearless race, loving freedom no doubt as his tribesmen of the Moroccan deserts today love it; and only in the desert could he enjoy it. Lifted again out of the thrall of slavery, which had fastened on him after his great journey from Florida, and given command of some three hundred savages to discover the cities of argent traceries and turquoise doors, he had made his tour like an Oriental chieftain, or like a Moorish prince before the Conquest, with pomp and display and the revels of power. Gifts were brought him and tribute was exacted. His tall, dusky body soon flaunted robes dyed with the colors of the rainbow. Tufts of brilliant feathers and strings of bells dangled from his arms and legs. He carried a magical gourd, decorated with bells and with one white and one scarlet feather; and sent it ahead of him to awe the natives in each town where he demanded entrance. A score, perhaps, of Indians formed his personal retinue and bore on their shoulders the provisions, the turquoises, mantles, and feathered ornaments accumulated on the road. Flutes of reeds, shell fifes, and fish-skin drums played his march across the sunlit mesas. And an ever-increasing harem

of gayly bedecked young women swelled the parade of Estevanico, the black Berber chief, on his way to the city set in
silver and blue. Perhaps, as has been suggested, the belled and
feathered gourd was "bad medicine" to the Indians of Hawikuh; for, when Estevanico's messenger presented it with the
announcement that their lord was come to make peace and
cure the sick, the Indians became enraged and ordered the
interlopers out of their country on pain of death. Estevanico,
disdaining fear, went on. Just outside the walls of Cíbola he
was seized. The "sun was about a lance high" when the men of
Hawikuh suddenly launched their arrows upon his followers.
Some of those who, fleeing, looked back, thought they had seen
Estevanico fall beneath that thick hail of darts.

"It is to be believed that a long time ago, when roofs lay over
the walls of Kya-ki-me, when smoke hung over the housetops,
and the ladder rounds were still unbroken in Kya-ki-me, then
the Black Mexicans came from their abodes in Everlasting
Summerland . . . . Then and thus was killed by our ancients,
right where the stone stands down by the arroyo of Kya-ki-me,
one of the Black Mexicans, a large man, with chilli lips [lips
swollen from chilli peppers] . . . . Then the rest ran away,
chased by our grandfathers, and went back toward their country
in the land of Everlasting Summer." So, in part, runs the Zuñi
legend, today, concerning the coming and the death of Estevanico, the Black.

Half a century after this event in the New World, Spain's
still restless government and military class were suspect by
the whole of Europe, fearful of a developing new adventure
at home. The narrative scene is from the opening lines of
Chapter XV, "The Ominous Year," of *The Armada*, by
Professor Garrett Mattingly:[13]

As the year 1587 drew to a close, a shudder of apprehension
ran across western Europe. In part it was a perfectly rational

13 Garrett Mattingly, *The Armada*, 172–73.

apprehension. As the closing in of winter made it less likely that the fleet gathering at Lisbon would sail before the year's end, it became increasingly certain that come spring it would sail—against England. In fact, although Philip still wrote to his ambassadors that the armada's destination must remain a secret closely kept, although at Paris Mendoza maintained an enigmatic silence, meanwhile trying every security and counter-espionage device he could think of, although Parma attempted misdirection by putting it about that the obvious aim at England was only a blind for a sudden descent on Walcheren, the shape of Philip's plan was becoming unmistakable. Lisbon was always full of foreigners and the least experienced observer could tell that this vast mobilization of ships and seamen, soldiers and cannon was not meant just to protect the commerce of the Indies or stir up trouble in Ireland. Flanders was still a crossroads trade, and among her own people there were many whose sympathies were with the rebels. Parma had to carry out his plans under their attentive eyes, and it was hard to persuade the Flemings that an amphibious invasion of Walcheren required five leagues of new canals linking Sluys and Nieuport. When the new canals were finished a barge could pass from the Scheldt above Antwerp to Dunkirk Haven without once venturing out into the open water and, by Parma's estimate, a flotilla from Dunkirk with favorable weather could be off the North Foreland and near Margate between dusk and dawn of an April night.

By the end of November the master pattern, a cross-Channel operation by Parma's army, convoyed and supported by a fleet from Spain, was clear to Buys and Oldenbarneveldt, Burghley and Walsingham, and Dutch and English naval dispositions were being made accordingly. For that matter the pattern was hardly less clear to bankers of Augsburg and merchants of Venice and argumentative idlers in Parisian wine shops. All Christendom came to attention to watch the contest between

England, the traditional overlord of the narrow seas, and the new Spanish colossus, aspirant to the empire of the oceans.

The notable dissertation mentioned earlier is entitled in book form *Pueblo Warriors and Spanish Conquest*, written by Oakah L. Jones, Jr., and published in 1966. A summary of its intent, rather than quotation from its narrative of many theaters of action in the northern provinces of New Spain in the seventeenth and eighteenth centuries, is called for. That intent flows from the essentially narrative question, How could a skeleton force of Spaniards advance again and again in the wilderness of the Southwest in this early period? The historical answer is that it could not. The Spaniards had to have help (it has already revealed itself in Bolton's account of the early phases of the Coronado expedition). The Indian character of that help offers an interesting and valuable chapter in the story of European advance in the New World.

The problem such an account poses—*How did it happen?*—is a good deal more serious than appears on the surface. It is easily possible to tell in detail, without color or dramatic overtones, the solid but uninspiring story of Spanish skill in enlisting, equipping, even winning the loyalty of Indian auxiliaries drawn from one town after another as the Europeans moved farther and farther northward. But this is not the method by which history in its narrative genre succeeds. It requires judicious selection of detail, a strong feeling of narrative progression, and something more than a trace of suspense, if the reader is to achieve ultimate reality. That the truths of this history must emerge from the rhetorical skill of the historian writing must be apparent to anyone who is familiar with Spanish colonial documents, charged as they are with administrative minutiae and imbued with self-interest.

Everywhere in the landscape of history we find a threatening, often a seemingly overwhelming, mass of detail, as ominous as a superior military force ready to engulf the unwary researcher who has invited it out for a contest of wills. Unfortunately, the mere historian is limited in his choice of battle plans. He cannot attack it selectively and with the high disdain of a novelist discarding characters who might get in the way of his plot. He can only accept the theater of action as it is, the serried ranks as they appear coming over the horizon. But he does retain the primary advantage of initiative. He can deploy it in either of two ways: by a recital of events along largely chronological lines, or by a strengthening topicality. The former offers the prospect of minimal success, except in accounts of up-country marches, as in the examples cited from Xenophon and, a few pages back, Bolton's "Death of Estevanico." A strengthening topicality, on the other hand, affords the certainty of a breakthrough.

A strengthening topicality takes place when the historian recognizes and gives proper emphasis to significant developments in his narrative. The consequence is a rhythmical structure of action, its crests fully significant, its ascending and descending curves true to the rising and falling phases of human striving, individually and in the mass. This, even more than the often remarked command of arresting detail in the writing of Macaulay, Élie Halévy, Butterfield, and Mattingly, is what distinguishes the narrative historian who is master of his craft. Its challenge may perhaps be best understood from examples drawn from what, at first glance, appears elementary, Indian conflict on the western plains.

Our historical structure must cope with episodes in the

life of the Southern Cheyenne Indian tribe, from the opening guns of the Sand Creek massacre, November 29, 1864,
east of present Colorado Springs, when more than one
hundred Cheyennes under Black Kettle lost their lives in
the onrush of Colonel J. M. Chivington's Colorado volun-
teers, to the Battle of the Washita in western Oklahoma
on November 27, 1868, when Black Kettle and more than
one hundred of his tribesmen were killed by troops under
Lieutenant Colonel George Armstrong Custer. Between
these dates we have, in addition to the delimiting episodes
named, the retaliatory raids by the Southern Cheyennes and
their allies, the Southern Arapahoes and Brulé and Oglala
Sioux, and their northern kinsmen, the Northern Cheyennes, first along the South and North Platte rivers, then
past Fort Laramie, Wyoming, as far north as the mouth of
the Yellowstone in western North Dakota and as far west
as the middle reaches of the Tongue and Powder rivers
in eastern Montana. The Cheyenne raids lasted into November, 1865, when most of the bands began moving south-
eastward to the Smoky Hill River in western Kansas, later
shifting their winter encampments of 1865–66 from the
tributaries of the Republican to as far as the Cimarron.

The third large event after Sand Creek was the signing of
the Treaty of the Little Arkansas by Black Kettle and a
number of other Cheyennes on October 14, 1865, near
present Wichita, Kansas. (Black Kettle had not moved
north with the hostiles after Sand Creek, and he freely
admitted he could not commit the Cheyenne soldier societies, who remained as belligerent as ever.)

By late spring, the hostile Cheyennes were back in Kansas
to claim the Smoky Hill country, lost to them in the Treaty
of the Little Arkansas. Against detachments of the U.S.
Army, which they had fiercely engaged far to the north and

west, they resumed the field. Their opponents counted some of the best military talent of the post–Civil War period: General William Tecumseh Sherman, commanding the Military Division of the Missouri, Major General Winfield Scott Hancock, Lieutenant Colonel George Armstrong Custer, and, later, General Philip Henry Sheridan in command of the Military Department of the Missouri.

Thus, in the year from late spring, 1866, to June, 1867, Kansas became a battleground, with extensions into northeastern Colorado, southern Nebraska, and northern Oklahoma. Late in June, 1867, General Sherman ordered Lieutenant Colonel Custer and his force to Fort Wallace against the hostiles. Lieutenant Lyman S. Kidder, ten troopers, and Red Bead, a Sioux scout, were to carry the orders to Custer, who had been campaigning on the Republican in the southwestern corner of Nebraska. Kidder, his troops, and Red Bead never reached Custer: they were annihilated on Beaver Creek fifty miles north of Fort Wallace.

Clear recognition by the government that the hostilities generated by the Sand Creek Massacre would not cease of themselves led to the campaign for a new peace treaty with the Southern Plains tribes in 1867—and a still further constriction of the Cheyenne domain. At Medicine Lodge Creek near Fort Larned on the western shoulder of the Big Bend of the Arkansas, the Cheyennes signed the treaty on October 28, ceding their lands in Kansas and accepting the remainder of their previous holding, all of it lying in northern Oklahoma.

That their warrior societies would not cease to hunt far to the northwest became clear by 1868. They would also attack whites and army detachments. In August, 1868, General Sheridan sent his aide, Major George A. Forsyth and Lieutenant Frederick H. Beecher, "fifty hardy frontiersmen," and Surgeon John H. Mooers against the Cheyennes. In northeastern Colorado on a small overgrown island in the Arikaree Fork of the Republican, they were surrounded on September 17 by Cheyennes and Brulé Sioux, who either killed or wounded twenty-two of the fifty-two men on the expedition before the day was out. On the following morning, the greatest war leader of the Cheyennes, Roman Nose, was dead from battle wounds. The Forsyth command was finally extricated on September 25. One of its dead, Lieutenant Beecher, gave his name to the battle and the island.

A now thoroughly aroused General Sheridan began to put into operation a plan of unrelenting pressure on the Cheyenne bands. His pincers would utilize three separate units, one moving down the South Canadian River, another in the region of the upper Beaver and Wolf creeks, and his own moving south from Camp Supply. To Custer he gave field command of the Seventh Cavalry based on the latter post.

On the Washita near the Antelope Hills in western Oklahoma, with a foot of new snow on the ground and in bitter cold weather, which had immobilized Black Kettle's encampment of 180 lodges, Custer struck before daylight on November 27, 1868. The resulting slaughter signalled the end of freedom for the Southern Cheyennes.

Although the foregoing highly condensed summary suggests the topical crests of any historical narrative dealing with this phase of southern plains warfare, it does not account for two serious complications. The historian must face the first if he chooses to draw heavily upon both the white and the Indian eyewitness sources. The amount of detail which emerges from these sources is all but overwhelming, as the most authoritative accounts make evi-

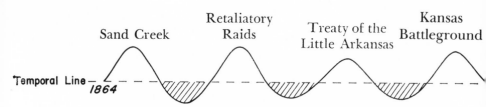

Sand Creek   Retaliatory Raids   Treaty of the Little Arkansas   Kansas Battleground

Temporal Line — 1864

dent.[14] The battleground was not only vast but shifting constantly. The Cheyennes were badly divided into peace and war factions. And conflicting policy frequently emerged from both Washington and the states and territories in the theater of action.

The second complication consists of the vexing problem of choice of focus. With whom do we march, the Indians or the army? That there is a choice is demonstrated by the connected account which emerged from one of its Indian (half-blood) participants, George Bent, whose less complex history allows sharply defined narrative crests for this five-year period.[15] In general, the white historian will place greatest reliance upon white (official) sources, using Indian testimony, when it has been preserved, as both countervailing and complementary evidence. This being so, he must find and rhetorically construct the cresting phases of his history. If he does not, he will have the straight line of *How it happened* but the *What happened* may forever remain obscure.

14 Wilbur S. Nye, *Carbine and Lance*, 43 *et alibi*; Donald J. Berthrong, *The Southern Cheyennes*, 195–334; Douglas C. Jones, *The Treaty of Medicine Lodge*; Stan Hoig, *The Sand Creek Massacre*; Rupert Norval Richardson, *The Comanche Barrier to South Plains Settlement . . .* , 283ff.

15 George Bent, *Life of George Bent Written from His Letters by George E. Hyde*, ed. by Savoie Lottinville, 137–327.

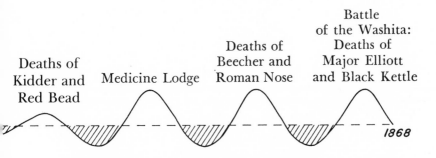

Deaths of Kidder and Red Bead   Medicine Lodge   Deaths of Beecher and Roman Nose   Battle of the Washita: Deaths of Major Elliott and Black Kettle   1868

The simplified topical crests of the history we have de-scribed, whether written from the Indian or the white orientation, appear in the accompanying graph.

What we have in such a graph is a temporal or chrono-logical line running through the middle. It is the base from which historical crests rise. We need to view the areas below the temporal line as containing almost as much as the areas above it. These lower areas are curves of condition, cause, or build-up to the crests above the line. When we speak of depth in a particular historical study, we should have the icebergs below the surface clearly in mind. They are masses of data, some of which may not even be expressed in the narrative, but their existence will condition what appears above the line nevertheless. It is from them that the topical or significant historical crests take their form. To be sure, they are anterior to the event or events of the crest action, and should be so understood.

But for him who essays narrative history there is no salvation—not in formularies or graphs or charts—except as he finds it in the resources of his own mind.

4. Continuity and Analysis

BY the time the historian approaches his first extended work—which may indeed be his dissertation—he has already written so many historical essays and reviews that his swift attainment of balance, proportion, and, above all, continuity would seem to be within easy reach. But continuity in the long form is more exacting than in the short form of the essay or article for a journal. It is also deceptive in that it is often assumed when, in fact, it is either absent or defective. Continuity, in the real sense, is won only after a good deal of painstaking effort, according to rules which, though straightforward enough, are frequently overlooked. They begin, and for many may be said to end, with the device known as a *hook*.

A hook is often chosen to close one chapter, forecasting the character of narrative action to come, a change in the theater of historical action or its chronology or both, a shift in the topicality of the historical construction, e.g., from government policy to its implementation by one or more administrative figures, or any other approaching development. The corresponding *eye* of the hook-and-eye pair will usually appear at the opening of the next chapter, thereby fastening the two chapters together and thus eliminating the discontinuity which so often vitiates the efforts of the beginner. If at first glance the technique of hooking seems an easy formulary, do not be misled. Its applications and variations require genuine imagination, as may be made clear from some overly simplified and some other more complex examples.

Sometimes the break between one chapter and its successor is so slight, from the point of view of time or place or action, that a transition is hardly necessary. After all, the convention of chapter breaks is so clearly understood by most readers that any transitional effort in these instances is unnecessary and if used will sound forced. Thus Alan Valentine's two-volume portrait of Lord North contains, for the most part, easy, nonhooking transitions from chapter to chapter. The following extracts taken, respectively, from the close of Chapter 10 and the opening of Chapter 11, exhibit the method, as the author describes North's kissing of hands as the newly appointed first minister at the close of the one chapter, and the political reception of that choice at the opening of the next:

In many ways North did not fit the traditional concept of a first minister. In appearance and manner he lacked *gravitas*. Contemporaries reported him "of the middle size, heavy, large, and much inclined to corpulency . . . a fair Complexion, regular Features, light Hair, with bushy Eyebrows, and grey Eyes, rather prominent in his Head . . . his Tongue being too large for his Mouth, rendered his articulation somewhat thick, though not at all indistinct . . . he saw very imperfectly" and was "to the last degree awkward."[1]

Those handicaps set off his talents in contrast, but it was not his talents so much as a combination of circumstances that made him the only expedient choice to head the government. But his new position was peculiar and far from secure. He was not to choose his own colleagues and form his own ministry,

1 Wraxall, *Memoirs*, I, 480, 481. [This and other internal footnotes, from the quoted authors' works, are included in my footnote series.]

but to accept his existing fellow ministers and the existing policies. In popular judgment he was merely a nominal first minister who would be dominated by the Bedford group and would shortly either be replaced by them or fall with them. Yet for all that, his selection as first minister was an impressive achievement for a man still in his thirty-eighth year. His appointment was announced without delay, and he kissed hands to become first lord of the Treasury and the King's first confidential minister.[2]

The opening of Chapter 11 is in itself dramatic enough, and the historical question it answers is logical enough, that any other approach might have seemed odd. It follows:

The emergence of North as first minister was "the astonishment of the nation" and a surprise even to Chatham. Seldom had the government been less entrenched in public estimation and party support.[3] But to the members of the inner circle North's elevation was no surprise, particularly since it was believed that he would not in reality be first minister. He had not formed a ministry; he had merely inherited one. The London *Chronicle* reported that "all the rest of the party resolved to keep their places if they could," and that "Lord North had a mere *Locum Tenens*." Weymouth wrote to General Townshend, lord lieutenant in Ireland, the day after North was installed, to offer assurance that "this arrangement does not make the least alteration in the King's measures, either at home or abroad."[4]

It is important to note that, while from one point of view, Valentine's break between these two chapters conforms to the accepted requirement of a breathing-pause, it in reality

2 Alan Valentine, *Lord North*, I, 189.

3 Annual Register (Jan. 28, 1770); Lucas, *Lord North*, I, 317; I. R. Christie, *The End of Lord North's Ministry*, 4.

4 London *Chronicle* (Feb. 1, 1770); BM, CHOP (1770–72), Vol. VI, No. 29 (Weymouth to Townshend, Jan. 30, 1770). Valentine, *Lord North*, I, 190.

ushers in a new phase in the career of a controversial English statesman. There must always be a better reason than a breathing-pause for chapter breaks. Logically, the break should be bridged by an implied historical question, by the beginnings of cresting action, or by both. Lurking in the opening paragraph of Valentine's Chapter 11 is the implied question, here of narrative character, would North really be in *locum tenens*?

Between 1932, the year in which the late Professor Allan Nevins of Columbia University, first published his *Grover Cleveland: A Study in Courage*, and 1950, when he published *The Emergence of Lincoln*, we have a span of eighteen years in the career of one of America's most productive and respected historians. (He wrote and edited more than fifty works in the fifty years from 1923.) These two studies contain contrasting solutions to the problems of continuity, in the case of *Grover Cleveland*, often as not a reliance upon old models, notably in the attempt at a hook at the close of Chapter XXXIII. Here the author has been dealing with the Pullman Strike of 1894, in which, acting on the advice of his attorney general, Richard Olney, Cleveland had sought and achieved an injunction, not only against physical violence and obstruction by the strikers but against the strike itself. Moreover the President and his Attorney General had ordered U. S. troops to Chicago. Here is Professor Nevins' hook closing the chapter:

> From Olney's unfortunate role in the Chicago strike we must turn to his equally unfortunate influence upon Cleveland in the Venezuela affair.[5]

The author then opens Chapter XXXIV with a long paragraph describing Cleveland's tendency to let his temper

[5] Allan Nevins, *Grover Cleveland: A Study in Courage*, 628.

flare under persistent irritation, in this case, and unique in his conduct of international relations, was his message on Venezuela, whose eastern boundary with British Guiana was an issue between the U. S. State Department and the British Foreign Office. The complexity of the issue, Secretary of State Walter Q. Gresham's preoccupation with it, and the untimely death of the latter require five pages before Olney re-emerges on the scene as Gresham's successor at the Department of State.[6]

This is hooking in its most unsophisticated form, and the eye of the hook-and-eye pair is clearly too large and cumbersome to effect a satisfactory fastening together of the two chapters.

But the author of the essay, "In Defence of History," which is one of the most profound and the most happily written that we possess in our language, had emerged by 1950 as a master of the techniques of historical construction. The following shows how the author now employs the device of the hook:

The time is 1858, in President Buchanan's administration, and the passage is the closing paragraph of Chapter 5 of Volume I of Professor Nevins' *The Emergence of Lincoln*:

Summer heat and humidity closed down on the Potomac. Congress had gone home; most of the great houses were shuttered; the President and Cabinet toiled with appointments and routine business. After the thunderclap of the Dred Scott decision, the season promised to be quiet. Most people forgot about the dark plot of Calhoun, Maclean, and Lecompte, and the outraged protests of Geary. The New York *Herald* and *Times* were busy praising Buchanan's Kansas policy, and together with the Washington *Union* were predicting its success. Only

6 *Ibid.*, 629–35.

the doubters waited anxiously for news from the valley of the Missouri.[7]

Chapter 6, which is entitled "Melodrama in Kansas," offers the following perfect fitting eye for the preceding hook:

Hundreds of people, a tense, expectant throng, had gathered in front of the Cincinnati House in Lawrence. The sun, just sinking in the west, threw its level rays on grimy farmers, wagoners, and blacksmiths in checked shirts and jeans, on storekeepers wearing aprons, on black-coated doctors and lawyers, and on women in sunbonnets holding children by the hand. Many stalwart fellows had knives in their belts or revolvers strapped to their waists. An impatient murmur arose, until "Governor" Robinson emerged upon the hotel steps with a portly, dignified gentleman of middle age—Frederick P. Stanton, former Congressman from Tennessee, now secretary and acting-governor of Kansas.[8]

As everyone knows who reads history, there are two kinds of it. The one, which we have been describing almost from the beginning of this book, is narrative; its vehicle is action in time. The other is analytical: its vehicle is interpretation. There is actually a third, a subspecies (if natural scientists will forgive us for drawing upon two genera to evoke it) which combines the characteristics of the foregoing categories. Analytical history and its subspecies require quite as high a regard for continuity as the narrative kind: they only seem to confer freedoms which are noticeable in the historical essay and collections of historical essays, with which, however, they have little structural relationship.

In almost any period of history—Classical, Medieval,

7 Allan Nevins, *The Emergence of Lincoln*, I, 147.
8 *Ibid.*, I, 148.

Renaissance, or Modern European or American—historians of both great and small stature frequently grow topical and analytical rather than narrative in their accounts. This is in part owing to the complexities which are to be found in many of these fields, partly to the demands of institutional and social and cultural understanding, and partly to the fact that, to account for France or England or the Netherlands at a point in time calls for little narration and much institutional interpretation. Thus the analytical approach, with its accompanying emphasis upon explication, is dictated by two factors: (1) the dominance of conditions other than time itself, as in complex political, social, and cultural movements, and (2) the fact that it is all but impossible to thread the various beads of these movements upon a more or less linear chronology. How, then, is continuity achieved under these dispensations?

For the author of a master-work, e.g., *The Later Roman Empire, 284–602: A Social Economic and Administrative Survey*, by A. H. M. Jones of Jesus College, Cambridge, an evident continuity is to be achieved from a plan well laid. For little more than three hundred pages in two massive volumes of some fifteen hundred are devoted to a narrative account of the period from the Antonines to the successors of Justinian (284–602); all the rest are descriptive—in Diocletian's time, to take one epoch, the status of the imperial office, the machinery of administration, the army, the courts, and so on. Dates are infrequent, not because we do not have good chronology for these times, for we do, but an understanding of condition, in the author's view, is more important than narrative time. Throughout these volumes, the reader will find the technique of topicality joined with explication developed to a fine point, as a man of Jones's superb learning might be expected to do. To take a typical problem with which he deals, how does he organize and give continuity to the descriptive topic of Education in this period? Its structure must rest upon two languages, in the first place:

> Culturally the Roman empire fell into two halves, the Latin-speaking West and the Greek-speaking East. The boundary was sharply defined. In Africa it lay in the desert separating the Romanized Punic cities of Tripolitania from the Greek cities of the Pentapolis. In Europe Greece and Macedonia and Epirus were Greek-speaking, as were the four provinces of Thrace south of the Haemus range, together with the cluster of old Greek cities on the Black Sea coast as far as the mouth of the Danube. North and West of this line, in the dioceses of Dacia and Pannonia, and in the Danubian provinces of Thrace, Latin prevailed. There seem to have been no surviving enclaves of Greek in the West; Sicily and southern Italy had been Latinised by the end of the third century. Conversely the Roman colonies in the East had long been assimilated by their Greek environment.[9]

But there were exceptions to the lines drawn in these boundaries, and the Roman deference to the superior antiquity and quality of Greek learning continued that language at many levels of education in the West until the fourth century, when Greek began to fall away, until the fifth century, when for most representatives of the upper class it became more ornamental than real. The Greeks of the East, on the other hand, never ceased to look upon the Romans and their literature as barbarous, and their use of Latin was more from self-interest in commerce and some professional callings than from respect.

The foregoing condensation suggests the character of

[9] A. H. M. Jones, *The Later Roman Empire, 284–602: A Social, Economic, and Administrative Survey*, II, 986.

Jones's management of continuity required in even the initial consideration of the language bases of Roman education. The larger pattern of his continuity flows from the cultural-educational questions to which he addresses himself in successive paragraphs and sections—the use of Latin in the eastern empire and Africa, Latin *versus* Greek in law, the dominance of the two languages as written languages, the survival values of other languages in the empire, the illiteracy of the masses, the structure of popular and higher education for those who were so fortunate as to be exposed to it, and Christianity and education. The rhythms as well as the logic of these discussions will afford the seeker after a developed expository style many of its benchmarks.[10]

Before other examples of historical analysis are given, some things need to be said about the subject as method. It is, above all else, refracted history. While it depends for its ultimate accuracy upon primary sources, critically examined, it differs from narrative history in that the historian who writes it accepts consciously the role of interpreter. And the difference between interpreter and narrator is vast. Avoiding large doctrinal issues, we can affirm with no difficulty at all the conviction that in analytical history, whether of the ancient world or of the economy of a modern state, after the reliability of sources, the prime desideratum in the historian's work is lucidity. Central to this lucidity are the order and continuity the writer gives to his presentation.

Once these ideas are understood, the doctrinal differences between a Theodor Mommsen and a J. B. Bury over the legitimacy of style in historical writing fall away. "The reputation of Mommsen as a man of letters," said Bury, "depends on his Roman history; but his greatness as a historian is to be sought far less in that dazzling work than

10 *Ibid.*, II, 987-97.

in the *Corpus* and the *Staatsrecht* and the *Chronicles*."[11] Whereas Johann Gustav Droysen could insist with almost equal persuasiveness that "History is the only science enjoying the ambiguous fortune of being required to be at the same time an art."[12]

While the doctrines and philosophies of history come and go with almost every decade, lucidity remains unchallenged and unchanged as both an intellectual and a stylistic objective in historical writing. It affords the indispensable lens for grasping the historical truth we are looking for, particularly in the writings of those who have committed themselves to the descriptive and analytical kind.

When we turn to the Medieval and Renaissance periods, the difficulty of finding satisfactory models of analytical history, from the point of view of modern rather than archaic style, is at once manifest. The development of an extended work calls for language resources and a paleographic command in the writer which are perhaps rarer today than even in Mommsen's time.[13] (Von Ranke was a comparative philologist before he became eminent in history; Henry Thomas Buckle learned nineteen languages; Droysen was both a philologist and a historian.) This barrier has held us to a fraction of the great syntheses which have appeared in other areas of history. It has not, however, restricted the flow of monographs, papers, and articles in learned journals, which are plentiful enough.

Not surprisingly, the French, slower developing as

[11] J. B. Bury, *History as a Science*, Inaugural Lecture as Regius Professor of Modern History, Cambridge University, 1902, in Fritz Stern, *The Varieties of History*, 214.

[12] Johann Gustav Droysen, Appendix to *Outline of the Principles of History* (1868), in Stern, *op. cit.*, 139.

[13] Theodor Mommsen, Rectorial Address, University of Berlin, 1874, in Fritz Stern, *The Varieties of History*, 194. Tr. Fritz Stern.

Medievalists and Renaissance historians in the nineteenth century than the Germans, are today, and for some decades past have been, in the forefront of historical investigation in these fields. One of their most gifted representatives was the late Professor Marc Bloch of the Sorbonne, whose two volumes on feudal society, published posthumously in 1949 (he was lost in World War II), are a study in lucidity as well as in the growth of the ties of social dependence and the place of social classes in political organization during the Medieval Period.[14]

In this author's quest for lucidity, one is at once struck by the highly organized fashion in which he develops his description, analysis, and interpretation. Even if it were not customary in French historical scholarship to be thus organized, it remains that, after the decline of Rome, the European world was a fragmenting one—vast, diverse, struggling, in spite of its apparent disintegration, to establish new social and political lines of dependence and of control. In the historian's craft, nothing short of integration can cope with such a historical landscape. It is filled with institutional realities demanding not only identification but explanation; myth and misinterpretation have often confused their true character and significance; and neither a traditionalist nor a Marxist approach to the exploitative character of feudal life will evoke the historical reality we need. Assuming the adequacy of his researches and the organized character of his presentation, what do we look for in Bloch's work?

---

[14] Marc [Leopold Benjamin] Bloch, *La Société féodale: la formation des liens de dépendance* (Paris, A. Michel, 1949); *La Société féodale: les classes et le gouvernement des hommes* (Paris, A. Michel, 1949); translated in one volume as *Feudal Society* by L. A. Manyon (Chicago, University of Chicago Press, 1961).

Continuity and Analysis

First of all, a real or an implied continuity is provided for almost at the outset:

The framework of institutions which govern a society can in the last resort be understood only through a knowledge of the whole human environment. For though the artificial conception of man's activities which prompts us to carve up the creature of flesh and blood into the phantoms *homo oeconomicus, philosophicus, juridicus* is doubtless necessary, it is tolerable only if we refuse to be deceived by it. That is why, despite the existence of other works on the various aspects of medieval civilization, the descriptions thus attempted from points of view different from ours did not seem to us to obviate the necessity of recalling at this stage the fundamental characteristics of the historical climate in which European feudalism flourished.[15]

After making this declaration of method, Bloch then establishes for us the existence of two feudal ages, the one beginning at the close of the invasions of Roman Italy and ending in the middle of the eleventh century, at which point the second feudal age began. From these bases, what in scholarship or French logic must come first if, as you propose, you intend to provide the reader a "knowledge of the whole human environment"? He identifies it at once as the density of population, from which he then moves to intercommunication "among these sparsely scattered groups," made strangers to one another by the collapse of central power and with it the maintenance of public works, including, obviously, roads. Thence the author moves to trade and currency, or rather the lack of the former and the extreme scarcity of the latter; the increase in European populations which made the second, and accelerating, feudal age possible; the modes of feeling and thought, including feudal man's attitude to nature and time, written and

15 Bloch, *Feudal Society*, 59.

spoken languages, the character of feudal culture and the classes contributing to it, and the religious mentality, with its superstitious fears as well as its devotion.[16]

The matter described above constitutes the first two chapters in Bloch's accounting of the environment of feudal life and the mental climate of feudal man. In successive parts and chapters he devotes himself to the features of kinship, vassalage and the fief; and in Book II to social classes, political organization, feudalism as a type of society and its influence, and, finally, the persistence of feudalism.

The second important feature of Bloch's presentation consists in the internal clarity of each section within a chapter, impossible to recreate in any summary of the type we are attempting here. For the learner, whether in American or European history, the lesson to be gained in this context is, however, almost self-evident. There can be no clarity, even with the most perfect of historical structuring, if the writer has not reflected upon his data. Nor can he convey what reflection tells him if his writing fails to involve the reader in the life he wishes to describe. For however pivotal certain historical events may be, it remains that the principal task of analytical history is, in our age as in those ages preceding it, one of accounting for the human condition.

The temptation to make things revolve around pivotal episodes is particularly strong in the Renaissance period, in which the enlivening influences of a host of developments seem evident. Science, art, music, letters, exploration, the questioning of religious authority, the re-emergence of national states, a many-sided commerce—all of these and strongly contested dynastic struggles and wars make the period from 1400 to 1650 not only rich but hazardous.

16 *Ibid.*, 60–87.

Except for textbooks, however, the searcher after the historical canvas of largest size will search in vain. The intellectual daring which would induce a Jacob Christoph Burckhardt in the nineteenth century to essay a portrait of the whole Renaissance (*The Civilization of the Renaissance,* 1860), or a John Addington Symonds to produce *The Renaissance in Italy* (1875–86), is now unknown or out of fashion, perhaps fortunately. What we have instead is a larger scholarship directed to smaller ends, some of which are entirely rewarding or brilliant. One of the latter is the late Professor Garrett Mattingly's *Renaissance Diplomacy,* which, from a stylistic point of view, is a testing ground for the relative claims of narrative history as against the analytical kind. It is also a testing ground for those who would like to combine, as Professor J. H. Hexter insists any reputable historian must, the techniques of narration and interpretation.[17]

The author's task, which began as a study of Anglo-Spanish diplomatic relations in the sixteenth century, moved instead, he tells us, to the growth of diplomatic institutions at the close of the Feudal Period and in the Renaissance. It therefore has its roots in that often baffling unity, the *res publica Christiana,* which bound Europe together in religion without discommoding its political divisions or its strife, and in the diplomatic practices, understanding, and laws now more precisely encompassed in international law. As the Renaissance dawned, the most important diplomatic institution, the resident embassy, would assume a sharply defined form. It would emerge from the Italian city-states, and in its functions it would not entirely deny Sir Henry Wooton's definition of its principal representative, an ambassador, as "a man sent to lie abroad

17 J. H. Hexter, *Doing History,* 167–70.

for his country's good." The following excerpt exhibits not only the author's method and style, but, for our immediate purposes, a sampling of his strong continuity:

One of the chief functions of the resident ambassador came to be to keep a continuous stream of foreign political news flowing to his home government. Long before 1400 the Italian city states had the opportunity to appreciate the value of such news to makers of policy. It came to them from two sources, from the consuls of their merchant communities abroad, and from the resident foreign agents of their bankers.

From the twelfth century onward Italian merchants began to cluster in colonies in the chief commercial cities of the Levant and to organize themselves under the jurisdiction of consuls. The consuls were often elected by members of the community and were primarily judges or arbiters of disputes among its members and the official representatives of its interests before the local authorities. From the first, however, the home governments of the colonists participated in the colonial organization and sent out officers with various titles to supervise and direct it. Later the consuls themselves acquired a more official standing and were frequently appointed by the governments of their native cities and were directly responsible to them. In a sense they represented not just the interests, say, of the Pisan merchants at Acre, the Genoese at Constantinople or the Venetians at Alexandria, but the whole power and dignity of the Pisan, Genoese and Venetian republics.

Strictly speaking, consuls were not diplomats. Their status depended not on the general principles of international law but on special treaties with the powers on whose territory they were. But they did in fact perform some of the services later performed by resident ambassadors. Although any really important message or negotiation would be entrusted to a special embassy, consuls did sometimes deliver messages on behalf of their governments to the local authorities, sometimes, therefore, to reigning princes. Sometimes they did negotiate in behalf of their governments. In some places they had positions assigned to them at public functions. And the consuls of some republics, those of Genoa and Venice, at least, were expected to report regularly of political as well as of commercial interest.

For Venice, anyway, a case might be made for her consuls having been the precursors of her resident ambassadors. One Venetian representative abroad, the *bailo* at Constantinople, performed both consular and diplomatic functions in the fifteenth century. Other consuls were sometimes given special diplomatic credentials. And all the surviving evidence indicates that by the latter part of the fifteenth century regular consular reports to the Venetian Senate had become an established custom. Apparently the Venetians themselves thought there was a close connection between the two institutions. When, in 1523, the Venetian ambassador was recalled from England, the Senate voted that, until he could be replaced, the interests of the republic should be confided to the Venetian consul at London, "according to the custom of former times."[18]

Even before Venetian consuls appeared in European cities, the merchant bankers of Lombardy and Tuscany had begun to maintain permanent resident representatives, the medieval equivalents of branch managers, at the courts or in the commercial centers where they did most business. Since much of that business was loans to sovereigns, the access of banking agents to the prince and his council could be as easy as that any diplomat enjoyed. In the correspondence of these agents the political news must often have been the most profitable part of the letter. When the bankers thus represented were members of the ruling oligarchy of their city, or the trusted clients of its tyrant, the reports of their agents could supply the basis for political action, and the conduct of the agents themselves might be guided, by political motives. When the banker reported to was himself the actual, if unofficial, ruler of his city—when, for example, he was Cosimo de'Medici—the diplomatic function

18 *Cal. Ven.*, III, 334.

of his foreign branch managers might become very considerable indeed. After 1434 it was progressively harder to distinguish between the resident representatives of the Medici bank and the political agents of the Florentine state.[19] But this is a late instance.

Before 1400, the tyrants and oligarchs of northern Italy must already have learned all that experience with consuls and branch banks had to teach. The earliest Italian diplomatic agents are to be found well before that date. They were not called "ambassadors" at first or entitled (as we shall see) to diplomatic honors and immunities. But they were received in the cities where they resided as the actual agents of their masters, and were charged with most of the duties later discharged by resident ambassadors. In northern and central Italy between 1380 and 1450 this kind of semi-official resident agent became increasingly common. Towards 1450 some of the earliest official residents of whom we have any certain notice began their careers as members of this ambiguous class, among them that Nicodemus of Pontremoli upon whom the consensus of recent writers has thrust, on somewhat slender grounds, the distinction of being the first resident ambassador.

We shall probably never be able to lay down with certainty every step in the period of transition before 1455. Many records have vanished. Those which have survived are largely unpublished and inadequately explored. Nor is it likely that any number of documents would enable us to assign with confidence respective weights to the influence of such antecedents as procurators, consuls, and banking agents on the invention of resident ambassadors. But the main outline of the story is clear. The new institution was Italian. It developed in the hundred years before 1454. And whatever suggestions, possible antecedents, and analogies may have offered, the development was, in the main, an empirical solution to an urgent practical

19 R. de Roover, *The Medici Bank* (New York, 1948), 5–18; B. Buser, *Die Beziehungen der Mediceer zu Frankreich* (Leipzig, 1879), 78–188 *passim*; C. S. Gutkind, *Cosimo de'Medici* (Oxford, 1938), 176–93.

problem. Italy first found the system of organizing interstate relationship which Europe adopted, because Italy, towards the end of the Middle Ages, was already becoming what later all Europe became.[20]

At this stage of our investigations of the techniques of sustained continuity, whether in the narrative or the expository kind of history, it would be a mistake to conclude that the tricks of style are the only business at hand. No one devoting himself to the modern period makes this more evident than the late Professor Élie Halévy (1870–1937) of the École des Sciences Politiques in Paris. Like many other scholars of Europe before him, he was something else before he undertook history. His two theses offered for his doctorate were devoted, respectively, to the psychological theory of the association of ideas, stimulated in part by an investigation of David Hume's writings, and to the life and thought of Jeremy Bentham.[21] When he was younger still, he had undertaken a comparative study of Spinoza and Pascal. His first book was entitled *La Theorie Platonicienne des Sciences*. His formative intellectual interests were therefore philosophical, tied closely to the development of ideas and their continuing influence.

From Halévy's interest in Hume and Bentham, the historical step into *La Formation du Radicalisme Philosophique en Angleterre* (3 vols., 1901–1904) was almost inevitable. For him and for us, it formed the indispensable groundwork for the multi-volumed *Histoire du Peuple Anglais au Dix-neuvieme Siecle* (6 vols., 1913–32). "He was," says R. B. McCallum, "the historian of ideas before

[20] Garrett Mattingly, *Renaissance Diplomacy* (Baltimore, Penguin Books, 1964), 58–60.

[21] His interest in and respect for Bentham were obviously undiminished a third of a century later, when I heard him deliver the Bentham Memorial Lecture in 1932 at Queen's College, Oxford.

he was the historian of events. And this speculative attitude is evident throughout the present work. He asks questions; and the accepted modes of French prose writing are more favourable to this method than is English prose. This interrogative approach has two great merits. It presents a problem more clearly than a merely expository style. It arouses the attention and expectation of the reader, who eagerly awaits the answer. It also discourages dogmatism and easy certainty. For if the question comes before the answer, then the answer may be less credulously accepted. Nor does Halévy always answer all his questions; at least he often provides imperfect and contingent answers, as he is too good an historian not to know that the final and conclusive answer may never be found. In this respect he has something in common with the English constitutional historian, Maitland, who had the peculiar gift of taking the reader into his confidence and sharing with him not only his knowledge but his doubts. A remarkable example of Halévy's interrogative method can be found in a long series of questions in which, almost satirically, he inquires wherein lay the superiority of the British Navy over the French during the revolutionary wars, and again and again he fails to find a conclusive answer. The fact of English superiority remains."[22]

A more conclusive example of Halévy's rhetorical method may perhaps be found in the British Army before and after Waterloo, in the author's first volume, *England in 1815*, a volume ostensibly analytical, embracing three parts: political institutions (including the armed forces), economic life, and religion and culture. The widely spaced interrogations, the unfolding of the tactical truth about the battle,

22 R. B. McCallum, Introduction to Élie Halévy, *England in 1815*, translated by E. I. Watkin and D. A. Barker (New York, Peter Smith, 1949), viii–ix.

and Wellington's dismaying candor are significant features of a highly developed analytical skill. When we view the Duke's admissions at the close of the passages quoted (some of which Halévy italicized for emphasis) and remember that Field Marshal Blücher, a determined commander but lacking tactical gifts in the real sense, had no grand plan, the victory remains something of a puzzle. The light Halévy throws on Wellington's part in it is, however, unmistakable.

Wellington had yet to confront Napoleon face to face. At Waterloo, Napoleon gave him the opportunity, and his military career closed with a brilliant victory. He did not, however, take any particular pride in his triumph. Before the battle he complained incessantly of the soldiers who had been placed under his command, and were not his old soldiers of the Peninsular War. "To tell the truth," he wrote to a minister, "I am not very well pleased . . . with the manner in which the Horse Guards have conducted themselves towards me. It will be admitted that the army is not a very good one . . . I am overloaded with people I have never seen before, and it appears to be purposely intended to keep those out of my way whom I wished to have."[23] In a letter written a few days later he employs stronger language: "I have got," he wrote "an infamous army, very weak and ill-equipped, and a very inexperienced staff."[24] Even when the victory had been won, he was annoyed to see it unduly magnified. In the efforts that he made to discourage men of letters from writing its history, there is evident, besides considerable irritation at the inaccuracy of accounts composed by civilians, the fear that the historians, if by chance they should

[23] Letter to Earl Bathurst, May 4, 1815 (*Supplementary Dispatches*, vol. x, p. 219).
[24] Letter to General Lord Stewart, May 8, 1815 (*Dispatches*, vol. viii, p. 66). He continues: "In my opinion they are doing nothing in England. They have not raised a man; they have not called out the militia either in England or in Ireland; are unable to send me anything; and they have not sent a message to Parliament about the money. The war spirit is therefore evaporating, as I am informed."

arrive at a knowledge of the real facts, would publish many instances of indiscipline and weakness best forgotten.[25] "I am," he wrote, "really disgusted with, and ashamed of all that I have seen of the Battle of Waterloo. The number of writings upon it would lead the world to suppose that the British Army had never fought a battle before."[26] He disliked the troops he had under his command and regretted the army he had led to victory at Talavera, Salamanca, and Vittoria, an army whose faults were now forgotten, and with which he would fain have shared his final triumph. When a few months after Waterloo he gave it as his opinion that "the best troops we have, probably the best in the world, are the British infantry," he is careful to add, "particularly the old infantry that has served in Spain."[27] Was it, then, the excellence of Wellington's strategy that secured the victory of an army raised in haste and of very inferior calibre? On the contrary, never had Wellington's strategy been more feeble than in the operations immediately preceding Waterloo. Perhaps the peculiar circumstances of his situation, neither at war nor at peace, unable on that account to reconnoitre the enemy and ascertain his position by "view,"[28] made it very difficult for him to receive information as to the move-

[25] Letter to ——, Esq., August 8, 1815 (*ibid.*, vol. viii, pp. 231–32). "The history of a battle is not unlike the history of a ball. Some individuals may recollect all of the little events of which the great result is the battle won or lost; but no individual can recollect the order in which, nor the exact moment at which, they occurred, which makes all the difference as to their value or importance. Then the faults or the misbehaviours of some gave occasion for the distinction of others, and perhaps were the cause of material losses; and you cannot write a true history of a battle without including the faults and misbehaviour of part at least of those engaged. Believe me, that every man you see in a military uniform is not a hero; and that, although in the account given of a general action such as of Waterloo many instances of individual heroism must be passed over unrelated, it is better for the general interests to leave those parts of the story untold, than to tell the whole truth." Cf. letters of June 23 and September 12, 1815 (*ibid.*, vol. viii, p. 163, 259).

[26] To Sir John Sinclair, April 28, 1816 (*ibid.*, vol. viii, p. 331).

[27] To Earl Bathurst, October 23, 1815 (*ibid.*, vol. viii, p. 285).

[28] To the Prince of Orange, May 11, 1815 (*ibid.*, vol. viii, p. 78).

ments of the French Army. But, on the other hand, he enjoyed the exceptional advantage that his theatre of action was the frontier of a country divided against itself and swarming with royalist agents, where therefore he could learn from spies all that his position made it impossible to discover by means of patrols. Whatever the reason Wellington scarcely foresaw an attack, and although on his arrival in Belgium at the commencement of April he entertained keen apprehensions on this score, they seem to have faded as it actually approached. If, indeed, he foresaw an attack at all, he expected that it would be "between the Lys and the Scheldt,"[29] or "between the Sambre and the Scheldt," or on both sides simultaneously, or perhaps "from the front."[30] And he persistently refused to credit the report that Napoleon would be on the frontier by June 13th. "I judged," he wrote, "from his [Napoleon's] speech to the legislature that his departure was not likely to be immediate. I think we are now too strong for him here."[31] And on June 15th he was engaged in arranging a combined invasion of France by the three allied armies, when he learnt that Napoleon had outflanked his left and attacked the Prussian outposts. The battle had now begun and these raw troops, who had never yet seen war, and were regarded with contempt by their own general, attoned, by a resistance worthy of the Peninsula veterans, for their commander's incompetent strategy. Napoleon's genius had not failed him. The plan he had formed would undoubtedly have given him the victory, could battles be won by plans. He thrust his army like a wedge between the left flank of the English Army, which he had taken by surprise, and the Prussian right flank. It was his intention to thrust Wellington's army to the left and Blücher's to the right, crush each in turn, and then march upon Brussels. But the spirit of his army was no longer what it had been ten years earlier, at Austerlitz or Jena. The

---

[29] Secret Memorandum, May 1, 1815 (*ibid.*, vol. iii, p. 51). To General —— (*ibid.*, vol. viii, p. 21).
[30] To Lieutenant-General Lord Stewart, May 8, 1815 (*ibid.*, vol. viii, p. 85).
[31] To General Lord Lynedoch, June 13, 1815 (*ibid.*, vol. viii, p. 135).

Prussians, far from scattering before the onslaught, kept up an obstinate resistance, and finally retreated in good order; and the French had so lost heart that they could not pursue nor even make sure of the direction of their retreat. The British Army came off even better, repulsed Ney's attacks, and retreated on Brussels only at the news of the Prussian retreat and to avoid isolation. Of the two generals, Wellington and Blücher, who combined the retreat of both armies to concentrate them in the rear? If it was Wellington, then it must be admitted that his plans contributed to the final success, but, after all, when Blücher joined him on the evening of the 18th the French defeat was already assured, after a day of promiscuous slaughter, the details of which, according to his own subsequent avowal, he had failed to grasp. "The battle," he wrote, "began, *I believe, at eleven. It is impossible to say when each important occurrence took place nor in what order.* . . . Repeated attacks were made along the whole front of the centre of the position by cavalry and infantry till seven at night. *How many I cannot tell.* . . . Napoleon did not manoevre at all. He just moved forward in the old style in columns, and was driven off in the old style."[32] Of the Allies 22,000 men had been slain or wounded, of the French 40,000. The campaign was concluded with a truly Napoleonic celerity. The French Army broke up after Waterloo, just as the Prussian Army had dispersed, nine years before, after Jena. On June 29th the Allies arrived for the second time beneath the walls of Paris.[33]

The present chapter, which began with a discussion of the hook-and-eye device in narrative historical construction, may appropriately conclude its analysis of the long-form of the book or dissertation with a demonstration of how a hook may close one volume and await an eye at the

32 *Ibid.*, vol. viii, pp. 244, 186. Letters to ——, Esq., August 17, 1815, and to Lord Beresford (ed. 1838), vol. xii, pp. 610 and 529.

33 The text and notes are quoted from the translation by E. I. Watkin and D. A. Barker of Halévy, *England in 1815*, pp. 89–92.

opening of any future volume the author may write. It is, again, from Élie Halévy's *Histoire*, Volume VI, which is, in French, Part II of the author's *Épilogue (1895–1914): Vers la Démocratie sociale et vers la Guerre.*

The European crisis created by the assassination of the Austrian heir apparent in late June, 1914, had led to the Austro-Hungarian declaration of war on Serbia on July 29 and the partial mobilization of Russia, looking to the defense of the Serbs. The German Imperial War Council meeting at Potsdam the same day cast the die for war with Russia and France, but a formal declaration awaited the outcome of Germany's continuing negotiations for British neutrality, which, far from being conditioned by Britain's regard for France, turned rather on the question of the neutrality of Belgium. With Russia's full mobilization on July 31, Germany sent its ultimatum to St. Petersburg, recognized a state of war with the Russians on August 1, and sent its troops into France August 2. At 7:00 P.M. on the latter date, Germany demanded passage through Belgium for its oncoming war with France, which it formally declared August 3. The German forces entered Belgium August 4.

The scene is in the House of Commons, with Sir Edward Grey, the foreign minister, and his Liberal colleagues convinced that war was unavoidable but still clinging to the hope for the safety of Belgium. In the government and among Britain's military leaders grave confusion reigned over ends and means; should troops be deployed in defense of the empire? Across channel? Or let the Navy win a Trafalgar-like victory against the German fleet?

. . . One thing was certain: war was inevitable.
This Grey made clear to Commons in the afternoon [of

August 3]. His speech, cool, measured, devoid of eloquence, won practically unanimous support from the House. A scattering of pacifists, of whom none could speak in the name of a party, nor even of a group, made their opposition heard. "Why say," asked Ramsay Macdonald, "that you are going to the aid of Belgium when, in fact, you are undertaking a great European war which will change the map of Europe?"[34] Listeners, coldly hostile, courteously heard them out. In the streets the crowd sang patriotic songs; young men queued up at the doors of recruiting offices. The following morning the Prime Minister [Herbert Asquith], without taking the trouble to consult the Cabinet in view of the tacit approval of the entire country, authorized a telegram from Sir Edward Grey to Sir Edward Goschen demanding of the German government the promise, before midnight, that the neutrality of Belgium would be respected. Could the German government even reply? The invasion of Belgium had already begun. Night came and England entered the War.[35]

When we turn from the long form of the book to the shortest form of all, the paragraph, in our search for the distinguishing characteristics of continuity, we have, fortuitously, two examples in the passages just quoted from Halévy. It is no fault of the translators' that the Waterloo paragraph goes on and on: it was Halévy's own breathless style. The fault, if we may identify it without a hint of *lèse-majesté*, appears often in the six volumes of the *Histoire* and *La Formation du Radicalisme Philosophique*. But with this master of historical method, it is not a question whether the analysis in the one case and the narrative in the second exhibit continuity. They do, indubitably. The question, rather, is whether at times the master might well have permitted the pauses between paragraphable matters which

34 *Parl. Deb., Commons, 1914*; 5th ser., vol. LXV, p. 1830.
35 Halévy, *Histoire* . . . , VI, 657–58. Translation *meus*.

would have given the reader time for retentive reflection.

Perhaps it is this pause that most fully justifies the creation of a paragraph in the first place. Provided the paragraph, in narrative construction, does what a paragraph should do, i.e., advances the narrative action; or, in analytical construction, conveys to the reader a recognizable step in the author's on-going interpretation. In either case, the brief pause at the end of the paragraph often affords the reader a degree of emphasis which is stronger than words. In this respect, the last sentence in Halévy's vignet of August 3, 1914, says all. There is no need to go beyond *"La nuit vint et l'Angleterre entra dans la guerre."* No second thoughts in the Wilhelmstrasse or in Downing Street. Nothing of decisions in the War Office or the Armiralty in London or orders hastily given. It all comes vividly in the imagination, as, in fact, it occurred in history.

What has been said often in this book may be said again about the character of a paragraph and the continuity that flows from it: it must result from thought—in fact, its best definition is that it is a *unit of thought*. It should also be *sequential*. Often the failure to understand these two simple rules-of-thumb gives us loosely related or unrelated matters within the same paragraph. The ensuing attempt by the writer to achieve continuity, as he moves to his next paragraph, is bound to be difficult.

A closely related problem is that of length. The mistaken rule that paragraphs should ordinarily be of about equal length may provide a purely mechanical rhythm while destroying unity of thought and the sequential character of good writing. If the homogeneity required in a well-constructed paragraph demands twenty printed lines, so be it; similarly, a good paragraph may extend no more than a single line.

As we have seen, paragraphs which close one phase of action in narrative history and forecast an oncoming development in the next chapter are crucial. They are equally important in analytical history, where the mere availability of sectional subtitles is often an invitation to the unskilled to avoid any suggestion, even, of transition from one subject to the next. A book needs to exhibit unity. Its transitional sentences and paragraphs are essential to this purpose. The architecture of its interior paragraphs will largely determine its success or failure as historical writing.

Here we are at the heart of style, which is the heart of continuity. The word itself is definable only in terms which rob it of its magic. It is more easily recognized than accounted for. In fact, those who achieve it and are asked to convey its mysteries to others usually end up with an invitation to hard work. They know and we should know that writing one sequential paragraph after another is labor—intellectual, to be sure—of the most exacting kind. The earlier the experience is begun, they tell us, the more likely that real skill will ultimately be achieved. "Write, revise, and write some more!" If the schools don't force you, force yourself. It will always be a lonely business, anyway.

Examples of sequential paragraphs are freely available— from H. L. Mencken's account of how he created *ecdysiast* to cover the need of a strip-tease artist who had written him in search of respectability, to James Thurber's ear-opening reception by Harold Ross, convinced that no one knew any English anymore because of the goddam women teachers, to the prose of Agnes Repplier's essay, "Horace," her own *monumentum aere perennius*. And some scores of others. But consider, in the history of science, the position Louis Agassiz took when *On the Origin of Species* was published in 1859. The writing is that of Paul B. Sears in *Charles Darwin: The Naturalist as a Cultural Force*:

Not the least spectacular opponent of Darwin was Louis Agassiz, Swiss-born zoologist and Harvard colleague of Asa Gray, and one of the most accomplished naturalists of his day. That he had an original, even bold, mentality is shown by his proof of continental glaciation.[36] Yet he would not accept the doctrine of evolution. There is a legend of the laboratory backstairs that, on his death-bed, he admitted this to have been a professional mistake. In his youth he had for a time been close to Cuvier. He was also, like many of the young continental scientists of his day, tinged with the romantic naturalism to which Goethe had given his blessing.

Springing from eighteenth-century natural philosophy, and with a lineage back to the idealism of Plato, romantic naturalism was more like its shaggy, undisciplined parent than its austere remote ancestor. But, like both, it regarded ideas as the reality, and what most of us call reality it regarded as their imperfect reflection. To its followers evolution was no problem. Do not ideas show varying degrees of difference and resemblance? What more natural than that their clumsy material expressions—the forms of life—should do likewise? To turn from discourse such as this to the lucid writing of Asa Gray is like moving from a muddy brook to a limpid spring. For Gray would seem as reasonable to a Greek, or, I venture, to one of our descendants ten centuries from now as he does to us. Gray asserted his belief in a personal God, but the relationship was one of high dignity where neither he nor God presumed to put words into the mouth of the other.

In fairness to Agassiz—and he deserves the greatest generosity, for he was generous—it should be said that he did not confine himself to *a priori* reasoning, but also stated reasonable

[36] But see R. F. Flint, *Glacial Geology and the Pleistocene Epoch* (Wiley, 1947), 2–5.

objections. He called for evidence of the plasticity of species—which we now have. He also called for something more constructive than natural selection, a creative, dynamic, driving force within life itself. On this last point he had, and today has, distinguished company. He was not too completely apart from Darwin himself in that respect, if we allow for the characteristic caution with which Darwin dealt with the mysterious problem of variation.[37]

[37] Paul B. Sears, *Charles Darwin: The Naturalist as a Cultural Force,* 43–44.

5. Portraiture's Heroes and Villains

Most men who play leading roles in history, unlike the Iron Duke, live to a considerable extent according to the principle of concealment. Their public lives, even in anger, are largely controlled by the notion of self-preservation. Ahead lies posterity, fully capable of applying the judgment of Claudianus, "Virtue is the only entitlement to power." It is a sobering thought, often effective in inducing outward behavior, if not admirable, then at least inoffensive. But no amount of contrivance will provide, in the end, a shield against the assessment of character, which is a good deal more than the sum of its virtues and vices.

Character, as a matter of fact, is a whole complex of evidence, almost impossible to conceal from a man's contemporaries, still less from the historians who come after him. Perhaps its best definition is that it is "the individuality impressed by nature and habit on a man." At every stage of his career, a figure large or small in historical significance will give himself away by his actions, judgments, and private relations. The light in which he accordingly stands will conform, in spite of any of his protestations to the contrary, to what nature and his habits of thought and action have made him. Here concealment is largely unavailing. And it may be added that few men know themselves well enough to be able to afford future generations safe guidelines in autobiographies and memoirs for estimating their lives and achievements.

These concepts, however, lighten the burdens of the historical portraitist hardly at all. They merely stand as little red flags warning the writer to proceed according to the rules of credibility of evidence. The green light in the darkness, obviously, is the incorruptibility of character— that complex of attributes which not even the principal himself can alter or conceal.

This principle is sufficiently strong that it shows up often in fiction. Few novelists and short-story writers have failed to encounter in their own work the character who insists on going his own way. Whatever place and course he may have been foreordained to occupy in plan and plot nicely ordered ahead of time, he will be found, sooner or later, moving at an oblique or even a right angle. If the writer recalls him to the straight line of his original development, he quite probably will end up a thin cardboard portrait of a man, unconvincing to the reader and unmourned at his demise. There is a better than even chance, on the other hand, that, given his head, he will achieve substance and credibility.

It is one thing to understand the attributes of a historical figure and quite another to adjust to the writing requirements for their development. The task, moreover, is complicated by two negative factors. The first is the tendency of the beginner to follow the rhetorical modes made respectable by a previous generation of historians—actually two generations, from the teacher's teacher to the graduate student. What we often get, therefore, is of a style half a century old or older, but owing nothing, unfortunately, to Henry James. The second factor is the overcontrol exerted by the student's fear of "fine writing," induced by lectures and essay critiques which indict this tendency. Writers of manuals, guides, and stylebooks mention this injunction.[1] It has been so little explained, however, that it must remain a mystery to most beginners. Worse still, from repetition from generation to generation, this unanalyzed concept has caused hundreds of degree candidates to react like frightened rabbits. They choose declarative sentences over compound and complex ones. They avoid description of scene, the physical and intellectual description of men and women in it, the nature of the landscape and climate in all of their moods, and even the expressed feelings and attitudes of important historical characters, when the documentary evidence for such description is abundantly available.

Professor Louis Gottschalk, himself one of the manualists noted, has been at some pains, however, to suggest that the past and its characters can scarcely be understood unless the writer of history appreciates what understanding means in human terms. We are entitled to realize that human experience is more or less continuous. This does not mean that we may see the past solely from the point of view of our current awareness; we must, in fact, divorce ourselves from that notion. But what people did and how they reacted in the past can hardly be dissociated from what they do and how they react today.

To achieve this understanding without offending the rule against "fine writing," then, calls for something more than we have usually been given in the mentions of this subject. I think what the manualists mean by fine writing

1 There are many, but the most useful is Homer C. Hockett, *The Critical Method in Historical Research and Writing* (New York, The Macmillan Company, 1966): cf. pp. 169–73; Louis Gottschalk, *Understanding History: A Primer of Historical Method* (New York, Alfred A. Knopf, 1963): cf. pp. 46–48.

is overblown expression, the use of alliteration, the misplacement of metaphor (not its avoidance), the use of indirect constructions when direct ones are clearly called for, and in general a striving for effect with words and constructions which are unfamiliar vehicles for the writer.

For the highly skilled, the difference between fine writing and good writing in portraiture and characterization, which concern us in this chapter, the manualists' injunction has no meaning. Hardly a professional historian, no matter how traditional in his thinking, would fault Sir Herbert Butterfield's account of the Napoleonic battlefield after Jena, excerpted in Chapter 2. It is scene-making which offers also a tangential view of an emperor and one of his principal generals. The same scene, peopled with the same historical figures, and accompanied by an alphabetical list of the words employed by Butterfield, could result, at the hands of a minimally gifted person, in a piece of fine writing. The difference between gold and iron pyrites is slight to the uninitiated. But method and models and experience can in time provide a certain expertness. The first place to explore for it may be in the wilderness.

There, in the open setting of the western plains and mountains, we find an Indian, accounted for by a contemporary half-blood. The Indian is Roman Nose, whom George Bent recalled after the Battle of Beecher's Island, in which, as we have seen, he lost his life:

Roman Nose had never before been wounded except by an arrow in a fight with the Pawnees, yet he was always in front in battle and rarely had a horse shot under him. Roman Nose was killed in the prime of life; he was strong as a bull, tall even for a Cheyenne, broad-shouldered and deep-chested. . . .
[He] was the most famous Cheyenne warrior of his day. Although Little Wolf (Okohm-ha-ket), or Little Coyote, had

counted more coups, he was not as widely known as Roman Nose. As a boy Roman Nose was called Sautie (the Bat); but when he became a warrior he was given the name Woqini, meaning Hook Nose, which the whites always interpreted Roman Nose. . . . Contrary to the general opinion, Roman Nose was never a chief, nor was he even the head man of any of the soldier societies. He was a member of the Hi-moi-yo-quis, or Crooked Lance Society, so called from the peculiar lance carried by the leader. This society is sometimes called the Bone Scrapers, from a peculiar piece of elk horn made in the shape of a lizard and used in the dances of this society. I also belonged to the Crooked Lances and it was at the ceremonies of this society in the North in 1865 that I first made the acquaintance of Roman Nose. At the time of the great wars in the 1860's he was known as a great warrior to all the Indians of the Plains, and his fame so spread to the whites that they credited him with being leader in all the fights where the Cheyennes were engaged. Thus he was reported as being one of the leaders in the Fetterman battle near Fort Phil Kearny, in December, 1866, though at that time he was living quietly with the Dog Soldiers south of the Platte. In the summer of 1866 he had come south with Black Shin's Sutaio and Gray Beard's band of Dog Soldiers and he never went back north again. He liked the Dog Soldiers, who were the wildest and most aggressive fighters in our tribe, and he continued to live with them until his death. I knew him very well and found him to be a man of fine character, quiet and self-contained. All of the Cheyennes, both men and women, held him in the highest esteem and talk of him a great deal to this day.

Roman Nose always wore in battle the famous war bonnet which was made for him up north in 1860 by White Buffalo Bull (or Ice Bear), who is still living at Tongue River Agency and is one of the most famous of the old-time Northern Cheyenne medicine men. This war bonnet was the only one of its kind ever made. When a boy, Roman Nose fasted for four days on an island in a lake in Montana, and in his dreams saw a serpent with a single horn in its head. This was the reason White Bull came to make this peculiar war bonnet. Instead of having two buffalo horns attached to the head-band, one on each side, it had but one, rising over the center of the forehead; it had a very long tail that nearly touched the ground even when Roman Nose was mounted. This strip was made of a strip of young buffalo bull's hide, and had eagle feathers set all along the length, first four red feathers then four black ones, then four red feathers again, and so on, forty feathers in all. In making this famous war bonnet, White Bull did not use anything that had come from the whites, no cloth, thread, or metal. Usually war bonnets required little medicine-making when going into battle, but Roman Nose's bonnet was very sacred and required much ceremony. In taking it out of its hide case, it was held over a live coal on which was sprinkled a pinch of powder from a medicine root; then the bonnet was raised toward the sun four times, next unwrapped from its covering and held up to the north, west, south, and east, after which Roman Nose carefully put it on his head. With the war bonnet went sacred medicine paint for the face, which was, for the forehead, Indian yellow, red across the nose, and black across the mouth and chin. A strict set of rules of conduct went with the war bonnet: certain things he was forbidden to eat; he must not go into a lodge where a baby had been born until four days had passed; and there were other rules. White Bull particularly cautioned Roman Nose never to eat anything that had been touched by metal, and was told that if he neglected this rule he would be killed in the next battle.[2]

Thus a Sioux woman, serving Roman Nose at a feast given by Sioux warriors a few days before the Battle of Beecher's Island (September 17–25, 1868), had lifted his bread with an iron fork, and thus he died in the ensuing battle. Such

2 George Bent, *Life of George Bent . . .* , 306–308.

is the testimony of his young friend, George Bent, himself a member of the great Cheyenne-Sioux raiding parties of 1865–66.

If we look back at Herbert Eugene Bolton's central figure, Estevanico, Carl Coke Rister's General Phil Sheridan, and Élie Halévy's Duke of Wellington, we can detect, without too great a tax on the imagination, what they share with the portrait of Roman Nose drawn by Bent, the son of Owl Woman. It consists in the abundance and richness of detail in all four and the skill with which the detail has been structured. It consists also in the visibility of the character narrated or described. This is the real objective of portraiture, without which history hardly can be told. And it may be added that it makes little difference whether the portrait is of a human or of an institution—a Lombard Street painted by Walter Bagehot or a League of Nations described by Carlo Schmid.[3] If it is of a human, we must see him physically. We must find out about his habits of thought and action, their antecedents, the opinion held of him by his contemporaries (there is Indian humor in Bent's statement about the whites' belief Roman Nose led all the fights against them), the institutions in which he placed faith, and the character of his written or spoken expression. If it is of an institution, it must stimulate in the reader a fully rounded awareness of what it is, why it is important, and the directions of its historical development. Just as, in law, a corporation is said to have personality, so also in the history of any institution it too must have personality. For it possesses a certain organic character, not independent, to be sure, of its human components, but capable nevertheless

---

[3] Walter Bagehot, *Lombard Street: A Description of the Money Market* [1873], Fourteenth Edition, reprinted, 1924 (London, John Murray); Carlo Schmid, *Vorträge* (Tübingen, Frühling, 1931).

of the growth, troubles, and the minor or major achievements found in the lives of individuals. A legislature groping in an unfamiliar area of social legislation or a regulatory agency grown incapable of change exhibits a fallibility all too human but organically different from the human kind. There are also social and cultural institutions, each with a life of its own—art, music, the theater, letters, religion, and philosophical thought—conditioned by the tides of popular taste and thought, as well as the creativity of leading minds.

Because it offers capsule characterizations of individuals and an often elusive kind of institutional interpretation, that of the spirit of an age, we can examine profitably part of the extension of Vernon Louis Parrington's account of the Gilded Age in the United States, first noted in Chapter 1.

The period, Parrington tells us, had been cradled in the great changes that had been shaping America since 1815. It had been developing for more than fifty years, witnessing in its progress the decline of a harsh domestic economy, the enthusiasms of the Jacksonian coonskin democracy, a heady conquest of vast new lands in the Mexican War, the excitement of the California Gold Rush and the pioneer thrust into the Oregon Country, the new freedoms discovered in the forties and fifties, and the maturation produced by the cruel years of civil war. "Everywhere was a welling up of primitive pagan desires after long repressions—to grow rich, to grasp power, to be strong and masterful and lay the world at its feet." How did some of the leading actors look in the age later to be known as Gilded?

Created by a primitive world that knew not the machine, they were marked by the rough homeliness of their origins. Whether wizened or fat they were never insignificant or commonplace. On the whole one prefers them fat, and for solid bulk what generation has outdone them? There was Revivalist Moody, bearded and neckless, with his two hundred and eighty pounds of Adam's flesh, every ounce of which "belonged to God." There was a lyric Sankey, afflicted with two hundred and twenty-five pounds of human frailty, yet looking as smug as a banker and singing "There were ninety and nine" divinely through mutton-chop whiskers. There was Boss Tweed, phlegmatic and mighty, overawing rebellious gangsters at the City Hall with his two hundred and forty pounds of pugnacious rascality. There was John Fiske, a philosophic hippopotamus, warming the chill waters of Spencerian science with his prodigious bulk. There was Ben Butler, oily and puffy and wheezy, like Falstaff larding the lean earth as he walked along, who yearly added more flesh to the scant ninety-seven pounds he carried away from Waterville College. And there was Jim Fisk, dressed like a bartender, huge in nerve as in bulk, driving with the dashing Josie Mansfield down Broadway—prince of the vulgarians, who jovially proclaimed, "I worship in the Synagogue of the Libertines," and who on the failure of the Erie coup announced cheerfully, "Nothing is lost save honor!"

Impressive as are the fat kine of Egypt, the lean kine scarcely suffer by contrast. There were giants of puny physique in those days. There was Dan'l Drew, thin as a dried herring, yet a builder of churches and founder of Drew Theological Seminary, who pilfered and cheated his way to wealth with tobacco juice drooling from his mouth. There was Jay Gould, a lone-hand gambler, a dynamo in a tubercular body, who openly invested in the devil's tenements as likely to pay better dividends, and went home to potter lovingly amongst his exotic flowers. And there was Oakey Hall, a clubman and playwright, small, elegant, and unscrupulous; and Victoria Woodhull who stirred up the Beecher case, a wisp of a woman who enraged all the frumpy bluestockings by the smartness of her toilet and the perfection of her manners; and little Libby Tilton with her tiny wistful face and great eyes that looked out wonderingly at the world—eyes that were to go blind in weeping before the candle of her life went out. It was such men and women, individual and colorful, that Whitman and Mark Twain mingled with, and that Herman Melville—colossal and dynamic beyond them all—looked out upon sardonically from his tomb in the Custom House where he was consuming his own heart.

They were thrown up as it were casually out of the huge caldron of energy that was America. All over the land were thousands like them, self-made men quick to lay hands on opportunity if it knocked at the door, ready to seek it out if it were slow in knocking, recognizing no limitations to their powers . . . .[4]

In short, it was the beginning of the "golden age" of free enterprise, and these were some of its prophets.

There are three kinds of portraiture: (1) the descriptive kind, of which we have seen several examples; it is characterized by author viewpoint. (2) The kind which is developed from the viewpoint of a figure contemporary with the principal chosen for portraiture. And (3) the kind which, in the absence of physical and other data, must depend upon the historical narrative to produce a recognizable human character. Our immediate business is the second kind. One of its ablest expressions is contained in Allan Nevins's *Hamilton Fish: The Inner History of the Grant Administration*.

Meetings in the large, bright Cabinet Room (so used from Andrew Johnson to Theodore Roosevelt) on the second floor of the White House, above the East Room; meetings in the President's office on the same floor; meetings at official receptions and dinners; meetings at Fish's own house, to which Grant sometimes strolled for evening exercise—at all these Hamilton Fish continued his friendly scrutiny of the President.

Physically, Grant was unimpressive. He was scarcely five feet eight inches tall, slightly stooped, and so retiring in man-

4 Parrington, *op. cit.*, III, 13–14.

ner, especially in a crowded room, that he gave an appearance of shyness. When the war ended he had been slender, weighing at most one hundred and forty pounds; now he was portly enough to fill out his shining broadcloth frock coat. His hair, brushed back from his forehead in a rough cowlick, was becoming grizzled, but his close-cropped beard and mustache were still a warm chestnut brown. His Cromwellian wart, just above the mustache on the right side, was becoming lost in lines engraved by time. A high, broad, squarish brow was the feature which first caught attention; a brow now corrugated by heavy horizontal wrinkles, which with the thoughtful droop of his left eye gave him a careworn and rather sad aspect. The eyes were arresting, not large, not widely-spaced, their steel-blue glint bespoke determination; yet they held a perplexed look. But his most striking features were his mouth and chin. The lips showed grim firmness, meeting closely in an almost horizontal line; the jaw was square, heavy, and in repose had a set rigidity that expressed his tenacity and force of character. Once during his Presidency he shaved his chin, revealing it as even longer, squarer, and grimmer than people supposed—the chin of a fighter. His voice was low-pitched but exceedingly musical, one of the clearest and most distinct imaginable, and so penetrating that it was heard at a surprising distance. In talking he was fond of two gestures; he stroked his chin with his left hand, or rhythmically raised and lowered his right, resting it at intervals on his knee. Despite his grim, careworn appearance, his nature was actually buoyant and optimistic. In social exchanges his eyes often lit up with a merry twinkle, and he would sometimes laugh heartily. Like Lincoln, he was essentially democratic, while sometimes silent, he was never brusque; he treated everyone, great or small, with courtesy; and though his acts might be autocratic, his speech and manners never were. It was possible for men who knew him well, as Fish soon did, to conceive a genuine affection for him; but no one knew him so well that he ceased to be a little of a puzzle.

Little by little Fish made up his mind as to the President. Grant's was a contradictory personality, and facile generalization upon him are to be avoided . . . .[5]

What we have in this example is near perfect command of contemporary-character viewpoint. Its continuation, also seen largely through the eyes of Grant's Secretary of State, gets into Grant's intellectual and administrative characteristics, his not infrequent naivete, his awkward self-constraint in the presence of men more learned than he, his carelessness with official papers, and his suspicion of "reformers." As Fish saw, he had little consultative talent: he had been and was a military commander—and a very good one, but not in the constricting confines of the Cabinet Room.

In general, viewpoint may be described as the vantage point taken by the writer for presenting his narrative or sections of it. For the most part, it follows Form No. 1, author viewpoint, somewhere between heaven and earth, high enough so that individual actions and the unified whole can be seen clearly. But to be only slightly more technical about it, we can call it "omnipresent" viewpoint, principally because a historian is not permitted to do what a novelist is fully entitled to do, that is, make himself, as narrator, part of the action. He never—or almost never—intrudes the personal pronoun "I" into his account. Omnipresent viewpoint is one of the two earliest forms of relating history and describing the figures in it (the other being, as we have seen, the narration of a participant, e.g., Thucydides).

[5] Allan Nevins, *Hamilton Fish* . . . , 131–32. Professor John S. Ezell, a first-rate historiographer, reminds us that such a thoroughgoing portrait as Nevins' may be compared with the familiar textbook variety, whose defects can only demonstrate what should not be done. Too often, he feels, the style of graduate students and young historians is influenced more by textbook style (perhaps unconsciously) than by the better examples which beginners should be pursuing. John S. Ezell to S. L., February 13, 1974.

Form No. 2—character viewpoint—when it is available, adds a new and sophisticated dimension to portraiture. By a curious failure on the part of even the most mature historians, it is little used; and this failure is all the more striking when it is realized that a very high percentage of all historical action, as distinguished from its principals, must be seen through the eyes of those contemporary with it. The impersonal document thus dominates the technique. In Nevins' portrait of Grant, he subtly shifts from omnipresent viewpoint to character viewpoint at the end of the first paragraph describing cabinet meetings, "at all these Fish continued his friendly scrutiny of the President." Then he reminds us, after the long interval of the second paragraph, with an opening to the third paragraph, that the viewpoint is still that of Fish: "Little by little Fish made up his mind as to the President." Going on from that point, he gives us Fish's determination of Grant's inner character, to complement the thorough-going physical description preceding.

A further device—and a very important one—is to be seen in the early lines of this third paragraph. It is indirect construction, that is, narration not taken directly from Fish's own words, but from Nevins' third-person retelling from Fish. Such construction requires changes in pronouns and tenses, e.g., from the following, as shown:

"[Grant] could be incredibly awkward—so awkward that, retiring from a dining-room with the second Duke of Wellington, he broke a long silence by remarking, 'They tell me, my Lord, that your father was also a military man.'"

In indirect construction, the passage becomes:

"[Grant] could be incredibly awkward—so awkward that, retiring from a dining-room with the second Duke of Wellington, he broke a long silence by remarking that he had been told that the Duke's father had also been a military man."[6]

Indirect narrative construction has first-rate uses when masses of documentary materials—letters memoranda, memoirs, reports, and the observations of contemporary figures—cannot be quoted satisfactorily or, because of their disconnected character, quotation *ad infinitum* from them is both uneconomical and tedious. Such construction, however, is best confined to portraiture of limited extent, scene-making, and settings which must, by their nature, depend upon direct observation of contemporaries. Once such indirect construction is settled upon, the writer should not vary from it until he brings the episode to a close. Nevins himself introduces direct quotation into his indirect narration, and from time to time shifts in midstream to author-viewpoint, but in the main he preserves rather admirably both character-viewpoint and indirect construction, when he adopts the latter as a natural accompaniment to the former.

Before we turn to Form No. 3 in portraiture, something must be said about legitimacy and illegitimacy in the employment of Forms No. 1 and No. 2. For those who take the trouble to read the continuation of the third paragraph quoted from Nevins' portrait of Grant, it will be found that the author builds characteristic upon characteristic in Grant, so that, without ever using the word psychology, he gives us, nevertheless, a firm basis upon which to understand the man and the peculiar conditions—I do not say conditioning—which affected the military figure now become president. But there is a fine line between the facts of a man's life and an effort to recreate his innermost self. The one is fully admissible in history or biography and the other

6 Nevins, *Hamilton Fish*, 134.

is something of a game, and as such will always be suspect. The exception is not the work of a historian but of a friend (Fish), associated over a long period of time with a person of significance, observing almost daily and recording what he expressly said and felt. Louis Mertins' account of Robert Frost, the poet, and S. N. Behrman's portrait in character of Sir Max Beerbohm, the novelist-essayist, are much above average examples of the latter.[7] An example of gamesmanship is the attempt to read more into the facts of Charles Dickens' married life than the record as such reveals. The Dickens case is an overreaching attempt to account for a certain loneliness in a man who betrayed practically none of it in his writing.[8]

Thus the rigid rules of evidence and judgment required by the historical writing process will always be put to their severest test in the portraits which appear in literary and intellectual history. For the scholar and his readers can never be satisfied with the literary output—or even the scientific output—of the man: his life and character, interesting perhaps in themselves, may also throw literary-critical light upon his writing. What often happens, however, is an almost overpowering impulse to conjecture. No one was less free of the hazard than William Faulkner:

And when I found that people read the books and got pleasure from them and found in them something of what I tried to put [in], I was very flattered. Though they found things in those books that I was too busy to realize I was putting in the books. They found symbolism that I had no background in symbolism to put in the books. But what symbolism is in the books is evidently instinct in man, not in man's knowledge

[7] Louis Mertins, *Robert Frost: Life and Talks-Walking*; S. N. Behrman, *Portrait of Max: An Intimate Memoir of Sir Max Beerbohm.*

[8] Edward Wagenknecht, *Dickens and the Scandalmongers: Essays in Criticism.*

but in his inheritance of his old dreams, in his blood, perhaps his bones, rather than in the storehouse of his memory, his intellect.[9]

In the history of science, it is easy to read more, for example, into Johannes Kepler's *Somnium* (written in 1608) than the known evidence will sustain. In his imaginary trip to the moon, based upon a science so prophetic that it has at last found support in the age of rocketry, are we to paint a picture of the scientist as social liberal (such doctrines as Kepler's were not entirely acceptable to authorities in his day), or are we to understand that he was merely having fun? Was he a daring young man on a political trapeze or was he expressing scientific hypotheses for which the world was not then prepared?

Unlike the attractions found in the personal lives of creative men and women, the careers of long-dead political and administrative figures leave little room for faulty recreations. For such people, the only resource of the historian is found in Form No. 3, in which, we may recall, in the absence of physical and salient character evaluations by contemporaries, the portrait of the man accrues, instead, from his decisions and actions. Thus, while we have one conventional likeness of Teodoro de Croix, painted during his ascendant phase in the Spanish manner, we must look elsewhere for this creator of much from little in Spanish colonial administration. What emerges from the Archives of the Indies—his reports, letters, and memoranda, and the various documents addressed to him from his superiors—is a figure of more than a touch of genius in the military organization of the northern provinces of New Spain, 1776–81.[10]

9 From Faulkner's Nagano speech, quoted in Joseph Gold, *William Faulkner: A Study in Humanism, from Metaphor to Discourse*, 19–20.

10 Alfred Barnaby Thomas, trans. and ed., *Teodoro de Croix and the Northern Frontier of New Spain, 1776–1783*, passim.

Or, to take another such figure, of whom we have no painting or artist's sketch, nor any physical or character description, we come away with an entirely human impression of Jacobo Ugarte through his actions between 1769 and 1791 in the same theater. He was a military man and his business was to contain, and if possible to remove entirely, the Apache Indian threat to the northern frontier of Mexico. He develops, through the documents (most of them his own), as a better desk man than a soldier, gifted, imaginative, mostly right when his superiors and often jealous colleagues were wrong. He displays a singleness of purpose. He proves himself tenacious and, often to the impatience of viceroys and military commanders, entirely stubborn. His official accounts were usually in order but his personal ones were almost always chaotic. Like a careless housewife, his liquidity was nil and his indebtedness constant. Yet he had it in him to lend (when he should himself have been borrowing) enough to his Indian charges to pay their imperial taxes. Because of these and other characteristics which emerge in his actions, we can be sorely tempted to believe that Don Jacobo Ugarte would have been attractive to a literary compatriot who had lived a century and a half before him—Miguel de Cervantes Saavedra. The reason is simple: he benefited none at all from the Spanish colonial vice of nepotism, and he refused to benefit his ensign nephew, passing him over entirely for advances in rank under his command. He was a medieval knight of honor in an often evil world.[11]

Institutional portraiture, because it recognizes the personality inherent in human institutions, requires an organic approach, very much as we have discovered it in the portrai-

[11] Max L. Moorhead, *The Apache Frontier: Jacobo Ugarte and Spanish-Indian Relations in Northern New Spain, 1769–1791, passim.*

ture occasioned by individuals. Why organic? Because the institution, much like the individual, exhibits a large degree of self-determined unity. It is the business of the historian to find it, whether in a parenthetical paragraph or in a volume or volumes. The man whom Lord Bryce called "the most original mind of his generation," Walter Bagehot, displayed a fine command of the technique in *Lombard Street*, an account of the London money market, with the Old Lady of Threadneedle Street, the Bank of England, at its center. In the memory of those now living, it was still an essay topic in entrance examinations for admission to Oxford, although it first appeared in 1873. (The tenuous relations between undergraduates, usually in arrears, and bankers and tradesmen, too often their sole means of support, may have suggested an added value to the exercise, which, however, seems never to have been realized.) It had not been on the bookstands long when it became recognized as a model of narrative and expository writing, so lucid and easy to grasp that not only the money market itself but the great English and imperial central bank could be understood by almost anyone. The Bank of England was then only twenty-one years short of its two-hundredth anniversary, but it had already long since achieved historical personality. Bagehot tells one anecdote from the financial community which bears out the fact:

The Bank of England had, till lately, the monopoly of limited liability in England. The common law of England knows nothing of any such principle. It is only possible by Royal Charter or Statute Law. And by neither of these was any *real* bank (I do not count absurd schemes such as Chamberlayne's Land Bank) permitted with limited liability in England till within these few years. Indeed, a good many people thought it was right for the Bank of England, but not right for any other bank. I remember hearing the conversation of a distinguished merchant in the City of London, who well represented the ideas then most current. He was declaiming against banks of limited liability, and some one asked—"Why, what do you say, then, to the Bank of England, where you keep your own account?" "Oh!" he replied, "that is an exceptional case." But no doubt it was an exception of the greatest value, because it induced many quiet and careful merchants to be directors of the Bank, who certainly would not have joined any bank where *all* their fortunes were liable, and where the liability was not limited.[12]

The general law of limited liability, enacted in 1862, would extend the same immunities enjoyed by Bank of England stockholders and directors to their counterparts in other joint-stock banks. But the value of Bagehot's anecdote, like Lord North's often repeated assertion that the Bank was "part of the British constitution," lies in custom and usage and acceptance which had clustered about the Bank and made it, if not an exception to the rule of the law, then at least the most informally organized among the great central banks of the world. It is just this quality which makes it one of the most inviting for historical study. Where that study has led may afford further illustration of its organic character.

Bagehot's is a long essay (the name he gives it) following on the heels of Thomas Babington Macaulay's account of the origins of the Bank. The history of the Bank, in the formal sense, came 251 years after its founding, with the publication of Sir John Clapham's two large volumes in 1945. They carry to 1914, with an epilogue extending to the close of World War II.[13] No one reading these volumes

[12] Walter Bagehot, *Lombard Street: A Description of the Money Market*, 94.

[13] There have been others, both long and short, but the full, abundantly detailed history is the one referred to: Sir John Clapham, *The Bank of*

can mistake the work and influence of persons, the Parliamentary concerns and enactments, the stresses brought on by wars, and the crises induced by domestic and foreign financial events. But the Bank is the unmistakable entity of the long history, as it is of English financial and economic life since 1694.

It was a privately owned joint-stock bank from the time of its charter renewal in 1709 until it became government-owned in 1946. As such it was an anomaly. But it was not less than the most effective central bank in the world during that time. Its internal rules were, often as not, understood rules, rather than enactments: the governance and operation of the Bank rested with its General Court of Proprietors (stockholders); its Court, consisting of twenty-four directors; the Governor of the Bank, chosen from its directors, normally serving for only two years; and the Deputy-Governor, similarly chosen and normally destined to succeed to the governorship. Its functioning rested early with a very small number of employees, later and now with more than one thousand. For the institutional portraitist, these facts about the Bank's public and private character and organization have significant value, for they establish at the outset of his efforts the need for a corporate rather than a personal interpretation. The highly condensed historical analysis which follows is essential to an understanding of the pragmatism in the Bank's founding and subsequent operations, the competitive nature of its early environment, and the course by which it became the custodian of English and world banking principle. These are some of the historical ingredients for the portrait of a particular institution.

The Bank had been created in 1694 largely for the

England: A History (2 vols., Cambridge, the University Press, 1945, and New York, The Macmillan Company, 1945).

purpose of remedying the financial plight of William of Orange, then on the British throne. Its vigorous competitors and severest critics early in the game were the London goldsmiths, who largely controlled money changing and lending after 1700. With the Bank's joint-stock status after 1709 and the restriction of all other banks to individual or partnership status, it had achieved a certain flexibility which could lead to a position of dominance, and from dominance to central-bank recognition. Central to the latter was the management of the public debt, control of the currency (a considerable part of which, until 1844, rested with private banks), management of the country's gold stocks, and the control of credit expansion and contraction achieved largely through Bank rate, or interest on loans. This evolution required most of the eighteenth and nineteenth centuries. In institutional terms, it was the period of learning how to apply the techniques of national monetary and credit management.

When Lord North said in 1781 that the Bank was "to all important purposes the public exchequer," he was not merely paying a compliment to that financial institution but recognizing what its evolution, as well as government and private banking practice, had given it, namely de facto indispensability. As long ago as 1730, private banks had begun to back away from banknote issues of their own in favor of the Bank's. But they had also invented the printed check, in virtue of which they were able gradually to close out their banknote issues. What this would ultimately mean to expansion and contraction of credit the Bank had to learn and cope with. It would also learn in the Napoleonic era what gold-drains would mean to its backing of its own banknotes and British Treasury notes. The lessons of competition were ever with it, for not even the Banking Act of 1844 (which separated its banking and note-issuing functions) would relieve it from being one bank among many, whatever the value of its entitlements and immunities. It could even sink if events conspired to that end, as indeed they did in 1860 when Overends, Guerney & Company raided its reserves, only to return its huge withdrawal in the form of banknotes cut in two, with its apologies. The Bank had raised the Bank rate and had refused to back down. Like a resolute individual, it had stiffened its back under the threat and had won. The Old Lady of Threadneedle Street had grown by principle, and she would survive by it. She would weather the storms of the later nineteenth century: the failure of Overends in 1866, the gold-drains to France and later to Prussia as a consequence of the Franco-Prussian War, a world-wide economic crisis in 1873, the gallant salvaging of Barings by the Bank between 1890 and 1895, and the strains of the Boer War.

Any institutional portraitist must raise for himself the question whether there is such a thing as institutional memory. For when the institution is less the child of law than of principle and practice, memory seems an essential condition of continuity—at least of the successful kind. The actions of the Governors and Courts of the Bank of England from 1730 onwards, as developed by Sir John Clapham's account, make clear that the critical lessons of the past were very much in the minds of management. But institutional memory of the negative kind—"We burned our fingers in 1898 but we have carefully avoided repeating the experience"—is commonplace in most business and industrial contexts. And it is almost always corporate, for the misjudgments of individuals tend, in the long run, to become buried in corporate responsibility. Institutional memory of the positive, innovative kind, on the other hand, appears historically to be much more difficult of development and retention. The exception, again, is found in the Bank, whose steady development of banking principle in 280 years traces to corporate thinking rather than to dazzling performances by individual governors or directors. A governor, after all, arrived at his elevation by seniority and by rotation, usually, as has been noted, for a term of only two years. Whatever his qualities of leadership—and they were often strong—it remains that positive action or innovative change flowed in actuality from the Court of Directors.

That the Bank accordingly developed institutional memory of the positive kind, even though it refrained in most instances from codifying it, is illustrated by its correspondence with developing central banks abroad. "Younger national institutions will often ask for its rules or its statutes, and are always told there is no book of rules; that its Charter would be of very little use to them; and that its relations with the Exchequer have never been codified from the relevant Acts of Parliament."[14] The institutional command of principle, moreover, was larger by a great deal than the Bank itself. For the Directors embraced most of the leading minds of the merchant City of London from the beginning.

However strong such inheritance may be, it remains that the national environment had a great deal to do with the lines of development the Bank took over the centuries. It was conceived and grew up in a highly stratified society, whose conventions, mores, and persistence in changing times set the conditions of continuity to be found nowhere else in Europe, or, indeed, in the New World. (The survival and continuing strength, socially and philanthropically at least, of the ancient guild organizations into the twentieth

14 Clapham, *The Bank of England*, II, 351–52.

century in England may throw more than small light historically upon the subject of such environment.) It was not always so, but the dignities admired in the City were part of an environment which ultimately accorded the Bank a position in financial respectability matched only by the See of Canterbury.

Stability, the condition to which, ideally, both inheritance and environment tend, is sometimes placed in jeopardy or fails. In such case, the institution becomes more understandable in human terms. Its controlled frights and struggles are, in fact, only once removed from the human kind. Their significance in terms of institutional portraiture is almost self-evident. For here error and extrication cut to the heart of things. The Bank and the British pound, closely tied to gold reserves and the convertability of banknotes to gold, had survived for a very long time. The pound was unassailable world-wide except during periods of extraordinary gold-drains from abroad and the exigencies of war, most notably World War I. But the changed climate of the economy at home and abroad, and particularly the threat of high inflation in England in 1919, caused the committee chaired by Lord Cunliffe, then Governor of the Bank, to recommend to the Treasury restrictions on currency and credit. The Treasury accordingly instructed the Bank to so act in 1920. Thereafter economic collapse occurred. Here, the Bank, as conservator of banking principles for the world, had itself acted too exclusively upon a single instrument of economic policy, as yet too little understood.

The unprecedented twenty-four-year reign of Montagu Norman as Governor, from 1920 to 1944, witnessed the long struggle of the Bank to cope with credit and currency controls in a much changed environment. The gold standard, suspended during World War I, was restored in 1925, relinquished in 1931, and not restored after World War II. The lessons learned and the new techniques developed by the Bank in this period made of it an institution coming abreast of modern, i.e., troubled, times. Yet it was ever the British banking personality. This, in quieter times and under other banking reserve conditions, Walter Bagehot had described convincingly three quarters of a century before:

> . . . You might as well, or better, try to alter the English monarchy and substitute a republic, as to alter the present constitution of the English Money Market, founded on the Bank of England, and substitute for it a system in which each bank shall keep its own reserve. There is no force to be found adequate to so vast a reconstruction, and so vast a destruction, and therefore it is useless proposing them.[15]

These are some of the data and a few of the concepts required in portraiture directed to institutional purposes. Nothing has been said about the young woman who ascended the throne of England in 1837 and the old queen who left it in 1901. Any similes that come to mind have no broad purpose, and it is somehow doubtful that "Victorianism" had much to do with the course of the Bank during nearly two-thirds of the nineteenth century. The proprieties had already been learned in Sir Robert Peel's time, even if there were confrontations yet to be met. If institutional analysis suggests that the Bank is an almost ideal case for portraiture, it must be said also that, however unique it may be, it is not without concrete lessons for the development of many other types of institutional portraiture, including even the Congress of the United States. The capacity of the latter for innovation may be less, but its negative

15 Bagehot, *op. cit.*, 310–11.

memory may be more. And wherever the institutional portraitist looks—to the business corporation, the U. S. Postal Service, or one of the established representatives of the arts—he must early be impressed with the existence of challenge and response in the institution. For in any extended institutional life public and competitive challenges are the order of the day and the responses to them the condition of survival.

6. Time, Place, and the Cultural Milieu

"THE STAGE," William Hazlitt observed of the successors of David Garrick, "is always beginning anew; the candidates for theatrical reputation are always setting out afresh, unincumbered by the affectation of the faults or excellence of their predecessors." Onstage for Hazlitt's critical appraisal of Massinger's *A New Way to Pay Old Debts*, which he published January 14, 1816, in *The Examiner*, were Edmund Kean for David Garrick, who had lain in Poets' Corner of Westminster Abbey these twenty-seven years, and Miss O'Neill for Sarah Siddons, whose farewell appearance in *Macbeth* four years before was triumphantly broken up by the audience at the sleep-walking scene, which she "carried to perfection." Garrick, the genius of Drury Lane, survives in the history of the stage, as does the incomparable Mrs. Siddons, but his times and ours have been less kind to Mr. Kean (Byron is said to have been convulsed by his performance as Sir Giles Overreach in Massinger's play), and Miss O'Neill must be searched for to be found at all.[1]

Historical writing, like Hazlitt's stage, is always beginning anew. Its candidates for historical reputation are always setting out afresh—no matter how many earlier writers upon the scene have reworked the research and produced

---

[1] William Hazlitt, *The Collected Works of William Hazlitt*, ed. by A. R. Waller and Arnold Glover, V, 272.

their analyses. The invitation to perfection leaves them unencumbered by "the excellence of their predecessors." As we have witnessed, however, it takes a very strong Mr. Kean to displace a long-dead Mr. Garrick. And in history, which can be seen and compared with other histories of the same events, the invidious example has far greater survival value than the remembered delights of inflection and gesture under the proscenium.

But there are other values to be found in the theater by the historian. From its opening scene a play and its players must strive for quick comprehension by the audience of the time and place of the action, and as the action develops it must convey an understanding of its cultural milieu. For these are the elements of situational command in the art of the playwright. If the play also achieves the quality of absorption, a phenomenon recognized by Hazlitt, Thomas DeQuincy, and Charles Lamb as "theatrical illusion," it has transformed its audience from a condition of inertia to a situation just short of participation. This condition is, as every theater-goer knows, an almost indescribable interchange between actors upon a shallow-dimensioned stage and the deep dimension the audience represents to its farthest seat.

When we turn from the stage in any period to the historical forum in our own, what we see invites critical analysis. Here, in historical journals and other periodicals, we find the situational devices of time and place frequently assumed rather than stated, and the cultural and social setting often passed over but lightly. Because the historical essay and the journal article are relatively short, they tend to reduce or leave out many factors which are useful in orienting their readers. It is assumed that the latter, being themselves professionals, will fill in these essentials of the larger historical canvas. The assumption is never justified, even in the shorter forms of historical writing; in the long forms of the thesis, dissertation, or book, it begs the questions which even highly specialized readers require for a rounded impression. With every piece of historical writing the assumption must be made that nothing is known and everything is new. The assumption is technically sound and it usually proves to be literarily rewarding. Theatrical illusion is our task too.

Aside from the basic assumption of many writers of journal articles, that only specialists will review their writing when published, there are three other patterns of thought or style which, seriously defective in the short form, can be close to disastrous in the long. The first of these consists in begging a long descriptive title for date or period, and often place as well. This course is presumed to relieve the writer of the necessity of orienting his readers early in the conceptual frame of his essay. If the piece is subsequently reproduced with a cover-title, not repeated at the head of the text, the result can be ludicrous. But this is a chance, not the main concern. Any piece of writing should be self-contained and wholly independent of its title, which in many cases is less than descriptive of its contents. Serious historical writing, moreover, which begs data from chapter titles (corresponding to journal-article titles) is far from uncommon. The mistake is usually traceable to the earliest forms of writing which the student tried to master—but unsuccessfully.

A second pattern (by now a formula which has hardened into majority acceptance) is the straw-man approach in article writing. It is at least half a century old but only now full-flowering. It sometimes takes the place of a conceptual opening paragraph, or it quickly follows it. The form is all too familiar: "Recent scholarship has tended to erase the distinction, set up originally in the nineteenth century, between cotton and tobacco culture in the South. Davenport, Smith, Wayne, and Garstenberg have all, in varying degrees, arrived at this conclusion. It will be the purpose of this article to show that . . ." What follows is an elaborate, heavily annotated demonstration that Davenport, Smith, Wayne, and Garstenberg were all, "in varying degrees," wrong. And because these peers of the article-writer are on the latter's mind, he assumes that he can avoid dealing with the obvious, i.e., simple or delimiting dates, places, states, subregions, and the larger agricultural environment in which the cotton and tobacco economy exists. Or, if he goes so far as to nod to specific or broad chronology, the act often enough lacks force.

The case is figurative but the formula is not. It scarcely crosses our minds that the latter is an invitation to tea of the fifth water, a rather grave dilution. But the extent to which the formula has taken hold is of more importance, in the long run, than what it produces. Quantification can help us at this point.

Of the sixteen articles appearing in *The American Historical Review*, Vol. 77, Nos. 1–5, inclusive, 1972, ten offer the formula described above in easily identifiable form. The presence of two senior scholars in the group, both of whom avoid the formula, provides a certain aspect of control to the critical analysis. Of twenty-three articles appearing in *The Journal of American History*, Vol. LIX, Nos. 1–4, inclusive, 1972–1973, fourteen offer the formula, with two articles by senior scholars, again staying clear of the formula and exhibiting writing of genuine roundness and excellence. In the two sets of articles, the management of time is at best spotty, with some notable exceptions, of which the articles by the senior scholars in each instance are exemplary. Place and milieu suffer similarly, but with the exceptions previously noted for senior scholars.

The wars over cause and effect in historical analysis are far from closed, but it is perhaps safe to say that the currency of the straw-man formula and the conceptual-analytical paragraph opening are traceable to the familiar dissertation abstract exacted by most graduate schools. Boiled down or not boiled down at all, it frequently reappears in journal articles, where it may haunt those who have insisted upon its survival. Only those who are more deeply engrossed in the psychoanalytical aspects of history than the present writer can say whether abstract-preparation has weakened the younger historian's grasp of the importance of early identification of time and place. But, with or without training, the suspicion can always cross one's mind.

The foregoing quantification will have identified the third defective pattern. It is the extent to which the straw-man formula commits the writer to a largely analytical type of construction. As earlier chapters in this book have shown, the case for analytical historical writing scarcely needs defense. But the kind of analysis which emerges from the straw-man concept is often deadly, particularly when it is applied to small ends, as must be the case in journal articles. There can be only one graver fault, i.e., the *a priori* approach with instant contradictions.

The English theater in the first quarter of the nineteenth century was chosen for the opening of the present chapter largely because the history of this cultural form will waive no neglect of its temporal and situational aspects. But the student of form will have to range very widely before he finds examples of excellence—indeed any examples at all— dealing with this and other cultural institutions in historical journals. Of the thirty-nine articles appearing in the two journals cited, none is concerned with art, music, the theater, or belles lettres, save one which deals with Florentine architecture in the Italian Renaissance. (Sex, which is represented in one article on the Progressive Era, might, by a stretch of the imagination, be thought of as a "cultural institution," but anthropologists can normally be expected to handle it better than historians.) The popular and the more critical areas of taste—in painting, sculpture, musical forms, plays, the novel, poetry, and, indeed, the writings of historians—are obviously significant components of any cultural environment in the nineteenth and twentieth centuries. Yet they have played small roles in most general historical writing, as any cursory review of the subject will confirm. As subjects of investigation and writing in their own right, they often fall (with the exception of historiography) to other disciplines or to gifted and inquisitive hobbyists. What this does to the historian who feels compelled to give some accounting of the environment at any given time is obvious: he must rely for the "feel" of society in its nonpolitical aspects upon professions other than his own. Such borrowing is not in itself a sin. The sin occurs when the cultural institution appears (in spite of the writer's best efforts) as an ornamental rather than a genuinely understood aspect of life in its historical context.

From the point of view of historical writing *qua* writing, there are two technical problems here. The first arises from the fact other disciplines employ analytical tools which do not serve sequential ends, primarily. The other, primarily the fault of the historian, is that cultural institutions cannot safely be thought of as general but must be viewed as individual and specific. Thus, in the first instance, the traditional literary historian is moved more by critical-analytical concepts than by the historical pursuit of successions. "The historian," Professor Higham tells us, "moves *between* particular experiences to learn how one begot another. But to establish these relationships he employs both the values of the artist and the inclusive propositions of the scientist; in his hands tested constructs and untestable values become functional to a narrative task."[2]

The second problem, that of specificity, often gets lost in overextended attempts to depict the spirit of an age, or in more limited writing veers from required facts to broad generalizations. It is not enough to write that "New York was enjoying a full season of opera in the winter of 1909–10," in an account of metropolitan growth. Two great opera organizations, the Metropolitan and Oscar Hammerstein's Manhattan Opera Company were competitively filling their respective halls with "divine sound." Competition in this area of the arts is in itself a phenomenon, but what kinds of operas did the cultural climate of New York demand in that era, and who were the divine voices?[3] In painting, the historian's concern for successions calls for specific evaluations, e.g., in this particular era, the place occupied by the Post-Impressionists. Were the museums and art galleries as hesitant about them as they had been about the Impressionists—Cézanne, Monet, Degas, Pissaro, and Miss Mary Cassatt of Philadelphia—thirty years before?[4] Styles are developed by creative artists, tastes by

2 John Higham, *Writing American History,* 29. The author's entire book will be found not only well balanced but highly stimulating, particularly in its approach to socio-historical concepts.

3 M. L. Cone, *Oscar Hammerstein's Manhattan Opera Company,* 208–74. At another level of popular taste, Lester S. Levy, *Grace Notes in American History: Popular Sheet Music from 1820 to 1900,* and the same author's *Flashes of Merriment: A Century of Humorous Songs in America, 1805–1905,* reveal in depth resources not easily available to the cultural historian.

4 Frederick A. Sweet, *Miss Mary Cassatt, Impressionist from Pennsylvania,* 104ff.

audiences. The extent to which the latter were subject to manipulation in any given period will always be a serious hazard in the writing of cultural and social history. But the long perspective, when it can be used, will often straighten out the curve of probability. The Impressionist paintings Miss Cassatt tried to interest her Philadelphia and New York friends in buying for $250 to $750 in the 1870's and 1880's were commanding hundreds of thousands in the 1960's. What perspective has done for the Impressionists it has done in lesser degree for American artists, early and late, like George Caleb Bingham, Thomas Moran, George Bellows, Charles Demuth, and (much later than she deserved) Miss Cassatt.[5]

The situational aspects of historical writing, whether in an article or in book-length, include the bad as well as the good. It is normal for historians, among other intellectuals, to look only for the good in art. But the bad also occupies the historical landscape, and it sometimes dominates, conditioning the lives of children as well as adults in strange ways. Equestrian statues of Civil War generals, swords drawn, occupy hundreds of town and city squares, while nearby the neo-classical courthouse, surmounted by a figure of Justice with balanced scales outstretched, casts its architectural shadow over a century or more of urban life. The serenity with which several generations of Americans have lived in the presence of such artistic phenomena is, in the historical writer's search for situational points of departure, worth remarking. Literarily, the period from 1870 to 1910

[5] John Francis McDermott, *George Caleb Bingham: River Portraitist*, depicts the artist's achievement; the values are reflected in an asking price of $95,000 of the National Gallery, which was considering the acquisition of one portrait a year after the publication of the book in 1959. Cf. Thurman Wilkins, *Thomas Moran: Artist of the Mountains*, 242; Emily Farnham, *Charles Demuth: Behind a Laughing Mask, passim.*

contains much besides the excellence found in Mark Twain, William Dean Howells, the brothers Henry and Brooks Adams, Henry James, Stephen Crane, and Frank Norris. Popular reading was besieged by the dime novel and cheap magazines, which constituted less a threat to morals than to narrative tastes and personal expressions in letters, memoirs, and journals.[6]

The specifics of historical situation are not merely a human scene but one identifiable in its social or cultural or political reality; not merely in chronological time but in seasonal time with its variant moods; not merely in geographical location but in the distinguishing characteristics of a particular place. The skill with which Allan Nevins incorporated these situational details as he moved from the scene in Washington in 1858 to Lawrence, Kansas, at the same instant is illustrative of transition, as we saw in Chapter 4. But it is also a demonstration of situational techniques, as we have defined them. Coming closer to our own day, Professor Arthur Link of Princeton, the premier scholar of the Wilsonian period in American history, has taken a period of little more than a year in his *Wilson: The Struggle for Neutrality*, covering 1914–15. The writing is of a high order. The author accepts a certain measure of topicality, as the structure of his book reveals, but he never lets this approach dominate his essentially narrative determinations. The skill with which he accomplishes his double purpose is nowhere so apparent as in his chapter openings, which reveal a measure of narrative continuity which can only be described as admirable. If we examine no more than the opening to his first chapter, it will be enough to

---

6 Albert Johannsen, *The House of Beadle and Adams and Its Dime and Nickel Novels: The Story of a Vanished Literature*, 3 vols. (Norman, University of Oklahoma Press, 1950, 1962), II, *seriatim*.

demonstrate what happens when the writer has situational command:

> Spring was coming to an end in Washington. Young cherry trees had long since blossomed feebly in the tidal basin, and the days were bringing heat that hung like an oppressive pall. Never since his inauguration as twenty-eighth president had the days been so crowded or the nights so restless for Woodrow Wilson as during late May and early June of 1914. The danger of war with Mexico raised by the American occupation of Veracruz in April now seemed safely past, but there were new perplexities in that strife-torn land. On Capitol Hill the two houses were mired in confusion over antitrust bills, and a furious debate raged in the Senate over some of Wilson's nominees to the new Federal Reserve Board. Nor could the President find relief by turning his thoughts away from Washington or inward to his family circle. The country was in shock over the outbreak of civil war in Colorado, the culmination of a bloody conflict between the United Mine Workers and mine owners, the appeals for action were pouring in daily upon the White House. More agonizing still was Ellen Wilson's failure to recover from a long illness and the gnawing fear that she might not get well.
>
> In the background, not yet urgent in the President's thoughts, was the mounting crisis in Europe and the threat of war. . . .[7]

Seven weeks later, on July 27, with domestic concerns still uppermost in his mind, Wilson would respond to reporters' questions whether he would tender his good offices towards a general European conference to preserve the peace. It was not the traditional policy of the United States, he

---

[7] Arthur S. Link, *Wilson: The Struggle for Neutrality, 1914–1915*, 1. (The work cited is the third volume of the author's ongoing multi-volumed biography of Wilson; with assistants, he has also edited *The Papers of Woodrow Wilson*, which had been advanced to sixteen volumes in 1973.)

said, to "take part" in political affairs outside the Western Hemisphere.[8]

Not surprisingly, the situational elements contained in this extract are ten in number. Time, which can be one of history's most treacherous passages, is represented by four, of which the "young cherry trees" which "had blossomed feebly in the tidal basin" is at once strikingly figurative and chronologically accurate. (The first eighty were Mrs. William Howard Taft's gift as recently as 1907, and three thousand more from Japan had been planted only three years before.) The crisis situational elements are six, one of which, personal in character, is the critical illness of Mrs. Wilson. From this situational base the swift narrative which follows takes its departure. We have seasonal scene, geographical scene, and, above all, a gathering urgency. That the new historical writer on the Washington scene will have to put his imagination to work is fully clear from the fact that both Mr. Link and Mr. Nevins have already entered a patent on the humid heat of a Capital summer. It is up to the newcomer to find some other way of saying it.

The Americanist's interests do not forbid him to look to other areas of history for situational models. One of these, published just over one hundred years ago, remains to the present day a respectable, even a brilliant, demonstration of milieu. John Richard Green in *A Short History of the English People* (1874) must face up to a greatly changed situation as the second Charles took the throne in the Restoration of 1660. The Puritan Revolution had run its course, its religious fervor and harsh morality depleted—at least in London—and the English people, weary of the restraints it had imposed upon their historic social and

8 *The New York Times*, July 28, 1914, in Link, *op. cit.*, 3.

cultural freedoms, longed for a return to the innocent pleasures as well as the monarchy they had known in other times. Cromwell himself saw the oncoming change, which many historians would later say signalized the beginning of the Modern Period:

If religious enthusiasm had broken the spell of ecclesiastical tradition, its own extravagance broke the spell of religious enthusiasm; and the new generation turned in disgust to try forms of political government and spiritual belief by the cooler and less fallible test of reason. It is easy to see the rapid spread of such a tendency even in the families of the leading Puritans. Neither of Cromwell's sons made any pretensions to religion. Cromwell himself in his later years felt bitterly that Puritanism had missed its aim. He saw the country gentleman, alienated from it by the despotism it had brought in its train, alienated perhaps even more by the appearance of a religious freedom for which he was unprepared, drifting into love of the older Church that he had once opposed. He saw the growth of a dogged resistance in the people at large. The attempt to secure spiritual results by material force had failed, as it always fails. It broke down before the indifference and resentment of the great mass of the people, of men who were neither lawless nor enthusiasts, but who clung to the older traditions of social order, and whose humor and good sense revolted alike from the artificial conception of human life which Puritanism had formed, and from its effort to force such a conception on a people by law. It broke down, too, before the corruption of the Puritans themselves. It was impossible to distinguish between saint and hypocrite as soon as godliness became profitable. Ashley Cooper, a skeptic in religion and a profligate in morals, was among "the loudest bagpipes of the squeaking train." Even among the really earnest Puritans prosperity disclosed a pride, a worldliness, a selfish hardness which had been hidden in the hour of persecution. The tone of Cromwell's later speeches shows his consciousness that the ground was slipping from under his feet. He no longer dwells on the dream of a Puritan England, a nation rising as a whole into a people of God. He falls back on the phrases of his youth, and the saints become again a "peculiar people," a remnant, a fragment among the nation at large. But the influences which were really foiling Cromwell's aim, and forming beneath his eyes the new England from which he turned in despair, were influences whose power he can hardly have recognized.[9]

What, then, of that new (for it was unlike the pre-Cromwellian) England, Milton's *Paradise Lost* soon to be the epic of a lost cause, the closed theaters reopened, the science of Francis Bacon rediscovered, the Royal Society established?

The Restoration brought Charles to Whitehall; and in an instant the whole face of England was changed. All that was noblest and best in Puritanism was whirled away with its pettiness and its tyranny in the current of the nation's hate. Religion had been turned into a political and a social tyranny; sobriety in dress, in speech, in manners was flouted as a mark of the detested Puritanism. Butler, in his *Hudibras*, poured insult on the past with a pedantic buffoonery for which the general hatred, far more than its humor, secured a hearing. Archbishop Sheldon listened to the mock sermon of a Cavalier who held up the Puritan phrase and the Puritan twang to ridicule in his hall at Lambeth. Dueling and raking became the marks of a fine gentleman; and grave divines winked at the follies of "honest fellows," who fought, gambled, swore, drank, and ended a day of debauchery by a night in the gutter. The life of a man of fashion vibrated between frivolity and excess. One of the comedies of the time tells the courtier that "he must dress well, dance well, fence well, have a talent for love-letters, an agreeable voice, be amorous and discreet—but not too constant." But to graces such as these the rakes of the Restoration added a

9 John Richard Green, *A Short History of the English People* [1874], 608–609. The edition here quoted is that of Harper and Brothers, New York, 1896.

shamelessness and a brutality which passes belief. Lord Rochester was a fashionable poet, and the titles of some of his poems are such that no pen of our day could copy. Sir Charles Sedley was a fashionable wit, and the foulness of his words made even the porters of Covent Garden pelt him from the balcony when he ventured to address them. The truest type of the time is the Duke of Buckingham, and the most characteristic event in the Duke's life was a duel in which he consummated his seduction of Lady Shrewsbury by killing her husband, while the Countess in disguise as a page held his horse for him and looked on at the murder.[10]

These are some of the social-situational elements in Green's approach to life in the last forty years of seventeenth-century England, but even the short excerpt is enough to indicate the human factors in what was to prove a vast transition.

It has been suggested earlier in this chapter that no situation can be conveyed historically without a careful management of time, the chronological metronome of action. Ordinarily in the work of beginning writers, however, it is less from lack of care for chronology than from excessive zeal in introducing dates that their historical constructions suffer. The problem may be traced to Professor Max Moorhead's now classic description of the intermediate fruit of historical research as "six shoe-boxes of note cards, every one of them dated." As each card is turned, a day, a month, or a year manages to slip into a fresh paragraph or, at most, a fresh page of often labored writing. In the next stage of the writer's career, both note-taking and chronology became less obsessive, so that his reader may search backwards and forwards for several pages in the text for some notion of time. The sin of overdating makes for dull reading, chronologically overcontrolled; the opposite sin of underdating

10 *Ibid.*, 607–608.

(sometimes by day of the week, more often by day of the month) may allow a freer narrative or analytical rein, but it can be equally exasperating. Histories are not always read sequentially; often they are used for quick reference, which can be effectively killed by indistinct chronology.

If we return to the opening of the present chapter once more, we can see that every event it contains bears its own date, yet there is only one day with its year mentioned. The narrative management of time is perhaps at its best when it is unobtrusive although fully present. This kind of management is successful, usually, when the writer is busy advancing the topical significance of his account, so that days or months or seasons emerge naturally from the story. Thus the emphasis is upon something other than time itself, which, while important sequentially, must always be secondary to action and significance in historical contexts. Arthur Link, in the excerpt earlier given, paints a seasonal picture before he introduces a year date, and he gives us the latter only after he has told us that the days were trying and the nights restless for the twenty-eighth President. The thousand uses of indirection can be found only with the exercise of imagination and restraint. Whenever the beginning historical writer finds himself impelled to deal with chronology instead of historical developments, he should back off long enough to determine where his emphasis should lie. Nine times out of ten it will lie with events.

The lacunae in historical developments, almost always clearly measurable chronologically, present a special problem and, at the same time, a special challenge. Charles W. Ferguson ran into it early in his *Naked to Mine Enemies: The Life of Cardinal Wolsey*, a book which any student should see without being invited to emulate, since the writing is largely unattainable. The Wolsey records break off for the early and even the Oxford years, which can be accounted for largely by two or three Magdalen College records, of Wolsey's kneeling for his degree in 1485 to his appearance in the college rolls as a Master of Arts and fourteenth in the list of fellows in 1497, and his ascent thereafter to the post of College Bursar. In ensuing years, to 1505, when he became chaplain to Henry VII, the facts are meager but they were propelling the cleric from Magdalen into the wider world of religion and politics. At page 67 in Ferguson's account we find the following:

> Casual accounts of Wolsey's life leave the impression that not much of importance had happened to him before he reached the court of Henry Tudor. Actually he had lived more than half his life, and all the forces that bent and shaped his ambition and oiled his abilities had already worked their effect. In a fixed society he had seen his father change from a rebel to a churchwarden, accepted for his property when he had been rejected as an alien. Thomas Wolsey had proved the power of words when he had determined for his degree at Oxford. He had shown his ability for something besides the scholar's life by engaging in the intrigues of the administration of his college. He had run head-on into the civil authorities, and to his sorrow, in his first parish. He had sampled the sweetness of patronage. At Calais he had shown that he knew how to do the world's work.

If we have been less than analytically attentive, it is only at this point, sixty-seven pages from the start, that we realize what a skillful reconstructionist has been doing with Thomas Wolsey's times rather than the facts of his early career, here tightly but honestly constricted.

Nineteenth-century America abounds in historical gaps—the earlier and much of the later life of Kit Carson, the closing vicissitudes of the aged Daniel Boone, river transportation on the Mississippi, Ohio, and Missouri rivers, and much else. Wherever and whenever the writer finds this confrontation unavoidable, he is thrown back upon "life and times," related exploration or industrial developments, the politics of a state or region, the religion or culture of a section—the situational aspects, in short, from which a figure or a social or economic force must emerge when, finally, the facts begin to make straight historical narration possible.

The place where historical action occurs, like its time, contains both opportunities and pitfalls. Place can be a building, e.g., the White House or the Capitol nearby, a town, a city, or that point on the Arkansas River between Sand and Adobe parks where Zebulon Montgomery Pike and his men had Christmas dinner in 1806.[11] Place differs from scene—that complex where human striving or achievement or defeat becomes visible against a background occupied by humans and only incidentally distinguishable by its geography or physical characteristics. It is simpler but, from some points of view, more exacting of writing skill than scene. Since it is usually secondary to historical action, it calls for almost instant identification in the reader's mind. The rules do not change even if he has never seen the place. They assign primary emphasis to symbol and imagery, very much as poetical techniques do. In the right hands, e.g., Paul Horgan's, they do their work swiftly:

In 1812, in Howard County, Missouri, on the Indian Frontier, there was a little United States community medieval in self-sufficiency and commonness of task. It was Cooper's Fort. Set in a clearing, with farms around its cluster of log buildings,

[11] Zebulon Montgomery Pike, *The Journals of Zebulon Montgomery Pike, With Letters and Related Documents,* ed. by Donald Jackson, I, 360–62.

a forest beyond, a well-worn road straggling in generally from the east, and a few paths beginning off toward the west, such a place was a little concentration of energy typical of its time. It was a tiny pinpoint on a map labelled Far West, a map that lived in people's thoughts, calling them like the promise of all lands they ever dreamed about.

Far West was a very faith; steamboats and children were named for it; promises were redeemed by it—a man to himself, a debtor to his neighbor, a lover to his bride. It had the grand commonness of all hopes.[12]

To Cooper's Fort in the Far West came families from back East, among them Harmon Gregg, his wife, and their children, of whom the youngest was Josiah, who would capture the Far West in a classic-to-be, *Commerce of the Prairies*, and in nine notebooks that other Far West beyond the prairies he left forever in 1840.

As others before me have insisted, literary dissection always destroys live specimens, but Horgan's symbolism and imagery together produce a living, not a dead, picture and the spirit of place and wider region. If we search it as specimen we find not fewer than seven metaphorical ideas, all evocative of place and the impelling hopes of those who dwell there. "Commonness of task" is not a concept we stumble past, unrecognizing. "Commonness of all hopes" intends to make the people of Cooper's Fort and us parties to a grand design at this time in this place.

The achievement of the result we have seen is not at all the consequence of formula. In such matters, the application of formula to widely disparate materials and situations can only result in stereotypes. It is the consequence, rather, of habits of mind which quickly assemble the elements of

12 Josiah Gregg, *Diary and Letters of Josiah Gregg*, ed. by Maurice Garland Fulton, with an Introduction by Paul Horgan, I, 3.

place, selectively sorting out the most significant among them, discarding the less valuable, and dressing them in the language of feeling and identification for readers anywhere.

Until the process becomes second nature to the beginning historian, he may find it useful to make a written inventory, the more telling details of place in the first column, the less telling in a second. For example:

The time is the late fall of 1813 and the winter of 1813–14. The place is western Holland. Following the revolt of the Dutch after the Battle of Leipzig, the provinces were groping for the return of the House of Orange until December, 1813, when the Prince of Orange agreed to return to form a constitutional monarchy. He would take the title of William I on March 30, 1814. The Napoleonic threat remains, however, and the cities of Haarlem, Amsterdam, The Hague, Rotterdam, and Utrecht, long the victims of economic depression, are in disarray. The winter, early in coming, descended upon the plains and estuaries with fury in December, 1813. Great sheets of ice sealed farmland and village, and the approaches to the ports of Rotterdam and the Hague saw blocks of frozen sea, which closed shipping so tightly that all commerce was brought to a halt. Into Janaury, 1814, the arctic winds from the North Sea lashed sturdy houses to their foundations.

The Hague	Devasted farmlands
Life from seven seas	A patient people
Idle ships, lost gains	View from a tavern
Merhant stores, bankers' slim hordes	Liberal hopes
	The Dutch inheritance
Fruits of rebellion	
Promise of Kingship	
Bitter winter's wait	

All of the items listed in the first column can be utilized in a single paragraph descriptive of the Hague and the larger world of Dutch concern. The historical art of place consists in the way they are assembled, even as we saw in Paul Horgan's notable example.

There are times when place assumes a larger role than a center of human life and events, so that, like a house or moorland in a gothic novel, it becomes almost a character in itself. The late Walter Prescott Webb recognized this phenomenon in *The Great Plains*[13] and again in his magazine assessment of the American West as a whole, whose lack of water has hung like an unhappy truth over its strivings for development.[14] Mining history, although as yet a sparse domain, can scarcely be conceived without the baleful effects of Rocky Mountain isolation and winter's white pall.[15] The historic struggle for oil resources in North America, again a neglected field of historical investigation, is in considerable part the story of a deep and reluctant earth.[16]

But in this as in the less active role of place, we have always to get at the human identification. It appears to excellent advantage in that evocative comparison the late Bernard DeVoto made between the familiar watered, grass-covered savanna east of the Mississippi River and the unbroken prairie land west of it, mysterious, unknown, forbidding to people in covered wagons, a land of the mind's eye and of imagining.[17] "Few men," Goethe said, "have the

13 Walter Prescott Webb, *The Great Plains*, *passim*.

14 Webb, "The American West, Perpetual Mirage," *Harper's Magazine*, May, 1957.

15 Rodman W. Paul, *Mining Frontiers of the Far West, 1848–1880*, 109–34; William S. Greever, *The Bonanza West: The Story of the Western Mining Rushes, 1848–1900*, 20, 93, 149, 233–34, 260, 267, 322, 331, 348–50, 368.

16 Max W. Ball, *The Fascinating Oil Business*, 55–70.

17 Bernard DeVoto, *Across the Wide Missouri*, 1–6.

imagination for the truth of reality" (*eine Phantasie fur die Wahrheit des Realen*), even though as historians they may be prepared to "challenge the power of time."[18]

[18] Ernst Cassirer, *An Essay on Man: An Introduction to a Philosophy of Human Culture,* 184, 204.

7. Bibliographies and Edited Documents

THE librarian's aphorisms that "a good bibliography is worth its weight in gold" and "any bibliography is better than none" have seemingly given smaller impulse to the energies of historians than they deserve. The corresponding respect librarians have for the editors of historical documents has found a better response in the profession—but not a landslide. The reasons in both instances may lie with the facts that these nearly indispensable tools for historical research require forms unfamiliar to the synthesist, unaccustomed precision, critical insights, and, in large measure, a selfless devotion to the work of others rather than to the creation of one's own. Further, in the case of bibliographies in volume form, there is no such thing as a "complete" or a "comprehensive" one. Every bibliography is, in a minor sense, out of date the day it is published. But if the paper on which it is printed is durable enough, it will see heavy continuing use a century or more after its original compilation. No reasonably competent bibliographer escapes immortality. The same can be said about the editor of documents. Comparatively, the author of a synthetic work usually sees himself displaced in a decade or, at most, in a quarter of a century.

The qualities required in a bibliographer—command of form, precision, and critical insight—are most readily found in two groups of bookmen in the United States, library cataloguers, who are obviously trained professionals, and collectors, who, in the main, tend to outdistance all others in critical and analytical command of a given field. To the latter we largely owe the principle that, in bibliography, mere title lists are all but useless, whereas critically described books and documents provide the guidance essential to scholarly research. To the dimensions of collecting many gifted individuals have added dimensions of scholarship which institutional scholars have too often overlooked— Carl H. Pforzheimer in English literature but particularly the Romantic Period; Arthur A. Houghton, Jr., in the Renaissance; E. L. DeGolyer in the history of science and technology, and he and his son, E. L. DeGolyer, Jr., in the Trans-Mississippi West and the Spanish Southwest; Fred Rosenstock of Denver, a great conservator of documents as well as a bookseller; and Ramon F. Adams, collector and bibliographer of the Frontier. To this personal list a round two dozen great assemblers of books, documents, manuscripts, maps, and memorabilia could quickly be added, but intent rather than numbers is the purpose here. In each instance intellectual interest preceded active collecting. And it is a safe conjecture that every consistent collector would have been that even if he had not been able to implement his interests with large cash reserves. The ultimate beneficiaries of collecting interest have almost uniformly been institutional libraries, with consequent intellectual endowments for the scholarly professions which are nearly incalculable.

Collectors like bibliographers, for the latter provide the checklists for the ongoing collections of the former. But for the historian as well as the collector, an inspired bibliography is a gift of the gods. Such a bibliography appeared at San Francisco in 1937, entitled *The Plains and the Rockies: A Bibliography of Original Narratives of Travel and Adventure, 1800–1865,* by Henry R. Wagner and Charles L. Camp. Its publisher was the Grabhorn Press, and its printers Edwin and Robert Grabhorn. The proofreading was Jane Grabhorn's. The volume contains only 428 numbered items, slight for a volume-length bibliography, but with related and peripheral references the index may run to more than nine hundred names figuring in book, pamphlet, and periodical titles. My copy, unnumbered, bought in 1939 at the published price of $12.50, inspired *The American Exploration and Travel Series,* in which sixty-three volumes have so far appeared.[1] The compilers and printers did just about everything "needful" in their production. Whatever the field of bibliographical inquiry, it still stands as an applicable model, indestructible in its excellence.

Each feature of *The Plains and the Rockies* illustrates a desirable bibliographical principle. Each title entry is numbered, the numerical series being arranged chronologically. The chronological arrangement is sound for obvious historical reasons, but for the beginning bibliographer the advantages of numbering each item become apparent in cross-referencing and in indexing. Cross-referencing thus gives the reader the number of the item. Equally, in indexing, item numbers take the place of page numbers, so that the indexed author-name carries after it an italicized item

[1] Although *The American Exploration and Travel Series* was inaugurated in 1939, its volumes 1 and 2 were brought into the series from the backlist of the University of Oklahoma Press, thereby creating a bibliographical puzzle for some. But this is the way it happened: I did it. Volume 3, Annie Heloise Abel's editing of *Tabeau's Narrative of Loisel's Expedition to the Upper Missouri* appeared in 1939 without the series title, which made its first appearance in John Francis McDermott's editing of Volume 4, *Tixier's Travels on the Osage Prairies,* which appeared in 1940.

number rather than a page number. Peripheral and related items not appearing in numerical series are given in the index in roman-arabic numerals, which again carry the reader back to the item numbers in series. The typographic arrangement exhibiting these features appears in the accompanying two-page illustration from *The Plains and the Rockies.*

However much this notable bibliography may vary in such matters as author identification, title management, and description (in the bibliographical sense) from the now elaborate and highly useful rules of Anglo-American libraries, it remains that what we have before us is quite adequate, splendidly visual, and informative.[2] It is the latter aspect, not 8° (for octavo) or measurements in centimeters, which concerns us now.

Messrs. Wagner and Camp had realized from two earlier editions of the bibliography (both prepared by Mr. Wagner) that their audience would consist of (1) collectors, (2) people both professional and nonprofessional interested in the history of the Trans-Mississippi West, (3) librarians, (4) book dealers, and (5) editors in book and journal publishing. Their critical-descriptive analysis of each item manages to satisfy, in most instances, the needs of these five categories, although the descriptions are necessarily tightly contained. Wagner's "Preface to the Revised Edition" and Camp's "Editor's Note" in the front matter of the book account directly or indirectly for the audiences envisaged and set geographical limits (west of the Missouri and east of the Sierra Nevada, Washington and Oregon, north of Mexico and Texas, and south of the Arctic Circle). Camp's "Note" also gives some account of the basis of author selection and

2 American Library Association et al., *Anglo-American Cataloging Rules: North American Text* (Chicago, American Library Association, 1967).

We do not find any more extended account of these two remarkable journeys until Mr. Irving printed in his "Astoria" a full account of both from journals in the possession of Mr. Astor, probably that of Hunt for the outgoing trip and Mr. Stuart for the return.

In the *Detroit Free Press*, June 28, 1856, is published a letter from Ramsey Crooks describing the return journey with Stuart. This is quoted in the *Oregon Hist. Soc. Quart.*, March, 1916.

W. R. Coe owns Stuart's original diary of this journey. It has recently been edited by P. A. Rollins; Scribners: 1935.   [10]

★ 1814 ★

HENRY MARIE BRACKENRIDGE

12. Views of Louisiana; together with a journal of a voyage up the Missouri River, in 1811. By H. M. Brackenridge, Esq. Pittsburgh, printed and published by Cramer, Spear and Eichbaum, . . . 1814.

8° 304 pp.

In the introduction Brackenridge says he went to St. Louis in the spring of 1810 and published during the ensuing winter a series of essays descriptive of the country, presumably in the *Gazette*. These form part of the "Views" in the present work. In the spring of 1811, at the solicitation of Manuel Lisa, and with the desire to join his friend Bradbury who had just gone up the river with Hunt's party, he started with Lisa and his party from St. Charles (April 2).

June 2 they overtook Hunt's party near Cedar Island. They went as far as Lisa's fort just beyond the Mandan Village, arriving there June 26, and remained till July 6. On the return with Bradbury he remarked that they made 1440 miles in a little better than 14 days.

In the appendix (No. 7) occurs "Extracts from the account of a Journey from Fort Clark on the Missouri, to the Salines on the Arkansas, by Mr. Sibley." Also (No. 8) "American Enterprise," our No. 11. At page 89 in the "Views" begins an account of the fur trade, which consists principally of Lisa's operations, including the expedition to the Yellowstone in 1807, formation of the Missouri Fur Co., and the second expedition to the forks of the Missouri. (For about all that is known of Manuel Lisa, see Judge W. B. Douglas' sketch of him in the *Mo. Hist. Soc. Coll.*, Vol. III, Nos. 3 and 4.)

A second edition of the journal separate, revised and enlarged by the

16

author was published in Baltimore in 1816 by Coale and Maxwell in 12° viii, 246 pp. The narrative in some places is rewritten with the inclusion of a few additional anecdotes, but in the main it is the same. Graff has a copy in printed boards with the binder's date 1816 on the boards and a title page date of 1815. Ayer has a Baltimore 1817 ed.

Henry M. Brackenridge was educated partly in Missouri before the cession and gives an interesting account of early times there in "Recollections of persons and places in the West," first published in Philadelphia in 1834 in 12° 244 pp. but more commonly known in the Philadelphia edition of 1868. He also published several books and pamphlets on South America and western American affairs, besides numerous articles in the newspapers. For another work similar to his "Views of Louisiana," see Major Amos Stoddard's "Sketches historical and descriptive of Louisiana," published by Mathew Carey, Philadelphia, 1812 in 8° viii, 488 pp.   [11]

[LEWIS AND CLARK]

13. History of the expedition under the command of Captains Lewis and Clark, to the sources of the Missouri, thence across the Rocky Mountains and down the River Columbia to the Pacific Ocean. Performed during the years 1804-5-6, by order of the government of the United States. Prepared for the press by Paul Allen, Esquire. In two volumes. Philadelphia: Published by Bradford and Inskeep ... 1814. 8° xxviii, 470; ix, 522 pp. Map and 5 charts.

MAPS: Map of Lewis & Clark's track across the western portion of North America. Fortification [opposite Bonhommie Island]. Falls and portages. Great Falls of Columbia. The Great Shoot or Rapid. Mouth of the Columbia River.

In 1893 Elliott Coues republished this edition in three volumes and a volume of Index with 3 maps, extensive critical notes, and a bibliography. Dr. Coues had access to the original journals and was thus able to supplement somewhat the narratives as prepared by Mr. Biddle. The maps consist of a copy of the map originally published with the 1814 edition, a new map of the route of Lewis and Clark, prepared by Elliott Coues for comparison, and finally a copy of the map made by Mr. Lewis at the Mandan villages and which was copied and elaborated, no doubt, types of material excluded, of which railroad promotions and scientific papers are notable. The temporal limits had already been set on the title page.

Like all of the other types of historical writing with which the present book has been concerned thus far, the compiler's description in a bibliography has a set of requirements. The first, which would seem to encompass all the rest, is that the compiler must know completely the title described. He must know also the bearing of this particular title upon other significant titles, and their bearing upon it. Implicit or explicit in any title description is the factor of worth, critically understood. He usually will confine himself to the first printing of the work in question, but in such case, if he is dealing with Francis Parkman, *The California and Oregon Trail*, he would need to give evidence of its (first) magazine appearance in the *Knickerbocker Magazine*, Vols. 31 and 32 (1848), its first volume form (1849),[3] and its almost constant revision during the remainder of Parkman's lifetime to a year before his death in 1893. What Parkman intended may be seen in its last revision. Its worth may more satisfactorily be judged in its first volume form, the less mature but also the less literarily self-conscious effort of a young man on the great and only western adventure of his life.

Or, to take another, near contemporary account, Washington Irving's *The Rocky Mountains; or, Scenes, Incidents, and Adventures in the Far West; Digested from the Journal of Captain B.L.E. Bonneville, of the Army of the United States, and Illustrated from Various Other Sources*, 2 vols. (1837).[4] Here the critical factor of worth requires first consideration by the bibliographer, simply in the inter-

3 New York, George P. Putnam, 1849.
4 Philadelphia, Carey, Lea, & Blanchard, 1837.

est of deciding whether the work is admissible at all historically. The historical profession has cast (I think unjustly) much doubt upon both *Bonneville* and *Astoria*[5] in a single phrase, which, from unanalyzed repetition, has become a cliché: "Washington Irving is a romanticist, not a historian." The phrase, however little it will stand etymological examination, tends to relieve most historians of the obligation to examine the book. But the case becomes more complex and more pressing when the bibliographer realizes that (a) the principal journal has disappeared, (b) the records of Bonneville's fur-trading expeditions of 1832–35 are at best fragmentary in the War Department archives, and (c) if Irving's account is to be stigmatized as "romantic" and therefore unreliable, how do we account for this early thrust by a military officer on leave into the Far West and, even more significantly, into California (under the detached party led by Joseph Reddeford Walker)?

The historian, guided by the cliché, may avoid the problem altogether, but the bibliographer of the Far West comes away from the above with the conviction that Irving's two volumes of 1837 must be included in his own compilation. The massive re-editing of *The Adventures of Captain Bonneville, U.S.A.* by Professor Edgeley W. Todd makes that decision obvious.[6] But a choice and a decision are not enough. The relevant expressions by Bonneville's companions and contemporaries must be applied—War Department Record Group 94, National Archives; U.S. Senate, RG 46, National Archives; Zenas Leonard, *Adventures of Zenas Leonard, Fur Trader*, edited by John C. Ewers[7]

5 *Astoria, or Anecdotes of an Enterprise Beyond the Rocky Mountains*, 2 vols. (Philadelphia, Carey, Lea, & Blanchard, 1836). Also No. 44 in *The American Exploration and Travel Series*, 1964, ed. by Edgeley W. Todd.

6 No. 34, *The American Exploration and Travel Series*, 1961.

7 No. 28, *The American Exploration and Travel Series*, 1959.

(Leonard was with the detached party to California in 1833, but Bonneville did not achieve his goal of getting there); Joseph Meek's recollections in Frances Fuller Victor's *River of the West*;[8] George Frederick Ruxton, *Life in the Far West*;[9] Thomas J. Beale, "Recollections of William Craig," Lewiston *Morning Tribune*, March 3, 1918; Stephen H. L. Meek, article in *Niles' Weekly Register*, March 25, 1837, Vol. 52, 50; George Nidever, *The Life and Adventures of George Nidever*, edited by William H. Ellison;[10] Joseph Reddeford Walker, account of the Bonneville and California expeditions, *Sonoma Democrat*, November 25, 1876; David Adams papers, Missouri Historical Society; Washington Irving to Major James Harvey Hook, March 27, 1836, in John Francis McDermott, "Washington Irving and the Journal of Captain Bonneville," *Mississippi Valley Historical Review*, Vol. XLIII, No. 3 (December, 1956), 459–67.

The foregoing are some but not all of the data needed directly or indirectly in shaping a historically useful title-description for a volume-length bibliography of the Trans-Mississippi West. The character of the resulting description can be seen in Item No. 67 of *The Plains and the Rockies*. Thus, even in the heavily worked field of western American history, a single title-description of an original narrative or journal becomes almost major in its research requirements. What happens in a field little developed is another story. Once told, however, it opens up historical opportunities little short of vast.

When a dozen Southern historians under the chairman-

8 Hartford, Bliss; San Francisco, R. J. Trumbull & Co., 1870.

9 Edinburgh and London, William Blackwood and Sons, 1849. Also No. 14, *The American Exploration and Travel Series*, 1951, ed. by LeRoy R. Hafen, with a foreword by Mae Reed Porter.

10 Berkeley, University of California Press, 1937. Original Manuscript in Bancroft Library, University of California.

ship of Professor Thomas D. Clark of the University of Kentucky met at Atlanta in April, 1943, it became apparent that a proposal to edit original journals and narratives of southern travel needed something more than the idea. A bibliography, one of those present suggested, would provide a firm and critically valid base upon which to proceed.[11] The six-volume bibliography which ultimately resulted from the committee decision affords not only the critical data for the selection and editing of individual accounts but a nearly indispensable reference tool for historical research for the South.

Travels in the Old South, in three volumes, *Travels in the Confederate States* in one, and *Travels in the New South* in two, embrace 2,703 numbered items described by sixteen historians, including the editor, Professor Clark. The first volume to appear was *Travels in the Confederate States,* compiled in whole by Professor E. Merton Coulter and published in 1948, five years after the Atlanta meeting. The sixth volume, published in 1962, brought the undertaking to a conclusion nineteen years from its inception.[12]

The compilers of this extended bibliography began their labors untrained in the formal bibliographical sense and ended them as professionals. The questions they had to ask

[11] The suggestion, as well as a purely hypothetical entry (including measurement in centimeters) which I drew up on a public stenographer's typewriter, seemed innocent enough. But a certain grimness in Thomas D. Clark's tone, as he recalled the incident in the course of a paper delivered twenty years later at the Salt Lake City meeting of the Western Historical Association, suggests that two decades extracted from a historian's life are no trifling matter.

[12] These titles, *seriatim,* are Nos. 11, 19, and 36 in *The American Exploration and Travel Series.* The compilers in addition to Messrs Clark and Coulter were Professors Alfred Barnaby Thomas, Hugh T. Lefler, Lester J. Cappon, John D. Barnhart, William B. Hamilton, Walter S. Posey, Culver H. Smith, James W. Patton, Charles S. Sydnor, Robert G. Lunde, F. Garvin Davenport, Fletcher M. Green, Rupert B. Vance, and Lawrence S. Thompson. They appear in the order given them in successive title pages.

themselves are covered in part in the editor's prefaces to five of the volumes. Most of them can be answered readily from Library of Congress Catalog cards, which most historians shuffle daily in their respective institutional libraries. The accompanying card with its identifying graphics may serve to illustrate what follows:

First, in volume-length historical bibliographies, arrange entries chronologically by year date of the first edition, if printed, numbering each entry serially.

Second, list by author's name, reversed, giving his inclusive years when known.

Third, below author's name give full title, followed after a period by place, publisher, and year date of publication. The year date may be presumed to indicate a first edition, unless a second or subsequent edition is the only known edition surviving, in which case list edition after title and before publication data. (Most economists and economic historians would prefer a title listing of the sixth edition of Thomas Malthus, *Essay on the Principle of Population* . . . , published in 1826, to the first edition, published in 1798; other historical

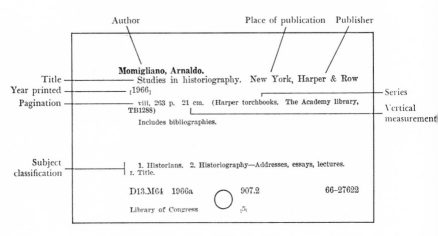

examples will readily come to mind; title description which then follows will account for the first edition by its year date as additional and necessary bibliographical information.)

Fourth, give pagination, enumerate illustrations, enumerate maps. Give vertical dimension of title page in centimeters. Indicate bibliography and index, if any. Indicate location of copy of the first edition examined, but do not attempt a census of copies known to exist.

Fifth, having regard for the five numbered audiences listed above for Wagner and Camp, *The Plains and the Rockies,* adapt a corresponding description of the title under consideration for the bibliography now being undertaken. The critical estimate of worth, the rarity of the item, and its bearing upon other and related titles and the historical climate in which it appeared are significant guidelines to adequate description.

Sixth, cross-reference by number of item.

Seventh, index by author and item number, italicizing the number, but leave in roman-arabic figures the item number when an author or other individual appears in an item description not his own.

The form in which titles are given is best confined to the style (principally lower-case) appearing in Library of Congress Catalog cards, for the reason that the idiosyncracies of title-page design in various ages give us little advantage when followed slavishly, quite aside from the riddle presented by an all-capitals treatment. The rules for foreign-language titles, as for all other important bibliographical practices observed by librarians in the United States and many other countries, are given in *Anglo-American Cataloging Rules* (North American Text), prepared by the American Library Association, the Library of Congress, the Library Association, and the Canadian Library Association (Chicago, American Library Association, 1967). A cautionary note may be added here that, however straightforward and sensible the procedures may be, as given in the foregoing *Rules*, no attempt should be made by the historian to master them. They run far beyond the needs he will encounter in the compilation of a volume-length bibliography directed to historical interests.

For historical purposes, a calendar is a chronologically arranged listing (most usefully with description) of documents relating to an individual, to an institution, or to a historical period. When it is of the descriptive type, its excellence will depend not only upon the adequacy of the form chosen by the compiler and his accuracy but upon the skill he is able to apply to the relevance and conciseness of his summaries. There is no place in descriptive calendaring for the historian who cannot write with flashes of insight and with an economy rare in a wordy tribe.

A descriptive calendar of original documents, like the critical bibliography of original journals, travel accounts, memoirs, and the like, is at once a highly valuable resource for the historical synthesist and a vehicle of primary importance to any author who compiles it. Whether the material calendared is in manuscript, printed, or a combination of the two (as is usually the case), the resulting work will see greatest use as a research guide. As in the descriptive feature of a volume-length bibliography, description in a calendar must be directed to the needs and interests of known audiences. Among the latter are obviously general historians, biographers, scientists, legal scholars, and political and social scientists.

The thrust towards calendaring is relatively stronger in Great Britain than in the United States, but older calendars have not only survived but have been reprinted within recent years because of their research value. Others have been superseded by large editing projects, e.g., *The Papers of Thomas Jefferson*, edited by Julian P. Boyd, in nineteen volumes.[13] The following calendars were in print in 1974: the correspondence and/or the papers of George Washington (exchanges with the Continental Congress), James Madison, Thomas Jefferson, Jefferson Davis, Joel R. Poinsett, Charles Darwin, Martin Van Buren, and James Monroe. Where the correspondence and other papers of a significant historical figure have not been edited and published, and particularly when the originals are widely scattered, the value of a good calendar is great. Such an undertaking is that of Irwin S. Rhodes in *The Papers of John Marshall: A Descriptive Calendar* in two volumes.[14]

Albert J. Beveridge, the most eminent biographer of Marshall, who did not have the benefit of such a calendar, had written that "Less is known of Marshall than of any of the great Americans." His pronouncement still remained in some part true after the publication of his four volumes (1916–19). It is therefore safe to say that until all of the known Marshall papers are published, Rhodes's *Calendar* must be the starting point for any future biographer of Marshall. From it any researcher can be guided to microfilm reproductions of such Marshall documents as he may need, as determined by the *Calendar* descriptions. Reproductions of facing pages 218 and 219, Volume II, indicate Rhodes's method. His management of the legal documents, many of which had not hitherto been utilized from Marshall's law practice and judicial services below the U.S. Supreme Court, owes much to his legal training.

Bibliographies and calendars of documents of volume length are fair game for any practitioner of the historical

13 Princeton, Princeton University Press, 1950–71.
14 Norman, University of Oklahoma Press, 1969.

Aug. 12
RICHMOND   *to Bushrod Washington*

Received box Washington correspondence copied at Richmond; original books returned; asks to have copy of letter to Col. Bouquet, July 29, 1758, and residue left uncopied by mistake; speaks of publishing correspondence. Acknowledges letter of Aug. 4. Plans for publishing separately introduction to *Life of Washington* as corrected; number of copies, consent and cost, putting reputation in work. DLC, Marshall Papers, Ac. 1780, 19. See letters B. Washington to C. P. Wayne, June 14 and Aug. 4, 1823, herein. Morristown National Hist. Park.

Sept. 26
RICHMOND   *to Joseph Story*

Check of $150 sent for advances to son Edward; $100 sent direct in August; sons in North spenders. Discusses Justice Johnson stirring of states rights opposition in South Carolina, his opinion published in *National Intelligencer* declaring act unconstitutional, violent reaction in South (state law prohibiting entry of freed Negroes held in violation of commerce clause). In Virginia case involving same law, J.M. avoided constitutional issue (*The Brig Wilson v. United States*, 1 Brockenbrough 423, herein 1820, U.S. Circuit Court, Va.). MHi, Story, 31. T. 33; DLC, Beveridge Coll.; Warren, *Supreme Court*, I, 626 (excerpt).

Sept. 29
RICHMOND   *to C. P. Wayne*

Acknowledges letter of Sept. 10. Interest in publishing second volume of *Life of Washington*, no pecuniary advantage, separate publication at own risk of historical portion, introduction and chapters 2 and 3 of second volume. Revision made of balance in two volumes; fate of separate volume determine publication of these. Morristown National Hist. Park.

Oct. 11
RICHMOND   *to Bushrod Washington*

Returned from upper country, answering letter of Aug. 29. Copies of letters (Gen. Washington's) to Washington in February; arrangement and selection. Letter from Wayne with cost of Small publishing "Introduction"; does not understand it. Plans printing 1,000 copies, advance cost of paper, balance from sales or will pay, 500 copies bound, Small to have preference. DLC, Marshall Papers, Ac. 1780, 18.

Oct. 12
RICHMOND   *to Joseph Story*
Shipping two barrels of family flour, not as white as desired; climate
and politics fickle. MHi, Story, 31. T. 34.

Oct. 31
NORFOLK   *to Polly Marshall*
Return home delayed by unfinished case; boarding at agreeable house.
VW; Mason, *Polly*, 246.

Nov. 4
RICHMOND   *American Colonization Society*
Selected president at organization meeting Richmond and Manchester
Society auxiliary to the American Colonization Society; not present. Meeting of Nov. 8, 1823, accepted presidency, and elected president at every
annual meeting through 1835. VHi; *Minutes of the Virginia Branch American Colonization Society*, Nov. 4, 1823—Feb. 6, 1859.

Nov. 6
RICHMOND   *to [John Lowell], Roxbury, Mass.*
Opinion of Court setting aside award of arbitrators not personal. VW
(incomplete).

Nov. 24
RICHMOND   *to Joseph Story*
Acknowledges letter of Oct. 19, thanking for attention to son, remit-
tance direct to Higginson. In Pennsylvania case, Story preparing opinion
for Court; not confident of own position. Two applications for *juris de
medietate linqua*, one rejected, other followed District Judge and New
York ruling of Judge Thompson because capital case; need for uniform
practice to be considered by Supreme Court. MHi, Story, 31. T. 35; DLC,
Beveridge Coll.

Dec. 6
RICHMOND   *to Bushrod Washington*
Sorry to hear of indisposition; sickly season; frost will help. Hopes
will meet "your brethren" in February. Chasm in correspondence copies,
mentioned in former letter; another by loss of few sheets at Mount Vernon,
those written before capture of Fort Duquesne, last one to Col. Bouquet,

craft, but finding aids normally call for long research experience, uncommon energy, and a generous regard for the needs of one's fellows. It is no accident that the two most consulted guides in American university libraries are the products of senior scholars: Professor Ray Allen Billington, "Guides to American Historical Manuscript Collections in Libraries of the United States," in *Mississippi Valley Historical Review*, Vol. XXXVIII, No. 3 (December, 1951), 467–96; and *Harvard Guide to American History*, compiled by Professors Oscar Handlin, Arthur M. Schlesinger, Samuel Eliot Morison, Frederick Merk, Arthur M. Schlesinger, Jr., and Paul Herman Buck.[15] Of a still more fundamental character is Library of Congress, *National Union Catalog of Manuscript Collections; Based on Reports from American Repositories of Manuscripts*, in twelve volumes (1959–74). It is obviously the fruit of institutional rather than individual research effort. Its descriptions are short but helpful. Another fundamental work is National Historical Publications Commission, *A Guide to Archives and Manuscripts in the United States*, edited by Philip M. Hamer (New Haven, Yale University Press, 1961).

However fundamental these works may be, especially when complemented by the institutional guides and catalogs compiled by such agencies as the National Archives and Records Service and the many historical societies and library collections, it remains that specific needs often have a different dimension. And satisfying them can afford almost endless careers in American history for those who are willing to dig and to analyze. What might be done in any era or area, for example, from the many and often voluminous bibliographies appended to the relevant monographs

---

[15] Cambridge, Belknap Press of Harvard University Press, 1966. A new, revised, edition of this work was in preparation, 1974.

and dissertations offered since the early fifties—roughly the date in which the above works were compiled? Bibliographical findings in the intensely worked area of American history are cumulative, and thus any future finding guides must reflect this fact. This in turn means that the finding guide eschews description and relies, instead, upon listings organized by subject, area, era, location (if unpublished document), and chronology.

While volume-length bibliographies and finding guides are of great value to the editor of historical documents, they do not always tell the whole story. The "document never before examined historically" is almost commonplace in the experience of those who search for primary materials in any area of history. Often the researcher bent upon a synthesis of his own will use original manuscripts without later returning to them for an editing project. The consequent loss to his publications record as well as to the corpus of historical sources in print is far from minor. Obviously, not all original manuscripts—letters, diaries, journals, narratives—are of such historical importance as to justify their being edited and printed in volume form. Nor are all previously printed versions, even those which are important but without proper annotation or connectives. But for United States history, there are scores of unpublished as well as previously printed documents which call for modern editing. *The American Exploration and Travel Series*, mentioned earlier in this chapter, affords extensive evidence of this fact. The sixty-three volumes it contains exhibit many of the requirements in edited documents, in contrast to the standards employed by a great pioneer of an earlier time, Reuben Gold Thwaites, in *Early Western Travels, 1748–1846*.[16]

16 Thirty-two volumes. Cleveland, The Arthur H. Clark Company, 1904–

There is not room in the present chapter to do more than deplore Clarence W. Alvord's estimate of Thwaites's achievement in the remembered phrase about the "fringe of the garment rather than the garment itself." Nor can we examine critically Alvord's implicit faith in "the science of history" or his own archaic style.[17] But there is room to compare briefly the work of Thwaites in *Original Journals of the Lewis and Clark Expedition* (8 vols., published in 1904–1905),[18] and that of Elliott Coues, who re-edited the Nicholas Biddle text of the Lewis and Clark journals in *History of the Expedition under the Command of Lewis and Clark* (4 vols., 1893).[19]

To take the two editors in reverse but chronological order, Coues, who possessed a wide-ranging interest and competence in natural science, saw in the Biddle version a call to do what Biddle in 1814 was little equipped to do, namely annotate the Lewis and Clark natural science, geographic, and ethnological findings from a modern point of view. The result is, in general, competent annotation, which constitutes a rather considerable extension of the journals themselves. (Many historians skilled in the diverse matters categorized above feel that Coues was too extensive and too leisurely in his annotations, facts which nearly appalled Coues' publisher, Francis P. Harper, as the edition moved towards galley proofs in the late summer and early autumn of 1892.)[20] But at heart the Coues undertaking—despite his

1907. The subtitle, rarely cited, even in the following abbreviation, is significant to the ensuing discussion: *A Series of Annotated Reprints* . . . .

17 C. W. Alvord, "A Critical Analysis of the Work of Reuben Gold Thwaites," Mississippi Valley Historical Association *Proceedings*, Vol. 7 (1913–14), 321–33. The quoted phrase is from p. 326.

18 New York, Dodd, Mead & Company, 1904–1905. Title above is abbreviated.

19 New York, Francis P. Harper, 1893.

20 Donald Jackson, ed., *Letters of the Lewis and Clark Expedition, with*

initial declaration that the Lewis and Clark journals, as presented by Biddle, must be "verbatim et literatim et punctuatim"[21]—became a bowdlerized version of Biddle's bowdlerizing of the fourteen volumes of "pocket journal" of Lewis and Clark. If this were not enough, when he discovered the existence of the original journals at the American Philosophical Society in Philadelphia, Coues proposed to Harper that "*after* our present edition . . . you will want to bring out another vol. reproducing the orig. mss. *verbatim.*"[22] Successful in borrowing the journals, he transported them to his home and in the process of copying them he freely inserted his proposed changes of wording in the originals. Coues died in 1899 and with him the project he had formed for what must have been a second bowdlerizing of the original journals. His insertions were not discovered by the American Philosophical Society until 1903.[23]

Between Coues the scientist-traveler-humanist and Thwaites the Wisconsin editor of historical documents, what is to be said? The discursive but charming annotations, usually accurate and informative, provided by Coues will always remain. But the Thwaites management of the original journals, practically tamper-free, is our working source today. Thwaites did not have Coues' gifts for natural science, geography, cartography, meteorology, or even ethnology, and he frequently stepped over or around annotation requirements in these fields. But the prescription for any modern editing of Lewis and Clark runs much beyond both Coues and Thwaites, anyway. Much of it appears in

Related Documents, 1783–1854 (Urbana, University of Illinois Press, 1962), 674.

21 *Ibid.*, 673.
22 *Ibid.*, 674.
23 *Ibid.*, 675.

Donald Jackson's *Letters of the Lewis and Clark Expedition, with Related Documents, 1783–1854,* to which the present discussion is heavily indebted, as the notes indicate. The object lessons to be gained from Biddle, Coues, and Thwaites, in varying degrees negative, concern the preservation of the integrity of original texts and the types and economy of editorial annotation in footnote form. The positive guidelines in scholarly editing of this type of material are principally the following:

1. Make no substantive changes in an original document.
2. Tamper as little as possible with its punctuation.
3. Reduce superior characters (i.e., letters raised above the manuscript line) and add a period to indicate abbreviation.
4. Use italics for words or passages underscored in the original, but italicize no passages for editorial emphasis. (This principle applies equally to matter quoted in a historian's synthesis from an original document.)
5. Where variations occur in abbreviated words, standardize the abbreviation.
6. Devise and provide ahead of the text a list of symbols for words or phrases inserted by the editor in the interest of meaning, missing or undecipherable words, conjectural readings, deletions by the original author, and deletions by the editor (confined to unrelated matter, a topic which needs clear explication in a preface or introduction).
7. Annotate in footnotes scientific, medical, geographical, place-name, historical references or allusions, and such other aspects of the document as may require explication.
8. Identify in footnotes all persons requiring identification, excepting the obvious, e.g., the Father of His Country.
9. Identify in the preface or introduction the chronological base used, whether old-style or Gregorian.
10. Annotate by item in a collection, e.g., of letters, or of letters and diaries or journals interspersed, placing notes at

end of item and starting a new series for the next item. Number each item serially, even in multi-volumed works.

11. In matter unbroken except, for example, by years, annotate serially by division, whether chronological or topical, as determined by the editor.

12. Place in appendices related documents or editorial condensations of them, when the work of an author or authors bears significantly upon the work at hand, or the editor finds grounds for historical interpretation or correctives to matter contained in the original document.

13. In broken matter, e.g., letters, it is permissible to place salutation on same line (left) with place and date, run in (right).

14. Observe the principle of economy of annotation, avoiding the editorial delights (as well as the pedantry) of extended commentary.

15. Work only from your own transcription of the original document or documents, proofreading the former against the latter.

After a century and a half of dishonor, we have in Jackson's editing of the Lewis and Clark letters and related documents a model of scholarly presentation. But back of the largely physical rules for managing these documents (roughly one-half of which had not previously been printed) are a dozen or more applications of the critical historical method in American research, attractively developed in an essay, "Some Advice for the Next Editor of Lewis and Clark" (*Bulletin of the Missouri Historical Society*, Vol. XXIV, No. 1 [October, 1967], 52–62). "But our nameless editor of the future," Jackson writes, "will need to satisfy himself about the matter [whether the Lewis and Clark journals were written in the field or on the explorers' return], and about all the earlier questions I have posed for him—plus countless other questions. He must transcribe once more all the cramped and scribbled prose in those notebooks, for no good editor wants to rely on another man's transcriptions. He must be thoroughly aware of all the research that has been done, and make use of it, but he must go far beyond it in his own studies. He must follow the routes of the expedition—before the Missouri River gets turned into one vast lake by all those dams—because the places these men camped, the trails they followed, have never ceased to fascinate us. Occasionally the historian becomes impatient with those who place so much emphasis on the campsites and routes, but it is a contagious condition—the coming month will find me out in the Wind River Mountains of Wyoming, dogging the footsteps of John Charles Frémont."

The critical historical method required for the satisfactory editing of historical documents is more than a good grade of historiography. It may consist of insights and applications in science, for example, for, dismissing its romantic overtones, the Lewis and Clark expedition was charged with scientific purpose, as Thomas Jefferson's instructions to its leaders make clear. Thus William Clark's entry on July 4, 1804, in his *Field Notes*, on first viewing the Great Plains, is time for a scientific pause. "The Plains of this countrey," he wrote, "are covered with a Leek green Grass, well calculated for the sweetest and most nourishing hay— . . ."[24]

24 William Clark, *The Field Notes of Captain William Clark, 1803–1805*, ed. by Ernest Staples Osgood (New Haven, Yale University Press, 1964), 69. This passage extended from William Clark's own writing, unattended by the refinements given some of Clark's other records by Meriwether Lewis, will explain why, in reality, the process of bowdlerizing the party's journals began even before Biddle, Coues, and others set eyes on them. Clark couldn't spell properly or punctuate, or choose capitals logically. Meriwether Lewis to Thomas Jefferson from Fort Mandan, April 7, 1805, is symptomatic: "You will also receive herewith inclosed a part of Capt. Clark's private journal . . . . This journal is in it's original state, and of course incorrect . . . ." (Jackson, *op. cit.*, 231). The reference is to Clark's "Statistical Table," *infra*.

In this observation and what follows, it is a fair inference that Clark was deeply moved, but the probable identity of the "Leek green Grass" was big bluestem (*Andropogon* sp.), though we cannot rule out Indian grass (*Sorghastrum nutans*). This determination, ultimately of practical as well as botanical significance, becomes the immediate concern of the scholarly editor. And thus also we cannot pass lightly over the ethnological data supplied President Thomas Jefferson by Meriwether Lewis with his covering letter from Fort Mandan, April 7, 1805. Jefferson thought the large table significant enough to include it in his ensuing message to Congress under the title, "A Statistical View of the Indian Nations Inhabiting the Territory of Louisiana and the Countries Adjacent to Its Northern and Western Boundaries."[25] Did the President have any bases for evaluating the data? As a relatively young member of the American Philosophical Society twenty years before, he had given thought to Indian tribal identities and linguistic affiliations.[26] His Secretary of the Treasury, Albert Gallatin, would later put a solid floor under linguistic classifications of the eastern tribes, particularly.[27] Many French fur men and not a few Englishmen had seen the upper Missouri River tribes before Lewis and Clark arrived among the

[25] Thomas Jefferson, *Message from the President of the United States communicating discoveries made in exploring the Missouri, Red River and Washita, by Captains Lewis and Clark, Doctor Sibley, and Mr. Dunbar,* in *American State Papers, Indian Affairs,* I, 706–707.

[26] [Thomas Jefferson], *Notes on the State of Virginia* [1785] reflects at many points Jefferson's ideas and information on the tribes with which he was familiar.

[27] Albert Gallatin, *A Table of Indian Tribes of the United States, East of the Stony Mountains, Arranged According to Languages and Dialects* (N.p., 1826); and Gallatin, *Synopsis of Indian Tribes within the United States East of the Rocky Mountains,* 1836, in American Antiquarian Society, *Archaeologia americana,* Vol. 2, *Transactions and Collections* (Cambridge, 1836).

latter. But the Voyage of Discovery gave Americans their first official view of these tribes and their numbers. From subsequent ethnological studies and from near contemporary data on numbers, we can tell quite succinctly and accurately the value of the Lewis and Clark "Statistical View."

For the scholarly editor of documents, there are, broadly speaking, two classes of materials: (1) connected accounts, more or less self-contained; and (2) collections of documents—journals, letters, orders, reports, and statistical summaries. Diaries, journals, and narratives by individuals are examples of the first class: they are usually chronologically arranged and thus exhibit sequence in the historical sense. The materials brought together in the second class must be made sequential by the historian. For the latter, the sequential arrangement plus editorial annotation of genuine cogency affords a type of narrative unfolding which is difficult if not impossible to duplicate in any but the most brilliant syntheses. Thwaites' *Early Western Travels* contains many first-hand accounts in journal and narrative form, as does *The American Exploration and Travel Series*. An exemplar from the latter, since we have been dealing with the Lewis and Clark Expedition, is Pierre-Antoine Tabeau, *Tabeau's Narrative of Loisel's Expedition to the Upper Missouri*, edited by Annie Heloise Abel from Rose Abel Wright's translation (1939). (Tabeau was the French-speaking *voyageur* who welcomed the Captains of discovery at Cedar Island, four miles above the mouth of the Grand River in present South Dakota, on October 10, 1805.) The account is important in itself, representing in lucid form the experiences and discoveries of French Canadians and other French entrepreneurs from the upper Louisiana country in the fur regions to and including the Three Forks of the Missouri in present Montana. But in its first printed form it also reveals the kind of annotation a modern scholar must bring to his task. Yet, curiously, Miss Abel a short thirty-five years ago was mildly criticized for the extent and completeness of her explanatory notes. It is doubtful if anyone would do it today. The critical re-evaluation of primary historical evidence of this type requires all the scholarship we can command. If we did no more than look at Tabeau's account of Indians of the Upper Missouri and compared it with Lewis and Clark's "Statistical View," noting the probable indebtedness of the latter to the former, we should have made a first-rate gain.

Exemplars from the second broad class of documents, in which the historian must bring sequential flow to many and often disparate documents, are abundant: *The Papers of Thomas Jefferson* in nineteen volumes, 1950–74, edited by Julian P. Boyd et al.; *Adams Family Correspondence*, two volumes, 1963, edited by Lyman Butterfield;[28] *The Papers of George Mason, 1725–1792*, three volumes, 1970, edited by Robert A. Rutland;[29] *The Papers of James Madison*, 1962–, nine volumes, edited by William T. Hutchinson and William M. E. Rachal, and by Robert A. Rutland and William M. E. Rachal (Vols. 8 and 9);[30] and forthcoming, *The Papers of George Washington*, in process of being edited (1974) by Donald Jackson. Among them may be noted interesting variations in editorial form. Boyd's *The Papers of Thomas Jefferson* is characterized by editorial notes at end of item not keyed by superior numbers to specific points requiring elucidation in text. Butterfield's *Adams Family Correspondence*, on the other hand, keys

[28] Cambridge, Belknap Press of Harvard University Press, 1963.
[29] Chapel Hill, University of North Carolina Press, 1972.
[30] Chicago, University of Chicago Press, 1962–.

notes at end of item to specific points. Rutland's course is like that of Boyd in *The Papers of George Mason*. But Hutchinson, Rachal, and Rutland, Rachal, *The Papers of James Madison*, keys notes. My preference and recommendation is notes keyed to specific points. The discursive coverage supplied by notes not keyed is imprecise and time-consuming for the researcher using collections of documents for his own research—and the latter is the principal post-compilation use of these collections.

There are obviously relative strengths in collected documents relating to individual careers. Some, notably the papers of statesmen, often deny straight-line narrative thrust, simply because political lives are multi-directional, even within the course of a week or a month. The task of integration in the form of annotations therefore becomes more exacting of the compiler, the more so when he realizes that chronology normally cannot be side-tracked in the interest of a significant as well as attractive line of development. Military and naval commanders, explorers, professional men and women, and regional diarists, among others, often exhibit in their papers a narrative thrust which greatly enhances their readability and interest. A good example is Zebulon Montgomery Pike.[31] Another and far more dramatic one is John Charles Frémont, teacher of mathematics, surveyor, and apprentice explorer and cartographer as a young lieutenant under the able French cartographer, Joseph Nicholas Nicollet (1838), who had earlier mapped the sources of the Mississippi for the U.S. government. Frémont's five expeditions, in 1842, 1843–44, 1845–47, 1848–49, and 1853–54, covered in part by his journals and

31 Zebulon Montgomery Pike, *The Journals of Zebulon Montgomery Pike, with Letters and Related Documents*, ed. and annotated by Donald Jackson, 2 vols., No. 48, *American Exploration and Travel Series*, 1966.

reports, extended by his *Memoirs*,[32] and supplemented by his own and related papers, provide a major opportunity to the scholarly editor. The heights to which it has been carried, in sequential weaving, critical interpretation in annotations, and bibliographical completeness, may be seen in Donald Jackson and Mary Lee Spence, eds., *The Expeditions of John Charles Frémont*, Vol. 1 (which carries the explorer's career through his second expedition), with its map supplement, and in Mary Lee Spence and Donald Jackson, *The Expeditions of John Charles Frémont*, Vol. 2, *The Bear Flag Revolt and the Court Martial,* together with its supplement, *Proceedings of the Court Martial.* The integration which the editors have thus far achieved in the documentary record of this controversial figure in American history makes the work of any future synthesist hazardous.[33]

It has taken us the better part of a century and three-quarters to achieve the principles and the scholarly insights required for the editing of original documents. And of the two, scholarly insights are more important than principles, for the latter have been with us in extended and well-developed form for half a century. They are contained in R. L. Poole et al, "Report on Editing Historical Documents," *Bulletin of the Institute of Historical Research,* Vols. I and II (1923–25), 6–25.[34] This carefully drawn set of rules is the product of the Anglo-American Historical Committee, appointed by the Conference of Anglo-American Historians in July, 1921. As Poole and the members of his committee made clear in the preamble to the "Report," their work was not considered final and might require

[32] John Charles Frémont, *Memoirs of My Life* (Chicago, Belford, Clarke, 1887). The author had planned two volumes, but only the first had appeared before his death in 1890.
[33] Urbana, University of Illinois Press, 1970 and 1973.
[34] London and New York, Longmans, Green & Company, 1925.

modifications in individual use. But it covers many of the points that a scholarly editor, on assuming a minor or major editing task, will find very useful. Like the volume *Anglo-American Cataloging Rules* referred to earlier in this chapter, the "Report" will run beyond the needs of most editors working upon American documents dating from the beginnings of the national period, but it leaves little to be desired, from the most complex to the simplest of editorial problems.

To all the other principles for the editing of original documents must be added the importance of personal searching of repositories. Relying entirely on finding aids, Donald Jackson tells us, is risky indeed. "Those aids are sometimes compiled from information submitted by busy archivists. In searching for grist for the [George Washington] project, we have found literally thousands of letters which could never have been located without a personal search. The problem becomes acute when the scholar is researching an event, rather than an individual."[35] Dozens, sometimes scores, of items bearing upon an event may be unearthed by the editor of documents, but no catalog would have cross-referenced them under the rubric at stake.

[35] Donald Jackson to S. L., June 28, 1974.

8. Criticism

"THE MORAL," Henry James concluded about the environment of the novelist, "is that the flower of art blooms only where the soil is deep, that it takes a great deal of history to produce a little literature, that it needs a complex social machinery to set a writer in motion." The environment James chose early in his career, in France, Italy, and England, offered him a detached view of his own society in eastern America and, at the same time, a sharpened set of values and the materials from which his international novels (a genre all his own) could emerge. In the last third of the nineteenth century, similarly, Americans in search of historical method and the more fully matured historiographical styles could find them in the most active theater of their development, Germany. What they learned at Göttingen, Heidelberg, Bonn, Berlin, and Tübingen they brought home, so that, a century later, some of the earmarks of von Ranke, Mommsen, Waitz, Bernheim, and their contemporaries and successors are still detectable in American historical writing.

Yet in any critical evaluation of depth, the American school stands on its own feet, one planted in a highly developed research method not easily matched elsewhere, the other in a competent if often unspectacular type of synthesis. Maturity has been achieved only after the intellectual

struggles which characterize advances in other fields—
social, economic, ethical, and legal among them. And like
maturity in other fields, historical maturity contains the
elements of antithesis as well as of synthesis. It differs today
from other stages in its development in the relatively more
rapid way in which intellectual styles and approaches to
the basic data of the past succeed one another. In this sense,
however infertile the craft of history may at times seem for
the working of other disciplines, it remains that the changes
in its outlooks are traceable in considerable part to the
emergence of new concepts in the social sciences, the dy-
namics of social change, new methods of measuring economic and political data (notably in statistical and computer
applications), and the seductive attractions of the doctrine
of advocacy in an otherwise objective enterprise. The
intellectual environment of today's historian is accordingly
many-sided, complex, and rapidly changing.

Whenever the historian lays aside his principal concerns
to respond to the invitation to critical estimate, he will be
writing within this historical environment, with its sometimes untested—indeed, its sometimes unrecognized—assumptions. What historical maturity has produced, on the
other hand—an exemplary method, a critical approach to
all the data of the past, and greatly sharpened conceptual
insights—will usually be almost second nature to him. Research, the basic ingredient of historical writing anywhere,
has become so thoroughly cultivated in our country that all
else tends to become secondary. This is from many points
of view unfortunate. Not that a reviewer should be content
with less than adequate digging by the man he reviews.
Rather that he should be looking for a roundness, an awareness of the unspoken assumptions of the historian's craft,
and something of intellectual brittleness mixed with good

humor. And if he finds style, that too rare commodity in the historical market place, and fails to assess it, he will not be serving criticism. The proposition that historical writing need not be pretty doesn't refute the notion that it ought to be attractive.

There are four kinds of reviews insofar as the interests of historians are concerned: (1) the critical examination of the as yet unpublished manuscript; (2) the professional review in a recognized journal; (3) the newspaper or popular magazine review for a general audience; and (4) the reappraisal of the historical work of the past. The methods employed in each vary rather markedly, but all four are guided by three questions: *How good is it? How much is it needed? What does it do for us?*

As yet unpublished manuscripts are reviewed by one's professional colleagues, at request and as a favor. Such reviews seldom produce the hard-boiled answers which are called for in the three hard-boiled questions given above. Most historians are extremely sensitive to criticism, even when it is constructively directed. Criticism is much better received from a publisher, the other reviewer of the unpublished work. If he is a general publisher, he will be far more interested in answering (to himself) the second question (*How much is it needed?*) than either of the other two. For in his craft need translates itself into money, the only known oil of solvency. If the general publisher is a scholarly publisher in disguise (an Alfred A. Knopf, let us say, or, in England, a Sir Basil Blackwell), he will answer all three questions to his own satisfaction, at least. But the far more likely application of these questions will be in a university press, whose sole reason for existing is serious scholarship. (We will see more of the university press people in Chapter 10.) Here the importance of the first question (*How good is it?*) demands not only a decision from the university press staff reader but detailed analysis from anywhere from one to three recognized scholars in the field to which the manuscript pertains. Such analysis is always anonymous even if recognizably informed and perhaps sophisticated. It will often prove quite helpful to the author if it contains suggestions for improvement in the work at hand.

The question *What will it do for us?* (meaning the publishing house) has high relevance in terms of list-making. Publishers' lists have to be kept in bounds, obviously. But the niche a given manuscript may be expected to fill in a general or scholarly list often weighs heavily in a publishing decision. Sometimes it is tied to prestige, a commodity which most scholars are unfortunately inclined to overestimate. Sometimes it is tied to list-balance. At others it is a factor in filling gaps in ongoing series or parts of a general list. In any case, the suggestions which accompany tentative acceptance of the manuscript should be given serious attention by the author.

The second kind of review, that which appears in a scholarly journal, is significant to the establishment of historical reputations—for the author being reviewed and for the author of the review. Here the questions one asks of the published book and its author are of a more professional kind. Most of them should have been stated, at least indirectly, by the author himself in his preface. This is where the reviewer begins:

1. Why was it important to undertake this episode in history?

2. What new light does this book throw upon the period undertaken?

3. How does the subject relate to periods or areas of history immediately preceding or succeeding it?

4. How important is the scope of the book?

5. In relation to the work of others upon the same historical topic, how successful is this new assault?

6. What does this account do for or against earlier estimates of individual figures, or, if it is institutional history, what does it do for the institution?

7. How adequate was the research as reflected in annotations and bibliography? What entirely new sources were found and employed?

8. Is the quality of the writing merely sound, above average, or brilliant?

It would be misleading to suggest that these criteria in professional historical reviewing today can be applied directly. When journals ask for reviews running to as little as four hundred words for single-volume works and five hundred for two or more volumes under one title, the criteria have no more than the most generalized application. But to have them in mind, at least, will make the reviewer's work somewhat less frustrating.

Except for the article-length review, the essay type has all but disappeared from the historical scene. Highly developed in England, it has traditionally provided an important vehicle for established historians and scholars in other humanistic fields. Its rewards for the professional historian as well as the lay reader are difficult to overestimate. Perhaps chief among these is the recognition by the reviewer that his obligation in this form is not simply to historical but also to literary values.[1] The genre has been far from neglected in one of the most influential of American literary weeklies,

[1] It would be difficult to find a British historian of the first rank who has not written the essay type of review for such general media as *The Times*, London, the *Manchester Guardian, The New Statesman and Nation*, and two or three others. Sir Lewis Namier's *Avenues of History* is essentially a collection of his essay-length reviews, many of which are in themselves notable contributions to history.

The New York Times Book Review, and in the *Saturday Review* of other years. It will be found often, even if in somewhat abbreviated form, in *The Times Literary Supplement,* London. The real home of the essay-review, however, is *The New Yorker,* which has set a high reviewing standard in recent years.

Admitting the space restrictions of the scholarly journal, which aspects of the review for it should the writer pursue or avoid? Clearly, the character of the author's original contribution and the literary-historical values he evokes are most important. One of the attitudes the reviewer should avoid is expressed with some dismay by those being reviewed as, "The reviewer analyzed a book I didn't write." Unfortunately the complaint is commonplace and for the most part justified. The tendency that produces it is an almost irresistible impulse to stand on another man's shoulders. It obviously has no merit though it is often hard to outgrow. Another fault to avoid is certainty, which turns out to be much too close to dogmatism for comfort. The absolutes that are sometimes claimed for history simply do not exist, any more than they do for science, which has a much better theoretical right to them. We will always be exploring a past that is in part unknown and unknowable. A sympathetic, tolerant, but not uncritical view of one's contemporaries is best. For the reviewer it takes the forms, "What was the author trying to do?" and "How well did he accomplish his objective?"

The preoccupation of the historical profession with methodology for most of the seventy-five years of the present century has produced recognizably important results. But reviewers today must view historical writing from significant new perspectives. In retrospect, the assumptions upon which national growth was based are seen, almost without exception, to have been limited; the interpretation of national and regional cultures must give way to a more realistic pluralistic analysis; the imperfect working of that "most perfect of documents," the Constitution, needs more attention from the historian and less from the apologist; and the now bulging economic and business data available to us must be set off against the generalizations of the past. Not a few foreign historians have tactfully advanced the notion that American scholars revolve too constantly in the U.S. national orbit, undeterred by more distant perspectives.

The popular review in a newspaper or magazine of general consumption, our third category, can scarcely avoid these and others of the deeper-running issues concerning the past. Here, however, the professional point of view is less obvious, even when it underlies whatever is written. The angle of view is simply much wider, embracing the far reaches of the national literate population. When the reviewer is an A. L. Rowse, a J. H. Plumb, or a John Fischer, the results may not only be significant to historical analysis but to popular taste from New York to California. The unforeseen consequences of a review of a historical work in the classical field by Joseph Alsop, writing for *The New Yorker*, can change radically the scholar's regard for nonprofessionals.[2] At this point it is worth noting that fully 80 per cent of scholars' books sold in quantities of twenty-five hundred copies or more are bought by the general public. (Scholars use books in libraries or acquire them by review but do not ordinarily buy them on a regular or sustained basis.) For all of these reasons, the popular review has an importance far outweighing traditional estimates of its worth by historians. Moreover it is much more likely to

2 Joseph Alsop, review of A. H. M. Jones, *The Later Roman Empire* in *The New Yorker*, August 28, 1965.

appear at or close to publication date than the review in a learned journal, which may require a year or more. (The comparison is not intended to be critical: learned journals are faced with more scholarly works than they can accommodate, at costs not covered by large advertising revenues.) That it will often run much longer than the journal review, cover more aspects of the historical book, and permit a more satisfying overview of both the book and the period with which it is concerned, are additional virtues.

The fourth type of review, which reappraises the work of the past, is far rarer in the United States than it is in the countries of Europe. Such reappraisal appears most commonly in formal historiographies, where critical evaluation is usually brief and almost certainly incomplete. And there are reconsiderations of past historians in scholarly biographies, in the introductions and annotations to historians' journals or documents, e.g., William Hickling Prescott, Francis Parkman, Frederic Bancroft, Hubert Howe Bancroft, Frederick Jackson Turner, and Charles A. Beard.[3] Article-length work of the type under consideration is welcomed by most journals. The problem is the disinclination of many young and some older historians to bring the writings of past scholars into clear relief in our own generation. But the deeper problem is a critical one, of looking past the

3 William Hickling Prescott, *The Literary Memoranda of William Hickling Prescott*, 2 vols., ed. by C. Harvey Gardiner; Francis Parkman, *Letters of Francis Parkman*, 2 vols., ed. by Wilbur R. Jacobs; Jacob E. Cooke, *Frederic Bancroft, Historian*; John Walton Caughey, *Hubert Howe Bancroft, Historian of the West*; Harry Clark, *A Venture in History: The Production, Publication, and Sale of the Works of Hubert Howe Bancroft*; Wilbur R. Jacobs, *The Historical World of Frederick Jackson Turner, with Selections from His Correspondence*; Ray Allen Billington, ed., *"Dear Lady": The Letters of Frederick Jackson Turner and Alice Forbes Perkins Hooper, 1910–1932*; Wilbur R. Jacobs, ed., *Frederick Jackson Turner, America's Great Legacy, Frontiers and Sections* (essays); Howard K. Beale, ed., *Charles A. Beard, An Appraisal*.

historiographical tags which have been attached to many writers of other times in order to find the larger truth or merit about them. The extent to which the reverse is true in literary-critical fields is a significant measure of neglect, at least insofar as the historical journal is concerned.

Retrospective analysis, in fact, has proved to be one of the most rewarding aspects of criticism in letters, philosophy, and the arts of music, the theater, and painting. To discover the place of a creative intellect in letters or one of the arts and to estimate his worth in the history of his medium or the spirit of his age is to add substantially to the record of a culture. In America, the long preoccupation with Frederick Jackson Turner's frontier thesis and its influence has tended to obscure rather than to define the tasks of individual reappraisal.

Implicit in all reviewing of scholarly work is the need for a well-grounded historical awareness on the part of the reviewer. Carl Becker, after reviewing what he subsequently described as a "book of some pretensions which unfortunately turned out to be largely pretentious," received from its author a sheaf of favorable reviews and an epigram, "Big men write books; little men review them."[4] The author's pique was little merited in Becker's case, but the epigram is sometimes not amiss in our era. Becker's further observations of the reviewer's craft continue to have a singular cogency:

"Critical reviewing, at its best, doubtless requires particular qualities: grasp and breadth of view as well as erudition; information mediated as well as catalogued; something of originality and constructive power." And with

4 Carl Becker, "The Reviewing of Historical Books," *Annual Report of the American Historical Association for the Year 1912* (Washington, 1914), 130. Subsequent quotations from Becker's articles are taken *passim*, 130–36.

a certain gift of prophecy he observed that "in our reviewing we look a little too much to the footnotes and the bibliography, and judge a book to be good if its techniques are
up to the mark.... We need a criticism that shall go beyond
technique." Of many reviews, he had to say that they were
essentially expanded bibliographical notes, even if in form
they affected "the mannerisms of the literary critique." To
fully satisfy the latter, he suggested that the reviewer would
serve himself and his readers better through the evaluation
of historical work which departs from conventional methods
of investigation or interpretation. Today, the search for
originality is as pressing as ever, and, admitting satisfactory
research technique, the reviewer must give greatly added
emphasis to this aspect of the historian's effort.

That American historical writing often lacks boldness
and dash, that its tendency to conformity seriously robs it of
character, and that, like a French spinster, it may be chaste
at the expense of being unloved—all of these negative
characteristics are tacitly admitted in historical circles. The
reviewer accordingly is not much better off in his search for
character in historical writing than his counterpart was
sixty years ago, when Becker was outlining the qualities the
critic should look for. Considered views of history, like considered views in politics or social analysis, are bound to be
debated. To choose a less than bold course is to miss both
the heat and the rewards of controversy.

There must be room in literary-historical criticism for
the realization that the historian's craft has been, and today
remains, one of the most conservative, in its professional
outlooks, in the United States and Canada. Yet the land-
mark historians—a limited company, to be sure—are precisely those who struck out boldly, their originality clearly
visible, the dust of the controversies they stirred still un-

settled. In the last half century they include Turner, Vernon Louis Parrington, Arthur M. Schlesinger, Charles A. Beard, Marcus L. Hansen, Oscar Handlin, Merle Curti, Howard K. Beale, Herbert Eugene Bolton, and Henry Nash Smith.

The historical voices of originality and imagination are a much larger company, though admittedly a less controversial one. Their works have continued in print from decade to decade, in original format and in many paperback reprints. Why? Originality, the reflective critic of historical writing may be assured, was not enough. It had to be joined with easily recognizable qualities of style, a command of narrative and analytical structures, and a fineness of interpretation. We tend too often to attribute successful performance to "balance," which is otherwise undefined. Our time might be better directed to something else—the author's convictions, which, if they have fully taken hold of him, are likely to take hold of us, provided he was sensible in arriving at them and we are not uncritical in pursuing them. For historianship is concerned less with periods than with problems, the historical depiction of which lies entirely in the hands of the writer.

G. N. Clark, the English historian, has considered the moot question of what should be done, in criticism, with the historical study lacking in any redeeming merit. His answer is that it should be ignored. There are too many good-to-excellent studies for the editor or the reviewer to spend time and space on the book that is clearly incompetent or mainly meretricious. It is a harsh judgment but a just one, as time, which ordinarily preserves what is worth preserving, will prove.[5]

A question equally difficult to confront but requiring an

5 G. N. Clark. "Historical Reviewing" in *Essays in History Presented to Reginald Lane Poole*, ed. by H. W. C. Davis, 119.

equally decisive answer is, Should conflict of interest cause a reviewer to decline a subject upon which he himself is at work? The answer is that he must. He should also decline to review the work of one of his colleagues in his own university (there will always be some doubt whether the reviewer can be truly objective in such instance, whereas any adverse criticism he might find it necessary to write must imperil departmental peace).

Equally, recommending reviewers of one's own work to the editor of a journal is to be avoided. Strange as it may seem, this practice is far more widespread than most scholars may realize. Fortunately, journal editors universally dismiss it without action, as do book publishers when authors suggest referees for their work.

In the area of small points in criticism, there is a large difference between the historian's *lapsus calami*—his slip of the pen—and historical error as such. The one is scarcely worth mentioning, unless it appears clearly as a pattern of carelessness; the other calls for analysis in historical terms. In my printing and publishing days, I used to assure authors that "every book must contain a minimum of eight typographical errors," a statement which I suspect the late Piet Peerenboom, who was at home at the House of Banta proofreading in classical Greek and Latin and half a dozen modern languages, would have concurred in. But there is a difference between a typographical error and a historical slip. David Livingstone for Robert R. Livingston is not a typographical error.

The very format of history suggests that the reviewer must be concerned with the accompaniments of scholarship as well as the scholarly synthesis itself. Any history of action which lacks maps is defective. If it contains one map or several clearly cannibalized from earlier publications, it is also defective. The historian today can claim no cartographical disabilities. He is expected to carry out the same quality of research in map depictions as that which went into his text. For it is too often possible to trace historical as well as cartographical errors back for twenty-five to fifty, or even more, years, simply by examining the ancestry of maps reproduced in current histories. (More detailed information on map preparation will appear in Chapter 10.)

From the point of view of the reviewer, pictorial illustration—paintings, drawings, photographs, and graphs, charts, and statistical data, when required—must be assessed. Here again, the research failures, half-measures, even the lack of responsibility by the writer must be set off against what, in other aspects, may have proved to be a satisfactory book. Because pictorial research is as yet so indifferently pursued by most historians, there are large margins for error, in identifications (of individuals or scenes), chronology, and authenticity and attributions. But the burden rests quite as much upon the person being reviewed, for an informed critic is scarcely relieved of the pictorial aspect of what, in text, are identifiable as "primary sources."

Reviewers no less than the authors they review suffer from certain disabilities. One of the most prominent of these, in scholarly circles, consists of the absolutes which the reviewer learned in graduate school and has never seen fit to modify. There will always be several ways of skinning a cat or preparing a bibliography to be appended to a scholarly volume. I think it is good for dissertation writers to adhere to the highly classified form of bibliography their supervisors wish them to know about. But many a fine historical volume has been concluded with a bibliography arranged alphabetically by author or agency. Battles have been fought (but none won) over the relative propriety of "foreword" or "preface." There is more room for discussion about the aptness of a title, or the propriety of using a title appearing on a slightly earlier publication (titles are not copyrightable, but they do lend themselves to legal considerations of fair competition). But library cataloguers will always have the last say in such matters. Figures don't lie, but it is a rare reviewer who takes the trouble to understand constant dollars. In areas of cultural, scientific, and intellectual history, the erudition required of the reviewer, as distinguished from his understanding of historical forms, will tax all of his resources.

And thus, in whatever area we evaluate historical criticism, we must be impressed with the seriousness of its demands. For it has the power to recognize excellence, to generate further scholarly effort, and to restrain mediocrity. At its best it will assure survival of the best historical writing and weed out the unfit. The Younger Pliny, we may recall, would permit even a shoemaker to judge a work of art, provided he didn't venture above the subject's shoetops (*Ne supra crepidam sutor judicaret*). His rule is a good one for journal editors and their reviewing scholars. A reviewer ought to have more than ordinary competence in the historical area of the work he is called upon to assess critically. If not he should regret.

9. Words

STYLE is a state of grace. It has little to do with the mastery of historical bibliography and methods, which are so effectively taught in American graduate schools. It is a personal acquirement and almost always reflects the literary-intellectual personality who uses it. People who regularly work at it for the purpose of making a living almost never talk about it among themselves. It can be analyzed, laid bare, and subjected to exegetical treatment, but it cannot be reconstructed.

Carl Becker, who knew as well as any of his day how to make words do pleasing work, set up the critical division between what a historian works with and how he achieves his results. And Barbara Tuchmann summed it all up tersely: "Research is endlessly seductive but writing is hard work." But there will always be the hope, particularly on the part of beginning historians, that some formula, some magical outline will somehow smooth the way to memorable results in dissertation, journal article, and monograph. There are many reasons why there can be no magical formula or outline. The most important of them is that style must be filtered through the intricate coils of the individual, matured, and filtered again. And back of that process is the necessary intellectual discipline of selective reading. I can't say anything of memorization, for the passages from poems, plays, and prose works that were customarily committed to memory in another age are no longer a part of the secondary-level educational process. "Relating" to one's fellows has taken their place. The trouble is that the writing of history can't avoid "relating" to the best expressions of meaning we possess in man's long struggle with language. A historian who has never really ventured through the frustrating barrier of meaning may have missed his calling.

We were late discovering that Immanuel Kant, in German or in translation, was very unclear about "a pure synthetic apriori proposition." But the historian of ideas can scarcely avoid that complex statement. Nor can any student of recent history avoid coming to grips with the popular commitment to "the good life," without some understanding of what is meant by the word "hedonism" and "psychological hedonism." There is even some merit in having, in the study of American political parties, a firm grasp on the concept of the indiscernibility of identicals. For wherever we turn we must encounter ideas which were persuasive in their time and fully capable, therefore, of surviving into our own era. Words made them so. Words, indeed, make history.

A respected graduate professor has suggested to me that any book with the title, *The Rhetoric of History*, must have something to say about words. "When I myself was a graduate student at Harvard," he said, "no one did anything for me in that vexed area. Today, I find the word problem more pressing than ever among graduate students."

This observation seemed to me an invitation to boil into a single chapter all the wisdom about grammar and usage that had been accumulated since Chaucer's time. I knew nothing good could come of his proposal. So did he. But it is one thing to write about the techniques of historical synthesis and quite another to appreciate the individual bricks and mortar—the words and usages which bind them together—in any edifice that is intended to last. Where do we turn for the right word, which, in Joseph Conrad's mind, is the essential building block of literate style?

Some people are quite sure that the Bible, if only one book could be taken, would be quite adequate for a long sojourn on a desert island. In the large savanna of history I should prefer *The Oxford English Dictionary*, organized "on historical principles," in thirteen volumes.[1] For much in our language, it traces usages and quotes passages dating as far back as the thirteenth century and carrying down to the present day. It is perhaps the best guide and the safest training vehicle for the person who will never become a philologist but must demonstrate some competency in historical synthesis. It is scholarly, correct, and full of surprises. We do not search far in it to discover, for example, that the much-used word *conceptualization* is really a bastardized expression, or that *rhetoric* is today used largely in a pejorative sense, however respectable its ancestry may have been. It offers little comfort to those who want an infallible referee of their word choices. The English language, the OED makes clear, is like the historian, it has always been in a condition of becoming. Words and phrases have come into and gone out of the language with what appears to be unrestrained abandon. In any age it is not the lexicographer who sets word acceptance but the people who write words and the public which accepts them or coins new ones.

---

[1] Sir James A. H. Murray et al, *The Oxford English Dictionary; Being a Corrected Reissue* . . . (13 vols., Oxford, The Clarendon Press 1961). With the exception of this work, reference works referred to in ensuing pages will not be described bibliographically in notes but will be found in the appended bibliography.

There are many times, obviously, when the OED will tell you more than you want to know. For these times the quicker references will be provided by the "international," or even the collegiate, volume of Webster. The only trouble is that most users of a dictionary never take the time to read the prefatory matter, the rules for pronunciation, the principles governing the division of words, and other important "using" data. Even more serious is the tendency of the non-language scholar to accept words "because they are in the dictionary." Indeed they are but they are often identified there as secondary spellings, obsolescent, or even obsolete.

The time was no more than forty years ago when marked differences in English usage and national divergences in dialects of English seemed to confirm the need for separate national dictionaries, especially those constructed along historical lines. Thus for the United States (and perhaps to a lesser extent Canada) *A Dictionary of American English* compiled by Sir William Craigie and James R. Hulbert and a staff of lexicographers and finally completed in 1944, took its place beside the OED. But we are less sure today. English tends, under the influence of television, moving pictures, the theater, and books, magazines, and newspapers of general consumption, to assimilate to a common written pattern, even if accents continue to vary. A good "median" English, therefore, will make the historian writing in that language understood almost anywhere English dominates.

The bypaths of English language can take the historian into many pleasant groves, but they are less professionally necessary than etymologically diverting. Any research library of size will contain handbooks of synonyms, acronyms, prepositions, word finders, and thesauri, etymological dictionaries, Joseph Wright's great *English Dialect Dictionary*, Eric Partridge's *A Dictionary of Clichés*, and, so help me,

Russell Rocke's *The Grandiloquent Dictionary*, a true guide for the pompous.

No one who writes English can afford to be without access to a good short English grammar. There are so many currently in print that any positive recommendation is unnecessary (see *Subject Guide to Books In Print*, together with its companion volumes, *Authors in Print* and *Titles in Print*, compiled and published annually by the R. R. Bowker Company, New York).

There is a certain irony in repeating today what foreign language teachers have been saying for generations, that the mastery of at least one language besides one's own is an end in itself but also of profound importance to the command of written English. If the American historian never pursued the French and Spanish documents for the Mississippi Valley, he would still stand to gain from intensive study of the one language or the other, ancillary to his professional study. My own conviction, of course, is that he had better not tackle that area without a command of two languages. Herbert Eugene Bolton, A. P. Nasatir, and Alfred Barnaby Thomas, among a considerable number of authorities on the Spanish documents for the Mississippi Valley, did not exhaust the vast documentary treasures in Spain, Mexico City, and Cuba. In French, the holdings of the Ministère de la Marine, Paris, contain thousands of documents little consulted and many complete books of a contemporary character, as yet unpublished.

In the end, even the Americanist, working only in U.S. documents, will find himself up against the need for French, Spanish, and German dictionaries—simply because the professional and the literary expressions in history contain many borrowings from these languages, quite aside from the appearance, infrequently, of untranslated passages.

The Rhetoric of History

English usage is language in action. Perhaps the best book currently available (it has been available since 1926) is H. W. Fowler's *A Dictionary of Modern English Usage.* Today's student of history, unlike his predecessors, will find it in some respects puzzling, for Fowler, as his only reviser in these fifty years admits, exacts of his readers a slower, more painstaking pace than is customary in those who run to the dictionary and run back again to their typewriters. "There are some passages," says Sir Ernest Gowers, "that yield [the desired sense] after what the reader may think an excessive amount of scrutiny—passages demanding hardly less concentration than one of the more obscure sections of a Finance Act, and for the same reason: the determination of the writer to make sure that, when the reader eventually gropes his way to a meaning, it shall be, beyond all possible doubt, the meaning intended by the writer."[2] Perhaps the distinguishing feature of Fowler's expository style is whimsicality, particularly in the articles on usage, of which there are some 150. Once understood in their whimsicality, however, these articles are unlikely to be forgotten. They extend from *absolute construction* to *worsened words*, with stops in between for *Americanisms, battered ornaments, elipsis, formal words, hackneyed phrases, hysteron proteron, pedantic humor, sequence of tenses,* and *sturdy indefensibles,* among the 150. For those who had liefer be right than be president, Fowler's grand lexicon may help, e.g., "The *per caput* consumption of beer in New Haven in 1973 was 56 gallons." If your dissertation director objects, refer him, as Winston Churchill referred his Director of Military Intelligence before Normandy, to Fowler. (The Prime Minister

2 Sir Ernest Gowers, "Preface to the Revised Edition" of H. W. Fowler, *A Dictionary of Modern English Usage* (Oxford and New York, Oxford University Press, 1965), iii, vi.

was concerned for his colleague's misuse of *intensive* for *intense*.)

Other books of which H. W. Fowler was joint author are *The King's English*, *The Concise Oxford Dictionary*, and *The Pocket Oxford Dictionary*.[3]

No one who writes regularly can afford to be without *The Elements of Style*, by William Strunk, Jr., and E. B. White, which is short, bright, and sensible. For learned writers it offers one rule which is a pearl above its price: If you must be obscure, be obscure clearly. The tendency of such writers to become mired in their own subordinate and conjoined clauses may be cured in specific instances, say Messrs. Strunk and White, very simply. Just back up and start all over again. (Which-mires characterize those who think in circles, not straight lines.)

Fowler, Strunk and White, and, not to be omitted, Porter G. Perrin in *Writer's Guide and Index to English,* together form a helpful company for the historian. Perrin is considered by most English departments in colleges and universities to be authoritative for their purposes. The objective (if only one may be selected) in all of these aids is to abolish wordiness in the serious writer's style. And wordiness owes much of its attraction for beginning writers to the adoption of phrases or clauses which are, as Messrs. Strunk and White phrase it, "the refuge of those who decline to cut, sharpen, and refine their writing." The tendency has something in common with Lyle Saxon's anecdote of the southern woman of advanced age who used to sit on her front porch chanting over and over again in a low voice, "Mesopotamia." When someone asked her why she did this, she replied, "It has such a comfortin' sound."

---

[3] In its obituary notice of Fowler, *The Times* of London said of his and his brother's *The King's English* that it "took the world by storm."

The choice of words, rather than the attempt to satisfy the graduate teacher's commands, "Be simple; be direct," becomes in the end a disciplined attitude of mind. Choice here means stylistic choice. There will be times when the everyday word *buy* will be better than *purchase*, but only the inept would discard the more formal word when the context requires it. For most scholars, however, the dangers do not lie between the classifications of simple and formal words. They lie in a conscious adoption of what would seem to satisfy the scholar's peers. This means at best words that lack juice and at worst a stilted, overgenteel vocabulary. The sound course is to write always to the tastes and interests of intelligent people everywhere, not merely to the members of the historical profession.

The lengths to which a truly disciplined mind will carry the process of stylistic choice are represented by Carl Becker's surviving drafts of Chapter V of *The Eve of the Revolution*, devoted in principal part to the thoughts and motivations of Samuel Adams and Thomas Hutchinson. His sketch of Hutchinson closes with a letter the Governor wrote describing Adams as a "Great Incendiary." As Charlotte Watkins Smith, Becker's most gifted literary-historical analyst, has shown, Becker quite apparently wrote with speed, both conceptually and structurally. But his first draft of the Hutchinson-Adams episode gave way to a second, and even to a third and a fourth, but what finally appeared in print bore substantial changes over Becker's fourth. There are successive deletions, word changes, and structural emendations. They are reproduced in Miss Smith's *Carl Becker: On History and the Climate of Opinion* and must be read in their entirety, as indeed all else in her Chapter V, "The Practice of Writing," must. Her Chapter IV, "The Art of Writing," is an equally rewarding analysis of Becker's ideas on that subject, drawn principally from his address delivered at Smith College in 1942, of which an earlier version had been delivered at Wells College in 1941 (the former appeared posthumously in Becker, *Detachment and the Writing of History*, edited by Phil L. Snyder, 1958).

Reminiscence can be a bore, but Becker's memory of his first encounter at age eleven with "literature" in the form of a sample copy of *Saturday Night* is entirely charming and interesting. When, two years later at the age of thirteen, he concluded after reading Tolstoy's *Anna Karenina* that it was "nearly, if not quite, as good as the stories in *Saturday Night*," he had arrived at his first independent critical judgment. The age at which he first found himself afflicted with the "literary malady" coincided with his wish to settle for a writing career. But his encounter in college with Frederick Jackson Turner and Charles Homer Haskins made a gentle curve in his decision, not a right-angle departure, Miss Smith tells us. (The University of Wisconsin in those days would have bent almost any twig towards history.) But, as time brought out, it was less the choice of a profession than a life-long commitment to reading, dating from *Saturday Night*, that gave form to one of the most satisfying historical stylists we possess.[4]

On style and the words that accompany it, Becker had definite and cogent ideas. As a student, he said, "the Rhetorics did not help me much because to the unformulated question I asked them they gave no answer. What I really asked the Rhetorics was, 'What must one do in order to learn to write well?' The Rhetorics all, without exception, replied,: 'Good writing must be clear, forceful, and elegant.' I have sometimes wished that I might acquire great wealth, and that the authors of all the old Rhetorics would come to

---

4 Carl Becker, *Detachment and the Writing of History*, 122–23.

me and ask, 'What must we do in order to acquire great wealth?' I would reply: 'Great wealth consists in a clear title to much money, forcibly secured in banks, and elegantly available for spending.' "[5]

Good writing, he suggested, is writing "that fully and effectively conveys the fact, the idea, or the emotion which the writer wishes to convey." Of the writer it demands, first of all, a dominant and persistent desire to write. Its second requirement is what he called "the inveterate habit of reading," the new and the old, the good and the bad, catching "the meaning and overtones of words and the peculiar pitch and cadence of their arrangement." One of the consequences of wide reading and the absorption of pitch and cadence, he believed, was the process of writing by ear rather than by rule.[6] In two of her analyses of Becker's writing, Miss Smith shows how biblical and Shakespearean rhythms ring clear in him.

Becker's third recommendation for those who would like to write well is to write. Having little or nothing to say is not a good excuse for not writing. Speaking properly, he reminds us, comes only with incessant practice.

The result? He mistrusted *style*, which, he said, "tends to fix the attention on what is superficial and decorative in writing, upon verbal facility and the neat phrase."[7] The idea, instead, is the thing. In the end it is quite as much substance as form. Style, however personal, has no independent existence aside from thought. It develops only when the writer quietly battles against an outside, imposed standard and wins the right to be himself.

Not even the writer of history, however, can divorce him-

[5] *Ibid.*, 124–25.
[6] *Ibid.*, 128–29.
[7] *Ibid.*, 132.

self from the notion that what he writes ought to find some-where a measure of applause. People don't write merely for the purpose of satisfying themselves. They write almost always with the corsciousness of an audience. In Walter Prescott Webb's case, it was at first an audience of one, but after gaining the interested attention of a small boy, Henry Woods, Webb, then a teacher in a one-room schoolhouse in the piney woods of East Texas, never stopped writing until his death.[8]

History, after all, is shared discovery. The requirement for sharing it, but even more importantly, the desire to share it well with readers, was never far from the thoughts of Edward Gibbon, as his letters reveal (he had, admittedly, an exceptional audience in such figures as David Hume, Horace Walpole, and Adam Smith, yet the last half of the eighteenth century was a time when Englishmen and Scots were learning to write again, even these figures among them).[9] William Hickling Prescott in his *Literary Memoranda*, Francis Parkman in his *Letters*, John Lothrop Motley in his *Correspondence*, and many more recent historians in various ways, revealed their responsiveness to an audience composed of both scholars and laymen. No one, perhaps, was more startled and pleased than Gibbon at the overwhelming success of the first three volumes of *The Decline and Fall of the Roman Empire*, the successive printings of which threatened the time he had reserved for the last three.[10]

[8] Savoie Lottinville, " 'Professor, That Was Purty,' " in Ronnie Dugger, ed., *Three Men in Texas: Bedichek, Webb, and Dobie.*

[9] Edward Gibbon, *Letters*, ed. by J. E. Norton, Gibbon to Georges Deyverdun, 7 Mai, 1776, II, 104–108.

[10] *Ibid.*, Gibbon to William Robertson, 3 November, 1779, II, 232–33; Gibbon to Dorothea Gibbon, 24 February, 1781, 260–61; G. to Dorothea Gibbon, 13 April, 1781, II, 265–67.

It would be difficult indeed for a writer to work effectively without some notion that what he wrote would ultimately be read by many people. Writing needs the stimulating feed-back of readers, even when their character and range are as yet not fully known. But if historical writing suffers today from a single malady, it is not so much that it lacks feed-back but that, in one of its most pervasive forms, it feeds back too much. It is the textbook, whose styles, organization, and concepts are the principal forms—sometimes the only forms—the undergraduate history major comes to know well. On to the Master's degree and the Ph.D., he has a hard time shedding textbook style. After all, he subconsciously reasons, it must be respectable: notable expressions of it were written by his major professors, who themselves are respectable. If the textbook is bad, why was it a principal vehicle for learning history?

In all truth, the textbook isn't bad. What we have today in the English-speaking countries is remarkably good. The textbooks we see in use are accurate, swift, and very much to the point. But they almost never exhibit the styles which are satisfying for original contributions in volume, much less article, form. In the latter, originality, a certain boldness, and a style intended to be arresting are prime requirements for success. A captive audience, as in textbooks, can never talk back except at examination time; a critical audience, on the other hand, will bite the hand that feeds it—usually for good reason.

Historical writing, perhaps more than some of the other learned callings, invites the familiar phrase. Graduate teachers today usually refer to it as the *cliché*, which traces etymologically to the French for a stereotype block or cast. Its appropriateness for the inappropriate is obvious. A better English expression is *hackneyed*. Etymologically it owes nothing to another language. A hackney is a horse, better still, a doubtful horse, a nag. English contains a very large stable of nags, but so does German, and that supposedly unflawed language, French, is not without its share. People, as a Yorkshire woman once observed, are "much of a muchness, only some is skinnier nor bonnier nor fatter as others." So equally with the languages they use.

More sinned against than sinning is the hackneyed phrase, which, like the formal word, is often picked up from an overacute memory or thin air. In introducing the foregoing sentence with a hackneyed phrase, I may have developed the only legitimate use of an old stereotype. Hundreds of such constructions are dredged up for use, as if they had a special validity, or an allusive quality, or perhaps to make up for words that won't come. When you feel impelled to use a hackneyed phrase, think twice. You can do much better on your own, if you try hard. Besides, you will have the pleasure of having your own original phrase used over and over again by others, so that it too in time will become hackneyed. To take in other hackneyed phrases from others' washings, we have the following as a very incomplete list, though a suggestive one:

General George Gordon Meade *slept the sleep of the just* after Gettysburg.

In this *feast of reason,* Thomas Jefferson found himself with a *surfeit.*

For Franklin Delano Roosevelt, devaluation by doubling the price of gold was *a consummation devoutly to be desired.*

All that was mortal of Brevet Major General George Armstrong Custer lay upon the now silent battlefield.

Napoleon at his best had *few equals and no superior* in the history of warfare.

Charles V wished above all else for peace and quiet in the Spanish Netherlands, but *it was not to be.*

Sir Robert Peel, in Victoria's eyes, had *the defects of his qualities.*

Politically, Wilson found, any attempt to change the temper of the farm bloc was *to be left severely alone.*

There was *balm in Gilead* as Cleveland and his campaign supporters met to celebrate the election victory.

Leaving *homes and loved ones,* the jaunty Texans marched off spiritedly to Santa Fe.

The Bank of England, a private corporation for more than two centuries by now, needed no justification except as an *act of supererogation.*

It was the irony of fate that Hannibal, most capable of generals, should have to face a doubting group of commanders that first night on the Po.

Raymond Moley, a highly trusted figure among Roosevelt's advisers, protested the action *more in sorrow than in anger.*

Mayor Lindsay was only one of five *young hopefuls* who let it be known that they, too, could *serve the nation* in its *highest gift of office.*

To the *eagle eye* of James Monroe, Jackson's action could hardly go unnoticed.

President Johnson was *seriously inclined* to accept House Majority Leader Carl Albert's views, but he still hesitated.

The *olive branch* so generously extended to the North Vietnamese fell upon *deaf ears.* (Here borrowing slips into the metaphor with an ease much too good to be true.)

Mixed metaphors, like the quick snatching of well-remembered phrases, almost always come in the heat of composition, when we are bent on sharing our delights with others. They are therefore easy to commit, embarrassing when they get into print, and unpardonable. But the best of writers and the worst of writers will on occasion get caught up in them. How they arise is less important than the principle that will keep them out of a piece of writing. That principle, as Fowler has told us, is to let well enough alone. If you have made a reasonably good metaphor, i.e., an undeclared comparison, stop before you spoil it with an unequal yoke-fellow. When we have a young man with his *nose to the grindstone and his ear to the ground,* we can be very sure that he may become a captain of industry but not an epigrammatist.

Such a phrase qualifies as a *reductio ad absurdum,* but we must not underestimate the lengths to which the mind is capable of going—not after the contagion caused by the Tom Swifty ("I'll take a double-martini," he said dryly) which had high currency only yesterday and a swift death at nightfall.

Although most writers of manuals for historical careerists tell us to use metaphors sparingly, if at all, I have suggested, at the point where extracts from Vernon Louis Parrington's writing were reproduced, that there is a real place for both the metaphor and the simile (which declares a comparison) in the more arresting type of writing. Parrington's metaphor of the railroads' binding the country together with steel bands is graphic and vigorous. His descriptions of some of the railroad barons shortly thereafter, rich in both metaphor and simile (the fat and the lean kine but not of Egypt), are demonstrations of what can be done with these forms.

A metaphor, as an undeclared comparison, is perhaps more difficult to deploy than a simile, which, as a declared comparison, usually begins with "like." The notes of birds singing in a Mexican forest, George Miksch Sutton, the ornithologist, wrote, "were on tip-toe." This is metaphor. Evelyn Grisso's description of a house tenanted by a tobacco-smoking bachelor, "It smelled like a snooker parlor," is simile.

Metaphors can sometimes be used incongruously to produce wit or a sufficient pause by the reader for reflection on what might otherwise have gone unnoticed. For example, I once listened to a debate in England on the subject of "Women in Politics." Using Miss Ellen Wilkinson, M.P., as representative of the species, a speaker might have said, deprecatingly, that she was a confused member of Parliament. What he actually said was, "she is the farrago intacta of the House of Commons."

But in truth figures of speech are refined devices requiring great care in use. The straightforward kind are easiest on both writer and his readers. "To the Indians on the heights above, the mounted troops on the valley floor looked like a long line of slowly advancing ants." Similes of such directness are best for beginners.

There is a common misgiving in historical circles about using words or phrases of classical allusion or literary piquancy. The reason given, that the classics and the literary depictions of character and motivation are old hat, is not, however, the best available. It is, rather, that the classics are largely unknown, even in translation when the original language is not English, and Dante, Shakespeare, Goethe, and Wordsworth are merely names. Moreover, in another era, when writing tended to be pretentious anyway, many allusions came in full-bodied, dragged by the heels. The effect was not the kind to inspire subsequent imitation.

The risk from another direction, i.e., in faddish words, is much greater. It is not easy to divorce oneself from what is current or currently popular. Madison Avenue, pouring its persuasive English into magazines, newspapers, and the television waves, accomplishes much more than a commercially propagandistic purpose. It shapes in subtle ways the usages and ideas of young and not-so-young people for whole decades. This language and these ideas tend inevitably to color and to shape the student's representation historically of times and peoples quite unconnected with our own. No working editor (and I was one perhaps too long) misses this type of flaw in countless manuscripts.

The pitfalls in half-remembered grammar are scarcely less serious. Most people who pursue history will instantly tell us that infinitives (to take a familiar case) are not to be split—that is, those who have not examined Carl Becker's notable locutions or Rudolph Bambas's stimulating discussion of to-verbs. "The exact truth of remembered events," Becker wrote in his Presidential Address to the American Historical Association, "he has in any case no time, and no need, to curiously question or meticulously verify." Val Lorwin, Becker's assistant at the time, tried to unsplit the infinitives (of which there are two) at proofreading time. But, Miss Smith tells us, Becker kept the splits, inasmuch as he knew that any other rendering would have been false.[11] Bambas's article on the split infinitive appears as an appendix to the present volume.

Most people outside English-language ranks don't know the difference between an infinitive and a compound verb. Their struggles to avoid placing necessary words, particularly adverbs, between members of a compound verb are accordingly fraught with hazards too frustrating to describe here (Fowler does it rather splendidly). "To really understand" is a split infinitive and it is better than anything else you can devise. "To really be understood" is a split

[11] The unsplit infinitives appear in the Presidential Address to the AHA at 246 in Becker, *Everyman His Own Historian: Essays on History and Politics.* Cf. Smith, *op. cit.,* 138–40.

infinitive and it doesn't say what you mean. "To be really understood" is not a split infinitive and it means what you wish to say—well. Again, Mr. Fowler will prove a splendid guide.

Some people do not like bread and butter. What is worse but comparable is that some graduate teachers of history do not like some words or expressions. Are the forms of "to be" suspect? Then what do you do with "To be, or not to be: that is the question."[12] From the same class are those who have ticks on the apparent (to them) irrevocable divorcement of adverbial and adjectival forms; whether (off the tops of their heads) certain words are comparative (fast, faster, fastest) or simply "more fast"; and the certainty that there is never a time when a preposition may close a sentence. "Lincoln found John Hay, his new secretary, one of the people worth talking to" thus gets prettied up in the form, "Lincoln found John Hay, his new secretary, one of the people to whom it was worth talking." We accordingly have Lincoln "evincing" an interest rather than simply (and correctly) "showing" it, thereby putting a screen ahead of his meaning. The English language is a deliciously flexible thing, if we will just let it alone or, alternatively, work very hard at letting it do its own good work.

Participles can give a sentence or even a paragraph a good fast start, unless, as too often happens, they are unattached. In a paragraph about Chester A. Arthur, we have the following: "Having shot his bolt, the party had to decide whether to accept it or find a new candidate." In the first place, the bolt which was shot was Arthur's, not the party's. In the second, the participial opening "having shot" has got to tie to the shooter, Arthur, not the party, which commands all

12 *Hamlet*, Act III, Scene 1.

the action after the comma in this false example. About the only way we can make it come off, then, is to recast it in direct terms: "Having shot his bolt, Arthur could only await the party's decision whether to accept it or to find a new candidate."

Structurally, historical writing tends to suffer from the fatal attraction of interposed conditions and explications. Instead of "He fought a desperate rear-guard action against his enemies all during July," we get a bundle of restrictive or nonrestrictive clauses, and subordinate or co-ordinate constructions.

"All during July, with the tenacity which he had already demonstrated as a Congressman, he fought a desperate rear-guard action, not in the sense of retreat but as a delaying tactic until Penrose could make up his mind about coming to his aid."

These contrasting sentences are clearly narrative in character. The one, however, is truly characterized by action. Its successor unfortunately sets out to tell all, and nearly does. In the telling it loses narrative thrust, quite aside from being awkward and breathless. Even in analytical historical constructions, the call is for large measures of uncomplex statement. Interposing conditions, extensions, or limitations destroys focus and divides attention.

Paul B. Sears in the chapter, "From Longhorn to Combine," in his study of the Great Plains, *Deserts on the March* (1935) demonstrated rather convincingly the merit of the technique we are considering. Its deceptively easy rhythms deal with successions in the short-grass and sagebrush country: moisture and drought, wind and calm, cattlemen and homesteaders, then back to cattlemen again, finally dry-land farming, overproduction, and drought, billowing dust, and the vast disaster of Depression. Many anthologies for schools continue to include it. And for good reason. It is genuinely good in itself but it may also help to raise up some sturdy practitioners of clear writing for all of us who wait upon the word.

10. The Mote in the Publisher's Eye

THE publication of Ray Allen Billington's editing of Nicolaus Mohr, *Excursion Through America*, in December, 1973, contained a significant overtone for scholars in practically all disciplines in the United States. The book had been "composed," i.e., set into type, by R. R. Donnelley and Sons Company, The Lakeside Press, Chicago, at the rate of one thousand characters a second. A character in printing is a letter of the alphabet, a punctuation point, a figure, or any other single symbol. The book, No. 71 in the *Lakeside Classics*, is, from a scholarly point of view, almost full-statured. It contains, in addition to its text, ample footnotes appearing at the foot of the page rather than at the end of book, and an index. It lacks only a bibliography, but all necessary bibliographical data appear in parenthesized form in the notes. Set as it was by an electronic device, it had to be free of all the niggling slips to which learned typescripts seem prone—transposed letters, strike-overs, misnumbered footnotes, misspellings, and omitted punctuation.

Corrections or changes are not forbidden by an electronic scanning device or any of its slower cousins, but they tend to nullify the great gains in time-saving and economy in book production made possible by this new development. Comparably, such changes correspond to a five-hour wait for transportation to one's hotel after a supersonic airplane flight.

It would be false to say that for the first time the scholar was running up against the realities of high technology. That had occurred long ago, in the eighteenth century and earlier, when nimble-fingered typesetters, picking movable type from wooden cases, had demonstrated with remarkable swiftness how irrevocable type can be—unless it is scrambled at the proof stage by the author. Mechanical typesetting, which in its dominant form produced all of the characters of a line of type in a single bar or slug, greatly increased the speed of composition and further reduced the freedom of the author to make changes in type set, beginning about 1900. The new technology, however, makes that of the last seventy-five years incredibly slow by comparison. It forecasts completed books in a week, two weeks at most. It also suggests that the scholar as we have known him is now in some senses obsolete. It may even be that the gifted but selfless men in gray and women in flat heels called publishers' editors are obsolete, too. Order and a much higher degree of perfection in the scholar's manuscript will have to come ahead of its submission to a publisher, scholarly or general. But I do not foresee that there will be no Maxwell Perkinses in the coming decades, any more than I can foresee that there will be no future Thomas Wolfes in need of them. It is, rather, that the priorities will change and the scholar's responsibility for the form of his manuscript will be greatly increased.

The change, long overdue even without the new technology, begins in most instances with the manuscripts which originate in American graduate schools. In ribbon copy as finally submitted for degrees, they have seldom left much to be desired from a purely mechanical point of view. Yet the thousands of theses and dissertations resting unpublished, sometimes unconsulted, in university libraries seem to me to constitute one of the largest areas of waste in American academic life. It is not that, in many instances, they lack promise. It is, rather, that there is no widespread understanding of what makes a manuscript worth the thousands of dollars required for its publication.

For more than half a century—roughly from the end of World War I to 1975—the divergence between what candidates for historical careers do in graduate schools and what they do in published form has gone largely unchallenged. Theses and dissertations are considered, quite justly, I think, to be necessary exercises in the pursuit of higher degrees. At the same time they are often spoken of, when completed, as "publishable" by those who have supervised them. Such judgments are, in a large number of cases, misguided. Few graduate teachers are entirely familiar with publishing canons. They cannot be for many reasons, some of which will emerge in the present chapter. But the important details a scholarly editor looks for must now become far more current in graduate circles than has been the case for most of our century. Both cost and competition will require it.

The first essential in the transformation of the thesis or dissertation into a book is obviously the encouragement of the graduate director to his student. I say "obviously" despite the fact that encouragement to publication in book form fails in many instances or is so little attuned to publishing reality as to be abortive. Encouragement too often takes the easy way out, i.e., for the author to break up his extended work into articles for submission to one or several journals. While the latter course is in some senses the "life of trade" for the journal editor, it can forestall the rich discipline which comes with the achievement of one's first book, to be followed by a second, a third, and perhaps even a fourth. If the one or two chapters in a dissertation which constitute the "contribution" have been siphoned off into journal publication, there is really not much left for a book publisher to offer his public. Many of us in scholarly publishing have had the experience of discovering, at time of contracting for a book, that *all* of its chapters had previously appeared in journal or magazine form. Needless to say (but I must say it even so) we can find no rational, and certainly no financial, justification for proceeding.

The second large essential at the graduate-school level is that the dissertation director who sees a genuinely publishable dissertation should pursue the subject with his former student for months, even years, to see that he doesn't rest on his degree laurels alone. The doctrine of "publish or perish" has been parroted unrealistically for at least two generations by deans and research scholars. For the recent graduate student entering upon his first (untenured) appointment, it should have a much more productive signification than it ordinarily conveys. It should be directed to the establishment of one's presence in the company of scholars. Nothing else really matters. Certainly not those unanalyzed jottings in the dean's office concerning books reviewed, journal articles accepted, conferences attended, and hours taught. Scholarship was never quantitative. Hence the enormous importance, qualitatively, of the student's first extended work—and the need of getting it before the scholarly world, if at all possible.

For the historian at any stage of his career, what are the publishing canons most likely to affect his progress? What standards must he meet? How does a publisher apply these canons and these standards?

FORM: The dissertation (less often the thesis) served up to a scholarly publisher according to the forms prescribed by a graduate school usually makes a bad first impression. It most likely bears a long descriptive title with no concessions to an audience much larger than the limited number of specialists who can be expected to profit in some degree from its publication. Footnotes, as required by graduate-school directives, will appear at foot of typescript page rather than at end of chapter so that they can be set into type as a separate operation and assembled at foot of the page of text. The acknowledgments will thank half a dozen or more professors for aid "generously given." And the dedication page will pay the tribute, "To my Wife but for Whom . . ." The text, footnotes, and bibliography will appear as a faint carbon copy or a Xerox copy fainter still.

Several things are wrong here. The most serious is that the author, the director of his dissertation, or both concluded (a) that the work is publishable, or (b) that the scholarly publisher will relay from his scholarly readers and his own impressions just how the work should be partially or fully revised. In either case, the main question is being begged. Neither the director nor the candidate for publication has made an honest attempt to answer it, and the publisher should not be asked to. In publishing we call this a "tentative submission."

The much better course is a decisive one. It provides a fresh new typescript, fully revised in the details outlined above and in the form of the text, ridding it of all evidences of midnight oil. And the footnotes have been sharply reduced to the essentials and placed at end of chapters. Sound scholarly practice, regardless of the many publishing variations from it today, insists upon footnotes as such rather than their placement somewhere else, to be kept track of by one's right thumb; but the typescript management of them here recommended permits all of the notes to be set in reduced type on a separate manually operated composing machine and then placed in proper position in the "make-up" process by a hand-compositor. Set by an electronic device, the process is at once more decisive, since a page of text and its accompanying footnotes emerge as a complete unit, and much swifter.

In typescript, everything should be double-spaced: text, quoted matter presented as extracts and indented both sides, footnotes, bibliography, and appendices, if any. Manual composition by Linotype, Intertype, Monotype, or other keyboard devices and electronic devices as well, demands double-spacing, and editors, who traditionally have done their corrective work by means of interlinear insertions, cannot work successfully in margins. The margins are normally reserved for the markings of typographers and designers.

Any typescript presented to a publisher should be as letter-perfect as the author or his typist can make it. This self-imposed requirement has at least three large values: (1) the impression that good order is likely to make on the publisher and his editorial readers; (2) in the event of acceptance of the typescript for publication, the relative ease with which it proceeds to bound-book form; and (3) a corresponding reduction in the margins for error, either by the author (to his ultimate chagrin) or by the publisher's copy-editor. Considering these points in order:

Any realistic portrait of a publisher must depict him primarily as a reader. If he sticks to his profession, he will become a fast-reader, but not in the sense in which that phrase is ordinarily meant: he reads; he doesn't merely scan. And he may polish off anywhere from three to ten book-length typescripts in a day. If, in his stack of typescripts, he encounters the too usual run of fourth-carbon copies and miserably retyped works and then suddenly strikes pay-dirt in the form of a physically well-prepared work—not brilliant but competent—he usually places it in the stack on the right, to be given further consideration or outright acceptance. Whereas the tentative submission, inviting a long letter (the author hopes) telling him just how to revise his dissertation or post-doctoral draft, inevitably conjures up in the publisher's mind a long-extended period of coaching. This manuscript falls into the stack on the left. So does the excellent, even brilliant work shot full of typing errors, interlinear scribblings, and parenthesized numbers for footnotes. It suggests disorderly work habits on the part of its author, but much worse, it means that the publisher will have to schedule from three to four weeks of a copy-editor's time to straighten things out. Not least, the poorly prepared typescript opens large vistas of author-publisher conflict at the galley or page-proof stage of its production.

In extension of this psychological analysis of the publisher, it needs to be said that a general publisher thinks in terms of profit, a scholarly (i.e., a university-press) publisher in terms of losses. When the editorial management of a given work runs beyond minimal requirements, the pleasure of publishing it must yield today to the realities of cost. Any less realistic publishing decision must result in the allocation of a disproportionate share of the scholarly publishing budget to a project which could have won its way with the application of stylebook and professional typing. Not even the senior scholar can escape the implications of counter-productive costs in today's inflationary climate or tomorrow's typesetting requirements, though admittedly any certain candidate for large sales will justify certain concessions by the publisher. The young scholar, as yet with no commanding reputation, must dig hard or die.

The second large value to be realized from the author's presentation of a well-prepared typescript—the relative ease with which it is set into type and made ready for presswork—has been borne out in hundreds of cases in my publishing experience. Somehow, the good typescript runs ahead of itself at all stages of its book production. Copy editors sail through it. Designers find it clean and easy to work with. Typesetters on digital equipment, accustomed to mixing roman, italic, and capital- and small-capital characters, ligatured letters, "standard" accents, symbols (&, $, etc.), and figures (both roman and italic), actually absorb the author's meaning as they work on a complex keyboard. Above all, proofreaders, with one eye cocked on the galley proofs and the other on the author's original copy, find sure footing for everything they do. The book thus beats its publication date by weeks, perhaps months.

The reduction of error, the third value realized from "clean" typescripts, can be amply demonstrated in any type-composing or proof room in America. The errors we are talking about now are not the common ones—transposed letters, words omitted in typesetting, and superior numbers in text (signalling footnotes at foot of page) out of sequence. They are usually winnowed by professional proofreaders, who have a still more delicate job to perform—watching for broken, burred, and wrong-font letters, which sooner or later will disturb the book reader who reads for long stretches. The reader may not detect the cause of his unease, but the proofreader glancing a long galley will. (To illustrate, two wrong-font *e*'s were set in the foregoing sentence. Find them if you can.)

The Mote in the Publisher's Eye

SCHOLARSHIP, a precious quality in any discipline, is a good deal easier to detect in a manuscript than most specialists realize. Historical scholarship is, in some considerable part, the result of attention to certain categories, each embracing a host of details: the originality of the undertaking (does it break new ground?); the relative weight of primary and secondary sources; the accuracy of citations; the fidelity of quoted matter to its originals; command of narrative and analytical techniques; sharpness of interpretation; and qualities of style. There are so many worth-while tasks for historians that the twice- and thrice-told tale in the American field, particularly, can only be viewed with misgiving by the publisher. New ground, original approaches to it, and a willingness on the part of the author to work deep in the archival underground are beginning to occupy primary position in his thinking. But his concern over citations, the accuracy of quotations, the admissibility of ellipses in certain instances, and other historical detail has occupied him for the better part of half a century. These are matters to which he is not supposed to be privy, but he is. Many journal and book publishers are appalled by the inaccuracies they find in citations from public documents, to take a single category. If a book publisher could afford the time and costs, he would check out every quotation to which he has access.

In the estimation of scholarship, the publisher has the benefit of readings by recognized authorities in the field to which a given work pertains. Because their anonymity is preserved, these readers can be entirely frank in their evaluations, and they usually are. A conscientious reader will often run far beyond the space provided in a publisher's reading forms, analyzing problems in the manuscript by page and line. These analyses are transmitted to the author only if the publisher senses that the work is salvageable.

ILLUSTRATION is a research function of the scholar. As I have earlier made clear, appropriate illustrations are an indispensable accompaniment of a work in history. They require much the same research effort and discernment as the historical text itself. Finding the right illustrations is not the task of the publisher, nor should it be left entirely to his discretion. As the historian conducts his research, he should not only be alert for portraits and scenes contemporary with specific parts of his text, but he should also go to great lengths to get them.

For example, in the presidential campaign of 1864, what we need is the face and figure and informal posture of Abraham Lincoln captured in that year, not the classic portrait of the President by Mathew Brady that Lincoln liked best. And when we have the tall Lincoln towering over General McClellan at Antietam, we have beaten the studio portrait all hollow. William Bent, the vigorous, hard-bitten, shrewd frontiersman of Bent's Old Fort, looks the part in an informal photograph made of him in company with Little Raven, the Arapaho chief, and the latter's two grown warrior sons and small daughter.

Painstaking study will usually give us a more rather than a less realistic artist's depiction of figures and scenes before the age of photography (1839). In painting, sculpture, and manuscript depictions, the range of illustrative choice for every period from the earliest times forward is both rich and historically satisfying. In European portraiture, one of the historian's tasks is to avoid idealization in his choices, when he can, and distortions when he knows they exist (El Greco).

In these and other aspects of historical illustration, the objectives are honesty and immediacy. Thus, surprisingly, we have vastly greater resources for depicting ancient Aztecs and Mayans than we do for ancient Scythians (the artistic remains of the ancient Americans were late in being discovered and slower in being dispersed and destroyed).

ILLUSTRATIVE SOURCES. The first and most obvious source is the range of relevant illustration which others have turned up and published in their own books. But if the candidate for publication rests there, as so many of his predecessors have done, he has sadly neglected his task as a historian. We have called the process cannibalizing. The process is stale and flat. Instead, the historian in search of illustration should use these previously reproduced pictures and their credit lines as a means of turning up pictures little or never used, in the same depositories from which the published ones have come. Try desperately for the unused.

Manuscript collections and other archival holdings almost always contain some pictorial materials, at least. Almost all state historical societies and libraries possess picture collections. What is said of them can be said with much greater force of national institutions, for examples, the Library of Congress, the National Archives and Records Service, the Bibliothèque Nationale in Paris, the British Museum in London, the national and provincial historical libraries in Germany, Italy, Spain, the Netherlands, Mexico, and so on. Many have published catalogues or descriptive lists of their holdings. Wherever the historian searches for primary materials, he should also search for primary pictorial materials: they will often be found side by side.

There are two categories of privately held historical picture resources: (1) the private collector as such, and (2) the pictorial service. The first may be prevailed upon to permit reproduction of one or more of his holdings, and the second, e.g., Bettmann Archive, Times Wide World, or Magnum is in the business of selling prints.

Additionally, the historian may find little-exploited pictorial materials in the "morgues" of newspapers, particularly the larger metropolitan ones, and in the picture collections maintained by some industrial and trade associations, for examples, the American Iron and Steel Institute, the American Petroleum Institute, the Association of American Railroads, corporations in all of these fields, in food processing, chemicals, and the like. Where else do you turn for photographs of early oil activity in Pennsylvania or drawings of the McCormick reaper, the narrow-gauge locomotive and its freight cars, the first iron and steel mill in colonial New England?

Finally, there are published copper, steel, and wood engravings, and non-book prints. You will find the former in books for the period to 1898, and the non-book prints in museums, archives, and art galleries.

Implicit in the task of gathering suitable illustrative materials is a fairly clear understanding of what can and what cannot be successfully reproduced by modern-day engraving methods. Photographs and photographic reproductions of paintings, drawings, and sculpture present no problems. Nor do line works, as in original copper and steel engravings. Glossy photographs of previously reproduced materials in photoengraving may give a conflicting dot-pattern and be all but useless. Subjects originally appearing in color may be reproduced either in black-and-white or in color. But color today, as in all ages past, is expensive, sometimes forbidding in historical works of relatively small sale.

The Mote in the Publisher's Eye

If we examine the reproductions in Billington's edition of Mohr's *Excursion Through America*, with which the present chapter began, we can see demonstrated, with great clarity, practically all of the types of illustration with which the historian is likely to be concerned—early photographs, line drawings, lithographs, paintings, and steel and copper engravings. For its pictorial research and its technically satisfying reproductions, Francisco de Miranda, *The New Democracy in America: Travels of Francisco de Miranda in the United States, 1783–1784*, edited by John S. Ezell and translated by Judson P. Wood, may also be consulted.

MAPS. If pictorial illustration remains one of the least satisfactorily developed areas in historical research, maps, by and large, leave still more to be desired. For the most part cannibalized in varying degrees from previously published books and journal articles, they reveal little of the "original research" on which the historical craft prides itself. The publisher, I should make clear, is not necessarily looking for finished maps to accompany a manuscript submission. He is looking for a draft form which is cartographically sound and well enough done to be interpreted by a cartographer. Trained map draftsmen can later turn out professional specimens to your publisher's order, usually at your expense. They cannot work to best advantage unless you supply them reliable data.

What should a map do? A map, even in its most complex form, is a diagram. In historical contexts it gives the reader the sites, routes, physical features, places, and distances which are of importance in the text. Why is it considered a diagram? Because, unless it contains raised surfaces, imparting a three-dimensional quality to what is seen, it is two-dimensional—length and breadth of the land, into which a third dimension, depth or elevation, must be read by imagination. Few historical maps actually require the techniques of depicting physiographic features, but most historical maps will benefit greatly if they are prepared from land-forms bases. The technique is simple: prepare your sketch map as an overlay on a land-forms map. A fine example of what may result can be seen in Frank Gilbert Roe, *The Indian and the Horse,* showing the historical dispersion of the horse among the Indian tribes of North America.[1] The base is that of Irwin Raisz, whose printed land-forms maps are available in most college and university bookstores in the United States and Canada. Even when physiographic features are not depicted, the transparent overlay on a land-forms map will keep the historian from putting an early fort on the wrong bank of a river or a town on a mountain peak. Perhaps 40 per cent of the map errors I have encountered arise from the failure to observe this principle. Other errors arise from the failure of the writer to regard map scales from which he has worked, or his tendency to forget entirely the bases he consulted.

The amount of detail which should be included in a map draft is governed by four factors: (1) the irreducible minimum needed for its successful use by readers; (2) the juxtaposition of place names, names of physical features, and the names of movements and the like; (3) the extent to which detail sacrificed in one map can be regained in a succeeding map or maps; and (4) the limitations imposed by the vertical format of a book.

It is always desirable to put into a map only as much detail as is necessary for properly complementing your text. Here, however, you must not leave out detail which will

[1] Publication data for this and other titles mentioned in the text of the present chapter will be found in the bibliography.

give quick orientation to the reader. Thus faint lines for states now existing but not yet formed at the time of which you write may be highly essential. Do not put in cities, towns, posts, roads, and railroads which were not there at the time.

When many place names and names of physical features begin to butt into each other, the nonprofessional cartographer solves his problems quite simply, by reducing their size. This will never do. Map names must be well adjusted to normal eyes. A series of names too small to be read in any map destroys the purpose for which the map was made.

Maps, when once drawn professionally, are relatively inexpensive to print. Therefore one map area may be disburdened of excessive detail when you have concluded that not everything needs to be said at this point but may be given supplementally in one or more additional maps. This alternative requires a more critical appreciation of book format than is customary even among scholars.

Because most historical works go into traditional book formats, whose vertical dimension is substantially greater than their horizontal, most bookmakers, geographers, and cartographers wish you to work to these dimensions. They will go to great lengths to avoid having the reader flop the book on its side, 90°, in order that one of its maps may be read. They work ideally so that you can use a book map just as you do a page of text, from top to bottom and from left to right. Maps with long horizontals are, for good or ill in bookmaking, an abomination. There are times when we must cope with them, unavoidably, but for the most part they can be got around without too much trouble. A skilled map-maker will juggle the area and the detail in such a way that he comes out with a vertically oriented map. Or, unable to escape a long horizontal, he arranges the map to be spread across two pages, splitting it (with no loss of detail) in the gutter of the book. Sometimes he will make two maps from the single map proposed, but for this purpose the data supplied him must be abundantly clear on rapid scrutiny.

The historian will sometimes attempt to escape his dilemma with a long horizontal by calling for one or more fold-out maps, possibly even the gate-fold kind, which, however delightful to look at, are not good solutions. Such maps are very expensive to insert in a book, since they call for hand-tipping or pasting in; they break along one or more of their folds; and, finally, as any historian knows who has tried to find a copy of Josiah Gregg's classic *Commerce of the Prairies* with its superb map of the Southwest intact, folding maps succumb to the collector and the criminally inclined.

Another poor solution is the endpaper map, which to too many people has seemed comfortable, decorative, and useful—all of these without regard for the facts (a) that such a map is not integral with the text of the book, (b) that on the first rebinding the map will be destroyed, and (c) that even during its short life the endpaper map will be defective at the gutter.

AUDIENCE: When a scholarly publisher has satisfied himself about the form and the quality of a manuscript, he still must answer the question, What are the audiences for the book? Ordinarily, its author will think only of that audience which consists of his colleagues in history. This is the smallest part of the market the publisher must look to. It may consist of only a few-score buyers. The institutional, i.e., library, market may account for five hundred to eight hundred copies, if the book has genuine historical appeal. Our total thus far may be twelve hundred copies. At a retail price of $10.00, discounted 40 per cent on average as the retail and wholesale booksellers' share, we are just half the distance to breaking even on an investment of some $14,000.

At the forks of the creek, in Westchester County, New York, or Bexar County, Texas, say, there are people with counterparts in hundreds of other counties scattered over the United States who provide salvation. They actually read history for pleasure. Some of them are active book collectors. Others developed their interests in consequence of the fact that higher education doesn't always fail. They are intellectually active and sometimes critically informed to a surprising degree. It is to this audience in part that any historian appearing in book form is addressing himself. And the estimation of this audience by the scholarly publisher is one of the highly important canons of his craft. He looks at it not at all as a popular "outlet" for the scholar's book. He sees it, rather, as a large and constantly changing reservoir for serious work in any field the historian cares to pursue. In both the short and the long terms, its existence usually provides the margin in a financial sense which makes the scholarly book possible. Its aggregate annual contribution to the scholarly book market far outstrips the subsidies provided scholarly book publishing by foundations and educational institutions. That the form and content of the historian's work must be conceived with some respect for it should be (but usually is not) axiomatic among historians.

The machinery of book distribution in the United States is as simple—some say archaic—as the workings of an old-time country store. The historian's book is sold ahead of publication to bookstores by the publisher's sales representatives. Put on display at publication time and after, the book is bought by people who constitute, in the best sense of the phrase, a noncaptive audience. Here the scholar will find both the rewards and the disappointments of free enterprise.

Book clubs small and large have added greatly to the market for historians' works during the last twenty-five years. For the book of above-average quality, the scholarly publisher will usually submit advance copies to two book clubs, sometimes more. But a selection is frosting on the cake, not a normal expectancy, for the mill run of those who write serious history. Perhaps the best way for the working historian to estimate the odds is to ask himself why Garrett Mattingly's *The Armada* became a best-seller in both the United States and England, whereas the same author's *Renaissance Diplomacy*, on which he pinned higher hopes, did not. In the process he may also note that the historical reading interests of his countrymen are far from confined to purely American subjects.

COSTS: The publication of scholarship has always been expensive, but by 1975, under much the same set of inflationary pressures which had so adversely affected the family food budget, publishing costs had severely constricted the lists and the criteria of manuscript acceptance among American university presses. The painstaking processes by which the scholar's work had been offered to his public, brought to their fullest flowering in the 1960's and in an academic atmosphere seemingly immutable, had to be re-examined in the light of cost-cutting. (Industry had much earlier faced up to the requirement as well as to increased production per man-hour.) On average, it had been costing the scholarly publisher a minimum of one thousand dollars spent on editorial time to put a "messy" typescript in order for setting it into type, five hundred dollars for a "clean" one, managed along traditional lines. Typesetting, as a plant charge, had gone up to fifteen dollars an hour, proofreading to ten dollars an hour, and presswork to twenty dollars an hour. Paper costs, along with cost of binding, had about doubled between 1969 and 1975. In the end, it was costing from fourteen thousand to twenty-two thousand dollars to produce and distribute (sell) a monograph in history. Printings were a minimum of one thousand copies, with two thousand the upper limit for the first run of a book with better than average sales outlook. (University presses, most of which can't show a profit and mustn't show a substantial loss, obviously have no means of financing long inventories of bound or unbound books.)

To continue our cost analysis along historical lines, by 1975 the scholar had witnessed the beginnings of a new phenomenon in publishing which promised help in the cost-cutting era. At widely spaced points, notably in California and New York, a cottage industry was emerging. Its skilled workers were learned typists capable not only of turning out a near letter-perfect typescript but of using coding keyed to OCR (Optical Character Recognition) equipment and produced on typewriters with "character recognition" faces. The typescript so produced (at the author's expense) could now brave the new world of high-speed typesetting, without further keyboarding, on OCR equipment that can "read" the typescript and convert into justified and "set" type. Only in its beginnings, the method was but a step removed from the meticulously typed results expected by graduate schools of their students. Revolutionary? Not at all. Painful? Yes, to all of us who have made some contribution to the arts of scholarly editing in publishers' workrooms. But clean manuscripts, whether they get a thoroughgoing editing or not, are long overdue. My conviction, strongly held, is that they are here to stay.

Who meets the costs? University presses, general publishers (the Macmillan Company, for example, met the large cost of publishing Edward Gibbon's letters in three volumes), universities, individuals other than authors, businesses, units of state and federal government, and (rarely) foundations. The scholar's book that far exceeds in sales the cost of its publication is not uncommon, but the average scholarly book sees the light of day because of seen and unseen subsidies, one of which we have discussed at some length in the preceding paragraph. Because of escalating costs which had begun to appear in their instructional and administrative budgets, some universities had begun, by 1968, to withdraw the aid they had earlier afforded their presses. The seasonal and annual publication lists of these presses were accordingly sharply reduced, some were operating minimally, and others had been placed on a caretaker basis or were in abeyance until better times should come. General publishers, long on profits in the 1960's, were no longer in a position to take up the slack, because of soaring costs and declining profit margins. Wherever we look, therefore, we are the more certain that the striving for excellence, which has been the burden of this book, is the scholar's most pressing requirement. Less than excellent performance may never be published.

STYLEBOOKS, DICTIONARIES, AND MANUALS: Much of the work of a copy-editor is directed to the need for giving a scholar's manuscript consistency in such matters as capitalization, the uses of italics, the management of quotations, spellings and abbreviations, the uses and placement of punctuation points, dashes, parentheses, ellipses, and hyphens, the division of words, footnoting, the arrangement of tabular matter, and the ordering of bibliographies and indexes. Some of these matters are prescriptively given in stylebooks, of which the most widely used is *A Manual of Style . . .* compiled and published by the University of Chicago Press. Others are given in Kate L. Turabian, *A Manual for Writers of Term Papers, Theses, and Dissertations,* Third Edition, Revised, also published by the University of Chicago Press.

A good stylebook not only enables the scholar or editor to give consistency to a work but decides his style options, e.g., whether he shall capitalize a title of honor and respect after as well as before a personal name. Under each of the topics noted in the preceding paragraph there may be a score or more of cases with decisive recommendations stylistically. Stylebook style, as distinguished from literary style, is devoted to matters which, for the most part, lie outside the scope of dictionaries, works on English usage, and thesis manuals. It is arbitrary, sensible, and specific.

The use of a stylebook by a historian can confer certain benefits. A potential publisher will spot the application of stylebook principles by the author after he has read half a dozen paragraphs of manuscript. His empathies tend to be more easily aroused and his editorial resistance reduced. But the qualities the author himself realizes from stylebook applications are far more important. A manuscript no less than an editorially stylized book tends to hang together better when it has met and overcome its inconsistencies. It has achieved and will always retain professional polish.

A stylebook is a reference work, not a body of principle which can be learned and applied from memory. The best course is to familiarize yourself with its contents, then keep it at your elbow as you write. Enough has been said in

Chapter 9 about standard manuals and reference works in usage, grammar, and the formation of style, but bibliography and methods, in spite of the heavy attention given them in graduate schools, are subjects which the scholarly publisher continues to find problematical.

FOOTNOTES AND BIBLIOGRAPHY. When it was first published in 1931, Homer C. Hockett's *The Critical Method in Historical Research and Writing* was considered a doubtful candidate for break-even sales. "The Macmillan Company," Professor Hockett wrote in his Preface to the thoroughly revised edition of 1948, "was persuaded, with some misgivings on their part, to publish the book. Its reception seemed to prove that it met a felt want." The author's second sentence above is understatement which perhaps only those engaged in the book trade can fully appreciate. The published record of the number of separate printings of this manual runs to ten. It is undeniably one of the most used and respected we possess. For any publisher it would have been a "property." Today no scholarly publisher can afford to be without it in his shelf of standard reference works. Any student who is making a career of history must number it among his possessions. Its uses as a research tool are both fundamental and far-reaching. As a guide to the management of citation and bibliography it has never been superseded. Any scholarly publisher of history must expect that an author who makes a submission to him is familiar with Hockett's principles and has taken some pains to apply them.[2]

Graduate schools are various in their requirements, so

2 Hockett's great manual had disappeared from the lists of its original publisher, The Macmillan Company, in 1974, nor had it reappeared in any paperback list at that time. However, it will be found in most research libraries, often in multiple copies. Its last printing was in 1968.

that the historiographical styles in citation and the management of bibliography may not be uniform in all details. But what Hockett lays down and what Miss Turabian has so succinctly outlined should do for most publication purposes. There is one major difference between dissertation practice and book publication, however, which should be familiar to the candidate submitting a manuscript to a book publisher for the first time. If the manuscript contains a bibliography, classified or alphabetically arranged, it need not (should not) incorporate bibliographical detail in the footnote citations, e.g., such parenthesized data as (New York, The Macmillan Company, 1948). For the subsequent searcher, these data can be found at end of book, in the bibliography. To incorporate them in citations is to duplicate them and increase book costs.

Equally important to cost-saving, when citations of original documents are frequent, is a list of abbreviations of collections or their repositories, best presented as part of the front-matter of the book. For examples: BC (Berg Collection, New York Public Library), PC (Pforzheimer Collection, New York City), NL (Newberry Library), etc. Admittedly, most readers, even the most learned, find these abbreviations awkward and difficult to retain, but the alternatives outweigh in cost any advantages they may confer.

For the skillful bibliographer, however, there is an alternative to footnote citations and an accompanying formal bibliography. It consists in a running account of sources, arranged by the chronological progression of a chapter, topically conceived. A close study of the technique may be undertaken in Madeleine B. Stern, *Louisa May Alcott,* and John Paul Pritchard, *Criticism in America: An Account of the Development of Critical Techniques from the Early Period of the Republic to the Middle Years of the Twen-*

tieth Century. The fact that both books are literary-historical does not vitiate the applicability of their bibliographical apparatus to general historical purposes. This method, which has gone largely unnoticed, has marked advantages over annotation schemes which, in the supposed interest of printing economy, throw things to the end of the book. It is exacting and in no sense an easy alternative to traditional methods. Its best applications occur when sources are relatively limited in number and, in traditional footnoting, would be referred to again and again.

COPYRIGHT is a subject which should be dealt with in at least one three-hour sitting in a history seminar, preferably by someone who knows at first hand publishing practice rather than statute and case law, merely. Because it rarely gets adequate attention either in graduate school or in a scholar's working career, it may remain a source of frustration and worry to the person who contributes, in the words of the U.S. Constitution, to "the progress and use of science and the useful arts." The first source of worry is the author's suspicion that someone may lift his concepts or his prose during editorial consideration of his work.

Manuscripts are protected by common-law copyright until they appear in some duplicated form and are offered to the public at or without a charge. Infringement of common-law copyright usually needs little more proof than the establishment of access to the work in question. People in the publishing business are highly sensitive not only to the ethics of their trade but to the implications of common-law copyright infringement.

The second kind of copyright is statutory, which takes the manuscript, at its publication, out of common-law copyright and surrounds the published work with the proprietary

safeguards which the copyright statute (1909), court decisions, and legal-administrative practices have given it—
provided all of the prescribed steps necessary to the achievement of statutory copyright have been taken either by the
author or by his publisher at the time of publication.

Who should secure copyright, the author or his publisher?
From a practical point of view, it really doesn't matter, assuming two conditions: (1) that the author, in permitting
his publisher to take out the copyright, has an antecedent
contract with the publisher securing the rights and entitlements important to him; and (2) that the publisher has a
record of responsible dealing and a reputation among
writers for integrity. Most scholarly books are copyrighted
by university presses; most books published by general publishers are copyrighted by their authors. Publishers can take
the necessary steps towards copyright in the author's name,
in his behalf.

The extent to which a scholar may draw upon another
scholar's copyrighted work, or any other writer's copyrighted work, is a frequent subject of correspondence between the scholar and his publisher. The legal doctrine of
fair use, flowing from the purposes of patents and copyrights
touched upon in the Constitution, for "the progress and use
of science and the useful arts," is simple recognition of the
fact that there is nothing new under the sun and that science
and humane letters and the inventive gifts of mankind must
draw upon the expressions of them in the immediate and
the more remote past. In literary or historical criticism, it
recognizes the impossibility of any criticism, favorable or
unfavorable, unless the matter criticized can be presented
with the author's critical analysis. This is why the materials
quoted in the present book fall under the doctrine of fair
use. The doctrine does not extend to an author's original

synthesis in the course of which he freely quotes and uses in extenso the writing of a predecessor still under statutory copyright. Nor does it extend to uses in anthologies, compilations, textbooks assembled from selections from copyrighted works, and the like. The degree to which verse is restricted is considerably more severe in practice.

How long does copyright last? In the first instance, under the U.S. Copyright Act of 1909, for a period of twenty-eight years, with the right of the author or his heirs or assigns, but not the publisher, to renew for a further period of twenty-eight years, making a total of fifty-six years. Copyright revision, which has been debated by one session of Congress after another for fifteen years, is now at that point where the term of copyright is proposed for the remainder of the author's lifetime plus fifty years (roughly the provision under British and some Continental laws), and for works copyrighted under the old statute, twenty-eight years plus fifty. (Copyrights expiring under the old statute have been automatically extended during the period of Congressional consideration of copyright revision.)

There are so many contingencies under copyright that the answers an author is likely to get from his publisher are "yes and no." The safest way for a scholar to proceed when in doubt is to consult Harriet F. Pilpel, *Copyright Guide*, Fourth Edition (New York, R. R. Bowker, 1969); Philip Wittenberg, *The Protection of Literary Property* (New York, The Writer, Inc., 1968); and, for the historical development of copyright, Lyman Ray Patterson, *Copyright in Historical Perspective* (Nashville, Vanderbilt University Press, 1968). For illustrations, George Chernoff and Hershel Sarbin, *Photography and the Law* (Philadelphia, Chilton Books, 1965) is authoritative.

The Mote in the Publisher's Eye

"MY WIFE DOESN'T CARE FOR RED": Publishers and their book designers are, generally speaking, highly skilled in the arts of book-making—far more so than most historians are likely to be. In hard-back form, their books exhibit qualities of design and choices of type, ornaments, and cloth which have become the envy of scholars and readers elsewhere in the world. It has been my good fortune to be associated with a number of gifted designers, and I myself have had the task of designing a good many books. My instinct has always been to keep hands off a designer's concepts, to avoid burdening him with any of my predilections or phobias. Yet, as the caption at the head of the present paragraph indicates, I have encountered many restrictive requests from authors in my day. Books turn out better when the people whose careers are dedicated to making them are given a free hand. For the bookmaker must move, in any case, within the narrow limits of traditional formats, which are dictated by highly practical considerations, and with some respect for costs, the availability of materials, and the historical relation of certain types to certain periods of history. As the late Will Ransom, a widely recognized designer, made clear, book design is a "modest art" but one that needs a lifetime for its mastery.

TRY, TRY AGAIN: We have looked at the publisher's psychology and the range of his complaints. What of the historian with his first manuscript? If he doesn't achieve a publishing acceptance the first time he submits it to a scholarly or general publisher, he should keep trying other publishers until he has exhausted the limits of rejection. The late Edward H. Faulkner's manuscript of *Plowman's Folly*, which would work an agricultural revolution in North

America in the twenty-five years after its publication in 1943, had been "everywhere" before I saw it and published it. I shall always cringe, on the other hand, when I remember that I let Roger Shugg at the University of Chicago Press publish Owen Wister's letters because I was hesitant, and Macmillan publish Edward Gibbon's letters because I couldn't find the money for three fat volumes. Vincent Starrett's account of the Chicago literary renascence had been resting in a drawer of his desk for eleven years when, on a tip from Edward Wagenknecht, I got hold of it and published it. And for the faint-hearted, it may be remembered (if any but a few of us knew) that H. R. R. Tolkien's *Lord of the Rings* achieved the vast audience it deserved only after Ballantine Books, whose editorial chief saw it for what it was, published it in paperback after it had failed on its first appearance in America. Publishing, even the scholarly kind, is a personal thing, enlivened by enthusiasms, restrained by cautions, balanced by experience, which must always see in a piece of scholarship more than meets the eye.

Bibliography

Alvord, C. W. "A Critical Analysis of the Work of Reuben Gold Thwaites," in *Mississippi Valley Historical Association Proceedings*, Vol. 7 (1913–14), 321–33.

American Library Association et al. *Anglo-American Cataloging Rules: North American Text*. Chicago, American Library Association, 1967.

Andrews, Charles McLean. *The Colonial Period of American History*. 4 vols. New Haven, Yale University Press, 1934–1938.

Bagehot, Walter. *Lombard Street: A Description of the Money Market*. New York, Scribner, Armstrong & Co., 1873.

Ball, Max W. *This Fascinating Oil Business*. Indianapolis, Bobbs-Merrill Co., 1940.

Bambas, Rudolph C. "Split Infinitive," an article hitherto unpublished appearing as an appendix to the present volume.

Barnes, Harry Elmer. *A History of Historical Writing*, Norman, University of Oklahoma Press, 1937.

Beale, Howard K., ed. *Charles A. Beard, an Appraisal*. Lexington, University of Kentucky Press, 1954.

Beale, Thomas J. "Recollections of William Craig," in Lewiston *Morning Tribune*, March 3, 1918.

Becker, Carl L. *Detachment and the Writing of History: Essays and Letters of Carl L. Becker*. Ed. by Phil L. Snyder. Ithaca, Cornell University Press, 1958.

———. *The Eve of the Revolution: A Chronicle of the Breach with England*. New Haven, Yale University Press, 1918.

———. *Everyman His Own Historian*. El Paso, Texas Western College Press for Academic Reprints, 1959.

————. "The Reviewing of Historical Books," in *Annual Report of the American Historical Association for the Year 1912*. Washington, 1914.

Behrman, S. N. *Portrait of Max: An Intimate Memoir of Sir Max Beerbohm*. New York, Random House, 1960.

Bent, George. *Life of George Bent Written from His Letters by George E. Hyde*. Ed. by Savoie Lottinville. Norman, University of Oklahoma Press, 1968.

Berthrong, Donald J. *The Southern Cheyennes*. Norman, University of Oklahoma Press, 1963.

Billington, Ray Allen. "Guides to American Historical Manuscript Collections in Libraries of the United States," in *Mississippi Valley Historical Review*, Vol. XXXVIII, No. 3 (December, 1951), 467–96.

Bloch, Marc Leopold Benjamin. *Feudal Society*. Trans. by L. A. Manyon. Chicago, University of Chicago Press, 1961.

————. *La Société féodale: la formation des liens de dépendance*. Paris, A. Michel, 1949.

————. *La Société féodale: les classes et le gouvernement des hommes*. Paris, A. Michel, 1949.

Bolton, Herbert Eugene. *Guide to Materials for the History of the United States in the Principal Archives of Mexico*. Washington, Carnegie Institution, 1913.

————. *The Spanish Borderlands*. No. 23, *Chronicles of America Series*. New Haven, Yale University Press, 1921.

Boorstin, Daniel J. *The Americans: The Colonial Experience*. New York, Random House, 1958.

Boyd, Julian P., et al. *The Papers of Thomas Jefferson*. 19 vols. Princeton, Princeton University Press, 1950–1974 and continuing.

Brooks, Cleanth, and Robert Penn Warren. *Understanding Poetry: An Anthology for College Students*. New York, Henry Holt & Co., 1938.

————. *Understanding Fiction*. New York, Appleton, Century, Crofts, 1959.

Butterfield, Sir Herbert. *The Peace Tactics of Napoleon, 1806–1808*. Cambridge, Cambridge University Press, 1929.

Butterfield, Lyman, ed. *Adams Family Correspondence*. 2 vols. Cambridge, Belknap Press of Harvard University Press, 1963.

Carritt, E. F. *The Theory of Morals*. London, Oxford University Press, 1952.

Cassirer, Ernst. *An Essay on Man: An Introduction to a Philosophy of Human Culture*. New Haven, Yale University Press, 1944.

Caughey, John Walton. "Our Chosen Destiny," Presidential Address, Mississippi Valley Historical Association, April, 1965, in *The Journal of American History*, Vol. LII, No. 2 (September, 1965), 239–52.

————. *Hubert Howe Bancroft, Historian of the West*. Berkeley, University of California Press, 1946.

Clapham, Sir John. *The Bank of England: A History*. 2 vols. Cambridge, The University Press, 1945; New York, The Macmillan Company, 1945.

Clark, G. N. "Historical Reviewing," in *Essays in History Presented to Reginald Lane Poole*. Ed. by H. W. C. Davis. Freeport, N.Y., Books for Libraries Press, 1967.

Clark, Harry. *A Venture in History: The Production, Publication, and Sale of the Works of Hubert Howe Bancroft*. Berkeley, University of California Press, 1973.

Clark, Thomas D., et al. *Travels in the Old South*, 3 vols. *Travels in the Confederate States*, comp. by E. M. Coulter. *Travels in the New South*, 2 vols. Norman, University of Oklahoma Press, 1948–1962.

Clark, William. *The Field Notes of Captain William Clark, 1803–1805*. Ed. by Ernest Staples Osgood. New Haven, Yale University Press, 1964.

Cone, M. L. *Oscar Hammerstein's Manhattan Opera Company*, Norman, University of Oklahoma Press, 1966.

Cooke, Jacob E. *Frederic Bancroft, Historian*. Norman, University of Oklahoma Press, 1957.

Craigie, Sir William A., and James R. Hulbert. *A Dictionary of American English on Historical Principles.* 4 vols. Chicago, University of Chicago Press, 1938–44.

De Voto, Bernard. *Across the Wide Missouri.* Boston, Houghton Mifflin Co., 1947.

Donovan, Timothy Paul. *Historical Thought in America: Postwar Patterns.* Norman, University of Oklahoma Press, 1973.

Farnham, Emily. *Charles Demuth: Behind a Laughing Mask.* Norman, University of Oklahoma Press, 1971.

Faulkner, Edward A. *Plowman's Folly.* Norman, University of Oklahoma Press, 1943.

Ferguson, Charles W. *Naked to Mine Enemies: The Life of Cardinal Wolsey.* Boston, Little, Brown and Company, 1958.

Fowler, Henry Watson. *A Dictionary of Modern English Usage.* Second edition revised by Sir Ernest Gowers. London and New York, Oxford University Press, 1965.

———. *The Concise Oxford Dictionary.* London, Oxford University Press, 1929.

———, and F. G. Fowler. *The King's English.* Oxford, The Clarendon Press, 1954.

———, and F. G. Fowler. *The Pocket Oxford Dictionary of Current English.* Fifth edition revised by E. McIntosh and G. W. S. Friedrichsen. Oxford, the Clarendon Press, 1969.

Frémont, John Charles. *The Expeditions of John Charles Frémont.* Vol. 1 and Map Supplement. Ed. by Donald Jackson and Mary Lee Spence. Urbana, University of Illinois Press, 1970. Vol. 2 and *Proceedings of the Court Martial.* Ed. by Mary Lee Spence and Donald Jackson. Urbana, University of Illinois Press, 1973.

———. *Memoirs of My Life.* Chicago, Belford, Clarke & Co., 1887.

Gallatin, Albert. *A Table of Indian Tribes of the United States, East of the Stony Mountains, Arranged According to Languages and Dialects.* N.p., 1826.

———. *Synopsis of Indian Tribes within the United States East of the Rocky Mountains, 1836,* in American Antiquarian Society, *Archaeologia americana,* Vol. 2, *Transactions and Collections.* Cambridge, 1836.

Gibbon, Edward. *The Decline and Fall of the Roman Empire.* 6 vols. London, 1776–88. New York, Modern Library, 1932 (3 vols.)

———. *Letters.* Ed. by J. E. Norton. New York, The Macmillan Company, 1956.

Gold, Joseph. *William Faulkner: A Study in Humanism, from Metaphor to Discourse.* Norman, University of Oklahoma Press, 1966.

Gottschalk, Louis. *Understanding History: A Primer of Historical Method.* New York, Alfred A. Knopf, 1963.

Green, John Richard. *A Short History of the English People* [1874]. American edition: Harper and Brothers, New York, 1896.

Greever, William S. *The Bonanza West: The Story of the Western Mining Rushes, 1848–1900.* Norman, University of Oklahoma Press, 1963.

Gregg, Josiah. *Commerce of the Prairies* [1844]. Ed. by Max L. Moorhead. Norman, University of Oklahoma Press, 1954.

———. *Diary and Letters of Josiah Gregg.* 2 vols. Ed. by Maurice Garland Fulton, with an introduction by Paul Horgan. Norman, University of Oklahoma Press, 1941 and 1944.

Halévy, Élie. *England in 1815.* Trans. by E. I. Watkin and D. A. Barker. New York, Peter Smith, 1949.

———. *Histoire du peuple anglais au dix-neuvième siecle.* 6 vols. Paris, 1913–32.

———. *La formation du radicalisme philosophique en Angleterre.* 3 vols. Paris, 1901, 1904.

Hamilton, Charles, ed. *Braddock's Defeat: The Journal of Captain Robert Cholmley's Batman, The Journal of a British Officer, Halkett's Orderly Book.* Norman, University of Oklahoma Press, 1959.

Handlin, Oscar, et al. *Harvard Guide to American History.*

Cambridge, Belknap Press of Harvard University Press, 1966.

Hawgood, John A. "The Pattern of Yankee Infiltration in Mexican Alta California, 1821–1846," *Pacific Historical Review*, Vol. XXVII (February, 1958), 27–38.

Hazlitt, William. *The Collected Works of William Hazlitt.* 12 vols. Ed. by A. R. Waller and Arnold Glover. London, J. M. Dent, 1902–1904.

Hexter, J. H. *Doing History.* Bloomington, Indiana University Press, 1971.

Higham, John. *Writing American History: Essays on Modern Scholarship.* Bloomington, Indiana University Press, 1970.

Hockett, Homer C. *The Critical Method in Historical Research and Writing.* New York, The Macmillan Company, 1966.

Hoig, Stan. *The Sand Creek Massacre.* Norman, University of Oklahoma Press, 1961.

Huizinga, J. "The Idea of History," in Fritz Stern, ed., *The Varieties of History from Voltaire to the Present*, 290–303. New York, Meridian Books, Inc., 1956.

Irving, Washington. *Astoria, or Anecdotes of an Enterprise Beyond the Rocky Mountains.* 2 vols. Philadelphia, Carey, Lea, & Blanchard, 1836. New edition, ed. by Edgeley W. Todd. Norman, University of Oklahoma Press, 1964.

———. *The Rocky Mountains; or, Scenes, Incidents, and Adventures in the Far West; Digested from the Journal of Captain B. L. E. Bonneville, of the Army of the United States, and Illustrated from Various Other Sources.* 2 vols. Philadelphia, Carey, Lea, & Blanchard, 1837. New edition, ed. by Edgeley W. Todd. Norman, University of Oklahoma Press, 1961.

Jacobs, Wilbur R. *The Historical World of Frederick Jackson Turner, with Selections from His Correspondence.* New Haven, Yale University Press, 1968.

Jefferson, Thomas. *Message from the President of the United States communicating discoveries made in exploring the Missouri, Red River and Washita,* by Captains Lewis and Clark,

Doctor Sibley, and Mr. Dunbar, in *American State Papers, Indian Affairs*, I, 706–707.

———. *Notes on the State of Virginia.* Philadelphia, Pritchard and Hall, 1788.

Jones, A. H. M. *The Later Roman Empire, 284–602: A Social, Economic, and Administrative Survey.* 2 vols. Norman, University of Oklahoma Press, 1964.

Jones, Douglas C. *The Treaty of Medicine Lodge.* Norman, University of Oklahoma Press, 1966.

Kant, Immanuel. *Kant's Werke.* 9 Bände. Band V: *Kritik der praktischen Vernunft. Kritik der Urtheilskraft.* Berlin, Druck under Verlag Georg Reimer, 1913.

Kipling, Rudyard. *In the Neolithic Age*, in *Rudyard Kipling's Verse; Inclusive Edition.* Garden City, N.Y., Doubleday, Page & Co., 1921.

Lambton, John George, Earl of Durham. *Report on the Affairs of British North America.* 3 vols. Ed. by Sir C. P. Lucas. Oxford, The Clarendon Press, 1912.

Larkin, Thomas Oliver. *The Larkin Papers.* 10 vols. Ed. by George P. Hammond. Berkeley, University of California Press, 1951–1964.

Leonard, Zenas. *Adventures of Zenas Leonard, Fur Trader.* Ed. by John C. Ewers. Norman, University of Oklahoma Press, 1959.

Levy, Lester S. *Grace Notes in American History: Popular Sheet Music from 1820 to 1900.* Norman, University of Oklahoma Press, 1967.

———. *Flashes of Merriment: A Century of Humorous Songs in America, 1805–1905.* Norman, University of Oklahoma Press, 1971.

Lewis, Meriwether, and William Clark. *History of the Expedition under the Command of Lewis and Clark.* 4 vols. Ed. by Elliott Coues. New York, Francis P. Harper, 1893.

———. *Original Journals of the Lewis and Clark Expedition, 1804–1806, Printed from the Original Manuscripts in the*

Library of the American Philosophical Society and by Direction of Its Committee on Historical Documents, Together with Manuscript Material of Lewis and Clark from Other Sources . . . Now for the First Time Published in Full and Exactly as Written. 8 vols. Ed. by Reuben Gold Thwaites, New York, Dodd, Mead & Co., 1904–1905.

————. *Letters of the Lewis and Clark Expedition, with Related Documents, 1783–1854.* Ed. by Donald Jackson. Urbana, University of Illinois Press, 1962.

Library of Congress. *National Union Catalog of Manuscript Collections; Based on Reports from American Repositories of Manuscripts.* 9 vols. Washington, The Library of Congress, 1962–74.

Link, Arthur S. *Wilson: The Struggle for Neutrality, 1914–1915.* Princeton, Princeton University Press, 1960.

————, and others. *The Papers of Woodrow Wilson.* Princeton, Princeton University Press, 1966–.

Macaulay, Thomas Babington. "History," in *Edinburgh Review.* Edinburgh, 1828.

McDermott, John Francis. *George Caleb Bingham: River Portraitist.* Norman, University of Oklahoma Press, 1959.

————. "Washington Irving and the Journal of Captain Bonneville," in *Mississippi Valley Historical Review,* Vol. XLIII, No. 3 (December, 1956), 459–67.

Madison, James. *The Papers of James Madison,* 9 vols. Ed. by William T. Hutchinson, Robert A. Rutland, et al. Chicago, University of Chicago Press, 1962–.

Mason, George. *The Papers of George Mason, 1725–1792.* 3 vols. Ed. by Robert A. Rutland. Chapel Hill, University of North Carolina Press, 1972.

Mathews, John Joseph. *Life and Death of an Oilman: The Career of E. W. Marland.* Norman, University of Oklahoma Press, 1951.

Mathews, Mitford M., ed. *A Dictionary of Americanisms on Historical Principles.* 2 vols. Chicago, University of Chicago Press, 1951.

Mattingly, Garrett. *The Armada*. Boston, Houghton Mifflin Co., 1959.

———. *Renaissance Diplomacy*. Boston, Houghton Mifflin Co., 1955.

Meek, Stephen H. L. Article in *Niles' Weekly Register*, Vol. 52 (March 25, 1837).

Mellenthin, F. W. von. *Panzer Battles: A Study of the Employment of Armor in the Second World War*. Norman, University of Oklahoma Press, 1956.

Mendell, Clarence W. *Tacitus: The Man and His Work*. New Haven, Yale University Press, 1957.

Mertins, Louis. *Robert Frost: Life and Talks-Walking*. Norman, University of Oklahoma Press, 1965.

Miranda, Francisco de. *The New Democracy in America: Travels of Francisco de Miranda in the United States, 1783–1784*. Ed. by John S. Ezell, trans. by Judson P. Wood. Norman, University of Oklahoma Press, 1963.

Missouri Historical Society, St. Louis. David Adams Papers.

Mohr, Nicolaus. *Excursion Through America*. No. 71, *Lakeside Classics*. Ed. by Ray Allen Billington. Chicago, R. R. Donneley and Sons Company, The Lakeside Press, 1973.

Moorhead, Max L. *The Apache Frontier: Jacobo Ugarte and Spanish-Indian Relations in Northern New Spain, 1769–1791*. Norman, University of Oklahoma Press, 1968.

Motley, John Lothrop. *The Correspondence of John Lothrop Motley*. 2 vols. Ed. by George William Curtis. New York, Harper and Bros., 1889.

Murray, James A. H., et al. *The Oxford English Dictionary*. 13 vols. Oxford, The Clarendon Press, 1933 (1961).

Namier, Sir Lewis B. *Avenues of History*. New York, The Macmillan Company, n.d.

———. *England in the Age of the American Revolution*. London, Macmillan & Company, Ltd., 1930.

National Historical Publications Commission. *A Guide to*

Archives and Manuscripts in the United States. Ed. by Philip M. Hamer. New Haven, Yale University Press, 1961.

Nevins, Allan. "In Defence of History," in Whit Burnett, ed., *This Is My Best*. New York, The Dial Press, 1942.

———. *Grover Cleveland: A Study in Courage*. New York, Dodd, Mead & Co., 1933.

———. *The Emergence of Lincoln*. 2 vols. New York, Charles Scribner's Sons, 1950.

———. *Hamilton Fish: The Inner History of the Grant Administration*. New York, Dodd, Mead & Co., 1936.

Nidever, George. *The Life and Adventures of George Nidever*. Ed. by William H. Ellison. Berkeley, University of California Press, 1937.

Nye, Wilbur Sturtevant. *Carbine and Lance*. Norman, University of Oklahoma Press, 1937.

Parkman, Francis. *The California and Oregon Trail*. New York, George P. Putnam, 1849.

———. *Letters of Francis Parkman*. 2 vols. Ed. by Wilbur R. Jacobs. Norman, University of Oklahoma Press, 1960.

Parrington, Vernon Louis. *Main Currents in American Thought*. 3 vols. New York, Harcourt, Brace & Co., 1927–30.

Partridge, Eric. *A Dictionary of Clichés*. New York, The Macmillan Company, 1940.

Patterson, Lyman Ray. *Copyright in Historical Perspective*. Nashville, Vanderbilt University Press, 1968.

Paul, Rodman W. *Mining Frontiers of the Far West, 1848–1880*. New York, Holt, Rinehart & Winston, 1963.

Paul, Rodman W., et al. Symposium, "California's Gold Rush and the Mother Lode," *Westways*, Los Angeles, Vol. LIX, No. 5 (May, 1967), 3–68.

Perrin, Porter G. *Writer's Guide and Index to English*. Fourth edition revised by Karl W. Dykema and William R. Ebbitt. Chicago, Scott Foresman, 1965.

Pike, Zebulon Montgomery. *The Journals of Zebulon Montgomery Pike, with Letters and Related Documents*. Ed. by

Donald Jackson. 2 vols. Norman, University of Oklahoma Press, 1966.

Pilpel, Harriet F. *Copyright Guide.* Fourth edition. New York, R. R. Bowker, 1968.

Prescott, William Hickling. *The Literary Memoranda of William Hickling Prescott.* 2 vols. Ed. by C. Harvey Gardiner. Norman, University of Oklahoma Press, 1961.

Pritchard, John Paul. *Criticism in America: An Account of the Development of Critical Techniques from the Early Period of the Republic to the Middle Years of the Twentieth Century.* Norman, University of Oklahoma Press, 1956.

Ranke, Leopold von. *Die Meisterwerke.* 12 Bände. Ed. by Willy Andreas. Wiesbaden, E. Vollmer Verlag, 1957.

Rhodes, Irwin S. *The Papers of John Marshall: A Descriptive Calendar.* 2 vols. Norman, University of Oklahoma Press, 1969.

Richardson, Rupert Norval. *The Comanche Barrier to South Plains Settlement* . . . . Glendale, The Arthur H. Clark Co., 1933.

Ritcheson, Charles R. *British Politics and the American Revolution.* Norman, University of Oklahoma Press, 1954.

Rocke, Russell. *The Grandiloquent Dictionary.* Englewood Cliffs, N.J., Prentice Hall, 1972.

Roe, Frank Gilbert. *The Indian and the Horse.* Norman, University of Oklahoma Press, 1955.

Rundell, Walter. *In Pursuit of American History: Research and Training in the United States.* Norman, University of Oklahoma Press, 1970.

Ruxton, George Frederick. *Life in the Far West.* Edinburgh and London, William Blackwood and Sons, 1849. New edition, ed. by LeRoy R. Hafen. Norman, University of Oklahoma Press, 1951.

Schmid, Carlo. Lectures. Tübingen, Spring, 1931.

Sears, Paul B. *Charles Darwin: The Naturalist as a Cultural Force.* New York, Charles Scribner's Sons, 1950.

————. *Deserts on the March.* Norman, University of Oklahoma Press, 1935.

Smith, Charlotte Watkins. *Carl Becker: On History and the Climate of Opinion.* Ithaca, Cornell University Press, 1956.

Stern, Fritz. *The Varieties of History.* New York, Meridian Books, 1956.

Stern, Madeleine B. *Louisa May Alcott.* Norman, University of Oklahoma Press, 1950.

Strunk, William. *The Elements of Style.* With Revisions, an Introduction, and a Chapter on Writing by E. B. White. New York, The Macmillan Company, 1972.

Sweet, Frederick A. *Miss Mary Cassatt, Impressionist from Pennsylvania.* Norman, University of Oklahoma Press, 1966.

Talbot, Theodore. *Soldier in the West: Letters of Theodore Talbot During His Services in California, Mexico, and Oregon.* Ed. by Robert V. Hine and Savoie Lottinville. Norman, University of Oklahoma Press, 1972.

Taylor, A. J. P. "Fiction in History," *Times* (London) *Literary Supplement,* March 23, 1973.

Thomas, Alfred Barnaby, trans. and ed. *Teodoro de Croix and the Northern Frontier of New Spain, 1776–1783.* Norman, University of Oklahoma Press, 1941.

Thwaites, Reuben Gold, ed. *Early Western Travels, 1748–1846.* 32 vols. Cleveland, The Arthur H. Clark Company, 1904–1907.

Tolkien, J. R. R. *Lord of the Rings.* 3 vols. New York, Ballantine Books, 1965.

Tompkins, Stuart Ramsay. *The Russian Intelligentsia: Makers of the Revolutionary State.* Norman, University of Oklahoma Press, 1957.

Turabian, Kate L. *A Manual for Writers of Term Papers, Theses, and Dissertations.* Third edition revised. Chicago, University of Chicago Press, 1967.

Turner, Frederick Jackson. *"Dear Lady": The Letters of Frederick Jackson Turner and Alice Forbes Perkins Hooper,*

1910–1932. Ed. by Ray Allen Billington, with the Collaboration of Walter Muir Whitehill. San Marino, Huntington Library, 1970.

———. *Frederick Jackson Turner's Legacy: Unpublished Writings in American History*. Ed. by Wilbur R. Jacobs. San Marino, Huntington Library, 1965.

Valentine, Alan. *Lord North*. 2 vols. Norman, University of Oklahoma Press, 1967.

Victor, Frances Fuller. *River of the West*. Hartford, Bliss; San Francisco, R. J. Trumbull & Co., 1870.

Wagenknecht, Edward. *Chicago*. No. 13, *The Centers of Civilization Series*. Norman, University of Oklahoma Press, 1964.

———. *Dickens and the Scandalmongers: Essays in Criticism*. Norman, University of Oklahoma Press, 1965.

Wagner, Henry R., and Charles L. Camp. *The Plains and the Rockies: A Bibliography of Original Narratives of Travel and Adventure, 1800–1865*. San Francisco, The Grabhorn Press, 1937.

Walker, Joseph Reddeford. Account of the Bonneville and California expeditions, *Sonoma Democrat*, November 25, 1876.

Wallace, Ernest, and E. Adamson Hoebel. *The Comanches: Lords of the South Plains*. No. 34, *The Civilization of the American Indian Series*. Norman, University of Oklahoma Press, 1952.

Watson, John, tr. *The Philosophy of Kant*. Glasgow, Maclehose, Jackson & Co., 1923.

Webb, Walter Prescott. *The Texas Rangers: A Century of Frontier Defense*. Boston, Houghton Mifflin Co., 1935.

———. *The Great Frontier*. Boston, Houghton Mifflin Co., 1952.

———. *The Great Plains*. Boston, Ginn & Co., 1931.

———. "The American West, Perpetual Mirage," *Harper's*, May, 1957.

Wilkins, Thurman. *Thomas Moran: Artist of the Mountains.* Norman, University of Oklahoma Press, 1966.

Wittenberg, Philip. *The Protection of Literary Property.* New York, The Writer Inc., 1968.

Wright, Joseph. *English Dialect Dictionary.* 6 vols. Oxford, The Clarendon Press, 1923.

Appendix:
The Split Infinitive,
by Rudolph Bambas

The term *infinitive* refers to one of the grammatical functions of a verb. In this function the verb can serve as a noun or as a noun and verb simultaneously. Thus, in the sentence, "He tried to do the right thing," the infinitive *to do* is a noun in that it functions as the object of *tried* and a verb in that it takes an object, *the right thing.*

As in the example *to do*, the infinitive is commonly a phrase, made up of a meaningful word, *do*, and a meaningless particle, *to*. In early English, this *to* was a preposition and governed the dative case form of the infinitive. It had the directional meaning of *toward* and could figuratively convey the idea of purpose. Thus, the early English equivalent of "He had plenty *to eat*" meant he had plenty in the direction of eating or for the purpose of eating. The prepositional force of *to* gradually wore out, and for centuries now the word has been merely an empty sign of the infinitive. This sign is commonly, but not always, found in infinitive expressions. It does not appear after auxiliary verbs, as in "I may go," "could go," "will go." *Go* is an infinitive in these verb phrases but is not accompanied by its sign, *to*. The sign is also omitted after some verbs, like *make*, for example: "I don't know what made me *do* it." *Do* is here a "bare" infinitive. Curiously, if we substitute a synonym for *made: caused, compelled*, or *forced*, the *to* reappears. "I don't know what caused me *to do* it." This inclusion or omission of *to* in infinitive constructions is a matter of idiom, of the way things are in English. Native speakers of the language are not ordinarily aware of inconsistency here, of a departure from the ideal ways of logic and analogy and are puzzled, amused, or annoyed when children and foreigners fail either to include or to leave out the *to* properly.

In the nineteenth century some stylists and grammarians decided arbitrarily and foolishly that it was an impropriety to "split" the parts of an infinitive, to insert an adverbial expression between *to* and its companion word. It is true that in hastily constructed sentences split infinitives sometimes appear that are clumsy or, worse, not immediately clear. In "He wanted *to* as quickly as possible *learn* French" it is awkward to postpone the completion of the infinitive phrase by the length of four intervening words. Grace, ease, and clarity are improved by putting the adverbial modifier, "as quickly as possible," at the end of the sentence. However, in absolutely prohibiting the split infinitive at any time, the grammarians of the last century ran counter to actual usage. All the skillful handlers of English from Shakespeare to Faulkner have split infinitives when it was convenient to do so, and in some expressions splitting, more than convenient, is impossible to avoid. For example, in the sentence: "He threw a rock at the dog, hoping *to just miss* it," the adverbial modifier *just* has to immediately precede (note split) the verb *miss*. If we write "He threw a rock at the dog, hoping just to miss it," we run the risk of being misunderstood to mean "he had no other hope than to miss it," which isn't what we mean at all. We can't put the adverb at the end of the sentence. To write "hoping to miss it just" just isn't English. Consider the sentence: "Since the water was dangerously low, he decided *to half fill* his cup." To put it "he decided to fill his cup half full" is a possible way to avoid splitting *to fill* but hardly seems worth the trouble. The use of both *fill* and *full* is awkwardly repetitive. Again, in "Some confirmed bachelors seem unwilling *to even think* of marrying," the split construction is the clearest and most effective variation.

Some adverbs, like *fast* and *hard*, regularly follow the verb and aren't likely to occur in the split position. We always say "to run fast" and "to breathe hard." In certain other expressions the adverb naturally follows the verb when we wish to stress the modifying idea, as in "The boy was asked *to behave properly.*" But in other expressions, when the verb contains the idea to be stressed, and the adverb is distinctly minor in importance, it is natural to let the verb occupy the later and more important position, as in "This affront he was sure *to properly resent.*"

The schoolbook proscription of the split infinitive was founded on the view that the parts of the infinitive formed, or should form, a tight logical and grammatical unit and that separating the particle *to* from its companion word would lead to an undesirable looseness in expressing thought. Curiously, however, it did not occur to the purists to object by analogy to the separation of the elements of other verb phrases. Thus, in "I will gladly contribute," or "He could easily finish the job by eight o'clock," the infinitives *contribute* and *finish* are separated from the auxiliaries *will* and *could* by adverbial modifiers. But such constructions were not considered split infinitives and passed unnoticed. Similarly, no one objected to the separation of prepositions and gerunds, as in "He ended the conversation *by suddenly shutting* the door."

Despite the stringency of the grammarians, the split infinitive continued to flourish in the usage of reputable writers, and today the unenforceable prohibition of it is disappearing from the school grammars and from editorial policy. The position of good usage now is that whether the infinitive is split or not is in itself a matter of no consequence. When we write we are aiming at clarity, proper emphasis, and grace. It is better to let a split construction stand, if it is clear and direct, than to make strained efforts to avoid it and be awkwardly "correct" according to the standards of an unnecessary and now happily outmoded "rule."

Index

Index

Index

Dictionaries: use of, 186, 222–24; foreign language, 187

Dictionary of American English, A: 186

Dictionary of Modern English Usage, A: 188

Dillon, Richard H.: 21–22

Dime novel: 127

Dissertations: instructions for, 38; fast acceptance of, 51, 57; continuity of, 64; abstract for, 123; journal publication for, 205–206; publishable, 205, 206; form of, 207–10; *see also* theses

Distribution, machinery of: 219–20

Documentation, in opening scenes: 28

Documents: editors of, 140; calendars for, 152; research of, 157–68; annotation of, 158; bowdlerizing of, 159; foreign, 187; *see also* edited documents

Donnelley, R. R., and Sons: *ix*; new technology of, 203

Double-spacing, of typescript: 208

Downey, Glanville: 29–30

Drawings, reproduction of: 214–15

Drew, Dan'l, in Parrington example: 101

Droyson, Johann Gustav: 73

Dryden, John: 13

Edited documents: guidelines for, 160–61; advice for editors of, 161; science in, 162–63; material for, 164–65; sequential flow in, 165–66; relating to individual careers, 166–67; principles and insights for, 167; rules for, 167–68; personal research for, 168; *see also* documents

Editing, cost of: 220

Edition, in bibliographies: 150

Editors: art of, 5; and bibliographies, 143; obsolescence of, 204; *see also* copy-editor

Electronic device, in printing: 203–205; footnotes for, 203, 208

Elements of Style, The, as guide: 189

Ellipses, admissibility of: 211

Ellison, William H.: 148

English language, flexibility of: 199

Engravings, reproduction of: 215

Episodes: uniqueness of, 4; emphasis on, 4–5; atmosphere of, 29; importance of, 49

Epistemology: 13

Errors: historical or typographical, 180; reduction in, 208, 210

Estevanico: in examples, 52, 53, 54, 55, 58; portrait of, 99

Evidence, rules of: 107

Ewers, John C.: 147–48

Explication: in opening scenes, 28, 29; and continuity, 70

Eyewitness accounts: 44–45; reliability of, 20; technique of in openings, 23

Ezell, John S.: *ix*, 215

Fair use, doctrine of: 227–28

Faulkner, Edward H.: 229–30

Faulkner, William: 107–108

Ferguson, Charles W., chronological management of: 133–34

Feudalism: 75, 76

Fiction: importance of to historian, 7; credibility in, 94

Figures of speech, use of: 196–98

"Fine writing," fear of: 94–96

Fischer, John: 175

Fish, Hamilton: 102, 104; portrait of, 105

Fisk, Jim: 101

Fiske, John: 9, 101

Flashback: in openings, 26, 29; variations of, 26–27; supports for, 27–28

Flaubert, Gustave: 7

Folk-memory: 44–45

Footnotes: in edited documents, 160; in electronic printing, 203; dissertation form of, 207; placement of, 207–208, 210; in typescript, 208; problems of, 224–26; bibliographical detail in, 224

Index

Pagination, in bibliographies: 151
Painting: as culture, 125–26; as book illustration, 212; reproduction of, 214–15
Paper, cost of: 221
Paragraphs: continuity for, 88–92; length of, 89; transition in, 90; examples of sequential, 90–92
Parkman, Francis: 146, 176; audience of, 193
Parochialism, sin of: 10
Parrington, Vernon Louis: 10; style of, 32–33; portraiture of, 100–102; originality of, 179; metaphors of, 197
Participles, dangling: 200–201
Partridge, Eric: 186
Patterson, Lyman Ray, on copyrights: 228
Paul, Rodman W.: 20
Peel, Sir Robert: 117; in cliché, 196
Peerenboom, Piet: 180
Perrin, Porter G., guidebook of: 189
Personal papers, of famous people: 166
Perspective: in narration, 43–44; in painting, 126
Pforzheimer, Carl H.: 141
Pforzheimer Collection (PC): 225
Photographs: as book illustration, 212; reproduction of, 214–15
Pike, Zebulon Montgomery: 135, 166
Pilpel, Harriet F., on copyrights: 228
Pissaro, Camille: 125
Place: in historical writing, 119–39 *passim*; and the stage, 120; defective patterns in, 121; straw-man approach to, 121–22; theater in, 123; aspects of, 126; techniques of expressing, 127–39 *passim*; command of, 128; and time, 132–39; management of, 135–39; human identification in, 138; *see also* situational elements
Plains and the Rockies, The: arrangement of, 142–46; audience for, 143, 151; title-description in, 148
Plato: 8
Pliny, the Younger (Caius Plinius Caecilius Secundus): 182
Plumb, J. H.: 175
Poinsett, Joel R., papers of: 153
Point of view: and conceptualization, 13–18; in openings, 20, 21, 22, 23
Political parties, history of: 10–11
Polybius: 45, 46
Poole, R. L.: 167
Portraiture: heroes and villains of, 93–118; credibility in, 94; examples of, 96–117 *passim*; "fine writing" in, 96–97; institutional, 99, 109–18; kinds of, 102; viewpoint in, 102–104; conjecture in, 107; from decisions and actions, 108–109; as book illustration, 212
Preconceptions, and history: 7
Preface: concepts for, 40–41; of edited documents, 160; or foreword, 181–82
Prepositions, at end of sentence: 200
Prescott, William Hickling: reappraisals of, 176; audience of, 193
Presswork, cost of: 221
Printing, electronic: 203–205
Pritchard, John Paul: 225–26
Proofreader, duties of: 210
Proofreading, cost of: 221
Publication: new technique for, 203–205; cost of, 205, 209, 220–22; standards for, 206–29; date of, 210; scholarship for, 211–12; illustrations for, 212–15; illustrative sources for, 213–15; maps for, 215–18; audience for, 218–20; copyright in, 226–28
Public documents, inaccuracies in citations from: 211
Publisher: in bibliographies, 150; as critic, 171–72; list decisions of, 172
Publishing, new phenomenon in: 221

Index